VISIONS OF SAINTHOOD IN MEDIEVAL ROME

VISIONS OF SAINTHOOD IN MEDIEVAL ROME

THE LIVES OF MARGHERITA COLONNA BY GIOVANNI COLONNA AND STEFANIA

Translated by
Larry F. Field

Edited and introduced by
Lezlie S. Knox and Sean L. Field

University of Notre Dame Press
Notre Dame, Indiana

University of Notre Dame Press
Notre Dame, Indiana 46556
undpress.nd.edu

Published in the United States of America

Library of Congress Cataloging-in-Publication Data

Names: Colonna, Giovanni, 1298?–1343 or 1344. | Stefania. | Field, Larry F.,
translator. | Knox, Lezlie S., editor, writer of introduction. | Field, Sean L.
(Sean Linscott), 1970– editor, writer of introduction.
Title: Visions of sainthood in medieval Rome : the lives of Margherita Colonna /
by Giovanni Colonna and Stefania ; translated by Larry F. Field : edited and
introduced by Lezlie S. Knox and Sean L. Field.
Description: Notre Dame : University of Notre Dame Press, 2017. |
Includes bibliographical references and index. |
Identifiers: LCCN 2017024313 (print) | LCCN 2017039588 (ebook) |
ISBN 9780268102036 (pdf) | ISBN 9780268102043 (epub) |
ISBN 9780268102012 (hardcover : alk. paper) | ISBN 0268102015 (hardcover :
alk. paper) | ISBN 9780268102029 (pbk. : alk. paper) | ISBN 0268102023
(pbk. : alk. paper)
Subjects: LCSH: Colonna, Margherita, 1255–1280. | Christian biography—Italy.
Classification: LCC BR1725.C548 (ebook) | LCC BR1725.C548 V57   2017
(print) | DDC 271/.97302 [B]—dc23
LC record available at https://lccn.loc.gov/2017024313

∞ *This paper meets the requirements of*
ANSI/NISO Z39.48-1992 (Permanence of Paper).

CONTENTS

INFORMATION ON COMPANION WEBSITE

A companion website to this book, with images, videos, genealogical tree, and other information related to Margherita Colonna and her two *vitae*, can be found at http://livesofmargheritacolonna.weebly.com. Although Web resources are inherently impermanent, Lezlie Knox intends to maintain and update this website for the foreseeable future.

PREFACE AND ACKNOWLEDGMENTS

Margherita Colonna (ca. 1255–80) belonged to one of medieval Rome's most powerful families. She led a dramatic life of ardent visionary piety, memorialized in two compelling hagiographic texts written shortly after her death. She was even belatedly beatified by the Catholic Church in 1847. Yet Margherita and the texts that record her life remain very little known, even to specialists. This volume offers the first English translation of her two "lives" and a dossier of associated documents, with the goal of making them accessible to scholars, students, and a wider reading public.

The two hagiographic *vitae* (saints' lives) are uniquely preserved in a fourteenth-century manuscript (Rome, Biblioteca Casanatense ms. 104) that languished in obscurity until the Franciscan scholar Livarius Oliger published an edition and study in 1935.[1] Our examination of the manuscript confirms this edition to be highly reliable. The present volume, in fact, owes a great debt to Father Oliger's work both as a historian and as an editor. For instance, it was he who demonstrated that the first life was written between 1281 and 1285 by Margherita Colonna's own brother, Senator Giovanni Colonna, and that the second was

---

1. Oliger, *DV.* Oliger credited the earliest description of the manuscript (which was unknown at the time of Margherita's beatification in 1847) and transcription of several chapters to Giuseppe Cascioli, *Memorie storiche del Santuario di Nostra Signora di Mentorella nella diocesi di Rivoli* (Rome: La Vera Roma, 1901). Oliger's work superseded this description, as well as those in A. Poncelet, *Catalogus codicum hagiographicorum Latinorum bibliothecarum Romanarum praeter quam Vaticanae* (Brussels: Société des Bollandistes, 1909) and the *Bibliotheca hagiographica Latina, Supplementum* (Brussels: Société des Bollandistes, 1911).

composed between 1288 and 1292 by Stefania, an otherwise unknown woman who must have been occupying a leadership position at San Silvestro in Capite, the female Franciscan community founded by Margherita's followers in 1285.

Yet in spite of Oliger's highly competent edition, these texts did not gain much attention from twentieth-century scholars. Giulia Barone produced several insightful articles in the 1980s and 1990s, while Robert Brentano made use of Margherita's example as part of his evocative studies of thirteenth-century Rome.[2] But the explosion of American scholarship on medieval holy women, perhaps best represented by the influential works of Caroline Bynum, passed over Margherita and her *Lives* completely.[3] Recently, however, signs of twenty-first-century interest have been appearing. In Italy, the Franciscan Attilio Cadderi (author of a pious 1984 biography of Margherita) produced a new Italian translation of the lives in 2010 as part of a volume designed to promote a new bid for Margherita's canonization. In Anglophone scholarship, Emily Graham's 2009 doctoral dissertation on Colonna patronage of the Spiritual Franciscans offered a new perspective on Margherita's career, and in 2013 Bianca Lopez published the first English-language article dedicated to Margherita's life and lives.[4] A great deal of research remains to

---

2. See the select bibliography for key works by Barone and Brentano, as well as those by Giuseppe Furitano, Edith Pasztor, and Lino Temperini in the same era.

3. For instance, Margherita Colonna did not appear in Bynum's landmark study *Holy Feast and Holy Fast: The Religious Significance of Food to Medieval Women* (Berkeley: University of California Press, 1987); more recently, she is not mentioned anywhere in the 700-plus pages of Alastair Minnis and Rosalynn Voaden, eds., *Medieval Holy Women in the Christian Tradition, c. 1100–c. 1500* (Turnhout: Brepols, 2010), including E. Ann Matter, "Italian Holy Women: A Survey," in Minnis and Voaden, *Medieval Holy Women*, 529–55.

4. See the select bibliography for the important recent contributions of Graham and Lopez. Cadderi's 2010 volume should help to bring Margherita to a wider Italian and Catholic audience, but (aside from the pleasant Italian translation itself) is not a major advance in scholarship, since it merely paraphrases Oliger's 1935 introduction and reprints his edition and most of his notes. Cadderi's 1984 biography offered a laudatory retelling of Margherita's life, based almost entirely on the two extant *vitae*, and already including long Italian translations from these texts (apparently a second edition exists, but we have not been able to locate a copy). Eileen

be done, however, concerning Margherita Colonna, her *vitae*, and her followers. We hope that the present volume will further that process.

This book results from a fruitful collaboration over several years. Larry Field first did the essential work of translating all of the Latin texts. Sean Field and Lezlie Knox then revised and edited the translation after checking the existing edition against the unique manuscript, added explanatory footnotes to the texts, and drafted the Introduction. Lezlie Knox also translated the excerpt from Mariano of Florence's Italian text. Along the way, a number of other scholars offered essential help. Emily Graham generously allowed us access to her (as yet) unpublished doctoral dissertation and supplied us with digital photographs of Biblioteca Casanatense ms. 104. She then continued to act as gracious consultant on specific questions about the Colonna family and San Silvestro in Capite. When it became clear that the editors' lack of liturgical expertise was slowing down the project, Cecilia Gaposchkin came to the rescue, going well beyond the normal call of scholarly duty by tracking down liturgical references to fill out notes for the *vitae*. She then kindly agreed to critique a draft of the translations and the Introduction. Anne Clark's perceptive reading of the translations saved us from several errors. Other colleagues kindly responded to specific questions—Michelina DiCesare on paleography, Claudia Bolgia on art history, and Kathleen Walkowiak on Roman social history. None of these scholars are responsible for any remaining errors, but all of them deserve credit for whatever strengths this volume may possess.

Lezlie Knox would like to thank the archivists and staff at the Biblioteca Casanatense and the Biblioteca Vallicelliana in Rome for assistance with manuscripts and incunabulae related to Margherita. Further assistance was obtained from the sacristan at Santa Maria in Aracoeli and the staff at the Galleria Colonna in the Palazzo Colonna. She also deeply appreciates the opportunity to spend five weeks in Rome during summer 2014 under the auspices of a National Endowment for the Humanities seminar, "Reform in Medieval Rome," organized by Maureen Miller and William North and hosted at the American Academy in

---

Kane, *The Church of San Silvestro in Capite in Rome* (Genoa: Edizioni d'Arte Marconi, 2005), 27–32, summarizes Margherita's life, based on *Vita I* and *Vita II.*

Rome. From that seminar, Emily Graham deserves particular thanks for focused conversations on the Colonna, as does Gregor Kalas, who was willing to drive through central Rome at rush hour the next summer in order to reach Margherita's relics in the Colonna countryside. Additional time in Italy was funded by Marquette University's Committee on Research and a faculty development grant from Dr. Jeanne Hossenlopp, vice president for research and innovation. Marquette's Interlibrary Loan staff did yeoman work obtaining materials, even as Milwaukee turned out to have surprising resources for medieval and early modern Roman history at both the Department of Special Collections at the University of Wisconsin-Milwaukee and the Franciscan Center Library at Cardinal Stritch University. Finally, she thanks her research assistants who contributed to this project at different stages: Claire Marshall, Glen Brown, Aaron Hyams, and Marisa Moonilal.

Sean Field would like to thank the members of his History 224 seminar at the University of Vermont in Spring 2015 for giving the translations a trial run. He is also grateful to the Interlibrary Loan staff at the University of Vermont Bailey-Howe Library, and to Paul Spaeth and the welcoming staff of the Friedsam Memorial Library at St. Bonaventure University.

We are particularly grateful to Stephen Little at the University of Notre Dame Press for his support of this project right from its inception, and to Rebecca DeBoer and her editorial team for their fine work. We also thank the press's two anonymous readers for helpful corrections and suggestions, and Elisabeth Magnus for first-rate copyediting.

Margherita Colonna's life and reputation were shaped first and foremost by her relationships with her siblings. Although we have neither senators nor cardinals in our families, the translator and editors would like to dedicate this book, with loving appreciation, to Michael Ward Field (in memoriam), to Sara Elizabeth Hook (née Knox), and to Nicholas Ezra Field.

NOTE ON TRANSLATION POLICIES

Our goal has been a translation that reads smoothly in English but remains close to the original Latin. Since neither Giovanni Colonna nor Stefania was a polished Latinist, and papal Latin can be notoriously flowery, at times this has been a challenging goal to meet. In particular, because chapters 1, 2, 6, and 9 of *Vita II* draw heavily upon earlier sources (identified in the notes), readers will likely notice rather sudden stylistic shifts in those spots.

Vita I and *Vita II* refer to Giovanni Colonna as Margherita's "older brother" or "other brother" and Cardinal Giacomo Colonna as her "more worthy brother." As an aid to the reader, we have inserted the corresponding name, in brackets, each time one of these locutions is used, or when it otherwise seems possible to identify which brother is being referred to. Similarly, in complex sentences with numerous personal pronouns we have often inserted a name, within brackets, in place of the pronoun, in order to avoid confusion. We also capitalize "Friars" and "Sisters" when the text uses *fratres* and *sorores* to refer to Franciscans or to Margherita's followers, and use lowercase "brothers" and "sisters" to designate Margherita's biological siblings.

We have generally used Italian forms for names of Italian men and women (e.g., Giovanni and Margherita rather than John and Margaret), except for popes, saints, and others who are well known to Anglophone scholarship under the English form of their name (e.g., Francis and Clare of Assisi rather than Francesco and Chiara). Biblical quotations appear in italics and follow the Douai-Rheims translation, with slight modernization; psalm numbering follows the Vulgate, and we refer to 1–4 Kings (rather than 1–2 Samuel and 1–2 Kings). Direct, substantial quotations from liturgical and other sources appear in quotation marks.

ABBREVIATIONS

AFH	*Archivum Franciscanum historicum*
AH	Guido Maria Dreves and Clemens Blume, eds. *Analecta hymnica medii aevi.* 55 vols. Leipzig: Fue's Verlag (R. Reisland), 1886–1922. Reprint, New York: Johnson Reprint Corp., 1961.
BF	J.-H. Sbaralea, ed. *Bullarium Franciscanum Romanorum pontificum, constitutiones, epistolas ac diplomata continens tribus ordinibus minorum, clarissarum, et poenitentium a seraphico patriarcha sancto Francisco institutis, concessa ab illorum exordio ad nostra usque tempora.* 4 vols. Rome: Typis Sacrae Congregationis de Propaganda Fide, 1759–1768.
Cantus ID	http://cantusdatabase.org/
Cantus Index	http://cantusindex.org/. The identification numbers for the Cantus ID and Index are consistent with each other and linked to René Jean Hesbert and Renatus Prévost, *Corpus antiphonalium officii.* Rerum ecclesiasticarum documenta. Series maior, Fontes 7–12. Rome: Herder, 1963.
CO	Eugene Moeller and Jean-Marie Clément, eds. *Corpus orationum.* 14 vols, Corpus Christianorum Series Latina 160. Turnhout: Brepols, 1992–.
DBI	Albert M. Ghisalberti, ed. *Dizionario biografico degli Italiani.* Rome: Istituto della Enciclopedia italiana, 1960–. 73 vols.
DV	Livario Oliger. *B. Margherita Colonna († 1280): Le due vite scritte dal fratello Giovanni Colonna senatore di*

	Roma e da Stefania monaca di S. Silvestro in Capite. Lateranum. Nova Series, An. 1, no. 2. Rome: Facultas Theologica Pontificii Athenaei Seminarii Romani, 1935.
PL	J. P. Migne, ed. *Patrologiae Latinae cursus completus.* Paris, 1844–64.
Vita I	"The Life of the Blessed Virgin Margherita of the Family Name Colonna," by Giovanni Colonna. Edited in Livario Oliger, *B. Margherita Colonna († 1280): Le due vite scritte dal fratello Giovanni Colonna senatore di Roma e da Stefania monaca di S. Silvestro in Capite*, Lateranum, Nova Series, An. 1, no. 2 (Rome: Facultas Theologica Pontificii Athenaei Seminarii Romani, 1935), 111–88. Translated in the present volume.
Vita II	"A New Statement on Margherita Colonna's Perfection of the Virtues," by Stefania. Edited in Livario Oliger, *B. Margherita Colonna († 1280): Le due vite scritte dal fratello Giovanni Colonna senatore di Roma e da Stefania monaca di S. Silvestro in Capite*, Lateranum, Nova Series, An. 1, no. 2 (Rome: Facultas Theologica Pontificii Athenaei Seminarii Romani, 1935), 189–222. Translated in the present volume.

TIME LINE

ca. 1255	Birth of Margherita Colonna.
1255	Canonization of Clare of Assisi.
ca. 1256/57	Death of Oddone Colonna, Margherita's father.
1263	Isabelle of France's Rule for the Order of *Sorores minores* (July); Urban IV's Rule for the Order of St. Clare (October).
ca. 1265	Death of Margherita Orsini, Margherita's mother.
ca. 1272	Giovanni Colonna attempts to arrange a marriage for his sister Margherita.
1273	Margherita Colonna moves to Mount Prenestino.
ca. 1274	Margherita receives permission to enter Santa Chiara in Assisi but decides against it.
ca. 1274–77	Margherita moves to Vulturella, then briefly joins the household of "Lady Altruda," and finally returns to Mount Prenestino.
1277–80	Pontificate of Nicholas III (Giangaetano Orsini).
1278	Giacomo Colonna is named cardinal. Margherita begins to suffer from an ulcer on her leg.
1279–80	Giovanni Colonna is named senator of Rome.
1280	Vision of "the pilgrim" (June); death of Margherita Colonna (30 December).
1281–85	"First Life" of Margherita Colonna, by Giovanni Colonna.
1285	Pope Honorius IV approves the move of Margherita's adherents to San Silvestro in Capite as an enclosed Franciscan community following the Rule of the

	Sorores minores (September). Translation of Margherita Colonna's relics follows.
1288–92	Pontificate of Nicholas IV (Jerome of Ascoli).
1288–92	"Second Life" of Margherita Colonna, by Stefania.
1288	Pietro Colonna named cardinal; Cardinal Giacomo Colonna named protector of San Silvestro in Capite.
ca. 1292	Death of Giovanni Colonna.
1294–1303	Pontificate of Boniface VIII.
1297	Outbreak of hostilities between Boniface VIII and the Colonna; Colonna cardinals stripped of their status and powers (May). Boniface VIII removes Giacomo Colonna as protector and Giovanna Colonna as abbess of San Silvestro (December).
1298	Boniface VIII transfers San Silvestro from the Order of *Sorores minores* to the Order of St. Clare (April).
1303	Pope Benedict XI lifts San Silvestro's excommunication, orders the return of its possessions, and allows it to return to the Order of *Sorores minores* (December).
1306	Giacomo and Pietro Colonna restored to the cardinalate.
1318	Death of Cardinal Giacomo Colonna; Pietro Colonna named protector of San Silvestro.
1326	Death of Cardinal Pietro Colonna.

Introduction

Margherita Colonna was born around 1255 to Oddone Colonna and his wife Margherita Orsini.[1] By the first half of the thirteenth century the Colonna were already amassing substantial ecclesiastical and political influence from their stronghold in northern Rome and in the hills east of the city around Palestrina.[2] Oddone Colonna had been senator of Rome

---

1. The estimate of Margherita's birth year is based on internal evidence in *Vita I.* She seems to have been quite young at the time of her father's death in 1257, and her family tried to arrange her marriage around 1272, which would suggest she was in her midteens at that point. See *DV*, 77–78. Oddone Colonna and Margherita Orsini married ca. 1233; see Giulia Barone, "Le due vite di Margherita Colonna," in *Esperienza religiosa e scritture femminili tra medioevo ed età moderna*, ed. Marilena Modica (Acrireale: Bonnano, 1992), 25–32, at 30n2. Margherita Colonna's mother's name is sometimes given as Maddelena, but see Robert Brentano, *Rome before Avignon: A Social History of Thirteenth-Century Rome* (1974; repr., Berkeley: University of California Press, 1990), 317n8.

2. For a modern survey of Colonna history and genealogy, see Sandro Carocci, *Baroni di Roma: Dominazioni signorili e lignaggi aristocratici nel duecento e nel primo trecento* (Rome: École française de Rome, 1993), 353–69; for a more evocative portrayal, see Brentano, *Rome before Avignon*, 173–83; *DV*, 68–75, addresses specific genealogical questions, and the brief narrative in Pio Paschini, *I Colonni* (Rome: Istituto di Studi Romani Editore, 1955) is still useful as well.

(1238–39 and 1241),[3] no doubt at least partly because of the influence of his uncle Giovanni (d. 1245), a powerful if controversial cardinal.[4] The Orsini family was equally illustrious. Margherita Orsini was sister to Senator Matteo Rosso Orsini and aunt to Cardinal Giangaetano Orsini, who became Pope Nicholas III (r. 1277–80).[5]

Margherita Colonna's siblings included five brothers. The eldest was Giovanni (d. ca. 1292), who married an Orsini cousin and was himself named senator of Rome (1261–62, 1279–80, 1290–91), as well as rector of the March of Ancona (1288–90).[6] The most illustrious ecclesiastical career was that of Giacomo (d. 1318), made a cardinal by his cousin Nicholas III in 1278.[7] Another brother, Matteo, became provost of St. Omer,[8] while Landulfo and Oddone followed secular paths.[9] Margherita also had at least two older sisters. One, Giacoma, married Pietro Conti, whose holdings east of Rome abutted the Colonna's. Another, whose name is unknown, married Oddone di Sant'Eustachio. A third sister, Aloisa, who may or may not have been younger than Margherita, married Richardo di Pietri de Iaquinto.[10]

---

3. Entry by Agostino Paravicini Bagliani in *DBI*, 27:394–96. On the fluctuating status, election, and power of the Roman senator or senators (there were generally one or two) at this time, see again Brentano, *Rome before Avignon*, 96–122.

4. Entry by Werner Maleczek in *DBI*, 27:324–28. Cardinal Giovanni di San Paolo (d. ca. 1215), who was a crucial early supporter of Francis of Assisi, is often referred to as "of Colonna," but recent scholarship has demonstrated that this label results from early modern confusion. On his interactions with Francis, see most recently Maria Pia Alberzoni, *Santa povertà e beata semplicità: Francesco d'Assisi e la chiesa romana* (Milan: Vita e Pensiero, 2015), 79–108.

5. Carocci, *Baroni de Roma*, 387–403. Orsini-Colonna connections are further detailed in Emily E. Graham, "The Patronage of the Spiritual Franciscans: The Roles of the Orsini and Colonna Cardinals, Key Lay Patrons and Their Patronage Networks" (PhD diss., University of St. Andrews, 2009).

6. Entry by Daniel Waley in *DBI*, 27:331–33.

7. Ibid., 27:311–14.

8. He was also canon of Beauvais, Laon, and Chartres, and died in 1327. See Carocci, *Baroni de Roma*, 366.

9. Ibid.

10. On these sisters, see ibid. The evidence cited there seems to suggest that Aloisa was older, though the genealogical chart implies the contrary. Carla Key-

The basic outlines of Margherita's life can be reconstructed from the two hagiographic texts translated in this volume (referred to here as *Vita I* and *Vita II*). After the deaths of her father (1256/57) and mother (ca. 1265), the young Margherita was placed under her brothers' guardianship, living in Giovanni's household while Giacomo left for Bologna to pursue his studies. When she reached marriageable age, probably around 1272, Giovanni sought a suitable husband for her. By contrast, Giacomo, while on a trip home from Bologna, urged her to devote herself to Christ in chastity. When Giovanni nevertheless arranged a betrothal, Giacomo received an angelic vision back in Bologna that confirmed Margherita's celibate destiny. And indeed Margherita then experienced her own vision of the Virgin and proceeded to vow virginity and flee to the family compound atop Mount Prenestino (modern Castel San Pietro) that overlooked the town of Palestrina.

There Margherita lived an ascetic life with a group of pious followers. She cut off her own hair and adopted a habit that resembled that worn by Sisters of the Order of St. Clare. This was an informal community, "with no abbess or superior," as Margherita herself remarked. It would seem, however, that the Colonna intended to found a more stable, traditional monastery—or at least so the hagiographic texts would have it. Thus when Giacomo returned from Bologna there were apparently efforts to build a monastery for Margherita and her companions. But for reasons not clearly explained in the texts this project was never carried out. And so Margherita and Giacomo turned to aiding the poor with the money that had been set aside for her dowry.

Margherita pondered several different spiritual paths. First she considered (or her family wished her to consider) entering the Order of St. Clare by becoming a nun at Santa Chiara in Assisi. The Franciscan

---

vanian, *Hospitals and Urbanism in Rome, 1200–1500* (Leiden: Brill, 2015), 276, says that Aloisa married into the Capocci family, but we have not been able to substantiate this claim. On Pietro Conti, part of the Poli branch of the family, husband of Giacoma (or Giacomina) Colonna, see Carocci, *Baroni de Roma*, 366. On Oddone of Sant'Eustachio, senator in 1293–94, see ibid., 411. See also the Colonna family tree in Andreas Rehberg, *Kirche und Macht im römischen Trecento: Die Colonna und ihre Klientel auf dem kurialen Pfründenmarkt (1278–1378)* (Tübingen: Max Niemeyer, 1999), 544–55.

minister general even gave his permission for this move. But "illness prevented her" from taking this step. Instead, Margherita briefly moved with her followers to the Church of St. Mary in Vulturella (modern Mentorella). The Conti lord of the area proved hostile to her intentions, however, and placed every obstacle in her way. Eventually Giovanni Colonna had to go and fetch her back. Margherita next briefly joined the household of a woman known as "Lady Altruda of the Poor" in Rome, doing menial chores while this lady went about her holy work in the city. But after "many days" Margherita allowed her brothers to persuade her to return to Mount Prenestino. There she spent the last years of her life, beset by a painful ulcer in her leg and dedicating herself to charitable work. Her final illness left her bedridden by Christmas 1280. She died, surrounded by her family, on 30 December 1280, when she was probably no more than twenty-five years old. Her body was buried at the Church of San Pietro at Mount Prenestino. Within just a few years, certainly before 1285, her brother Giovanni Colonna (the layman and senator) composed her first hagiographic "Life" (*Vita I*).

Margherita's followers at first continued to live some kind of communal life on Mount Prenestino. By 1285, however, they had taken formal vows and professed the Rule of the *Sorores minores inclusae* (Enclosed Minor Sisters), which had been written by Isabelle of France and approved in its final form by the papacy in 1263. The new nuns made these vows first to Cardinal Jerome of Ascoli, former minister general of the Franciscans, bishop of Palestrina, and a firm Colonna ally. By fall of 1285, Pope Honorius IV (r. 1285–87) had expelled the Benedictine inhabitants of San Silvestro in Capite—located in the heart of the Colonna neighborhood of Rome—and had given this monastery to the newly constituted community, while confirming it in its observance of the Rule of the *Sorores minores inclusae*. Margherita Colonna's remains almost certainly accompanied the new nuns from Mount Prenestino to San Silvestro, although the oldest extant narrative of this translation comes only from a sixteenth-century source.[11] When Jerome of Ascoli became Pope

---

11. Mariano of Florence, *Libro della dignità et excellentie del'Ordine della seraphica madre della povere donne sancta Chiara da Asisi*, ed. Giovanni Boccali (Florence: Studi francescani, 1986), 212–37 (on Margherita) and 235–37 (specifically on her

Nicholas IV (r. 1288–92), he named Cardinal Giacomo Colonna protector of the community. Thus San Silvestro in Capite was very much under Colonna patronage and was the center of efforts to preserve and promote Margherita Colonna's saintly memory.[12] Indeed, it was a leader of this community, Stefania, who, at the request of Cardinal Giacomo Colonna, wrote a second hagiographic text on Margherita's saintly virtues (*Vita II*), which was completed between 1288 and about 1292.

These two texts evidently were composed at least in part in hopes of sparking a case for Margherita's formal canonization, which must have seemed a real possibility during Nicholas IV's pontificate. Of course, such a canonization never occurred. But to understand what was at stake for her family and their allies, it is necessary to turn to the political and social history of medieval Rome.

FAMILY AND POWER IN ROME, CA. 1200–1305

The Colonna were one of the great baronial families who had come to dominate Rome politically and economically by the thirteenth century.[13]

---

translation). Mariano used *Vita I* and *Vita II* and may have had access to other documents no longer extant. *DV*, 85, cites a fifteenth-century inventory that lists among the relics of San Silvestro the "caput sancti [*sic*] Margarite de Columna in argento," so it is at least certain that her relics were transferred from Mount Prenestino before that inventory was made. On the modern fate (and continued veneration) of Margherita's relics, see the postscript to Cadderi's Italian translation in Attilio Cadderi (P. Carlo O.F.M.), trans., *Beata Margherita Colonna (1255–80): Le due vite scritte dal fratello Giovanni, senatore di Roma e da Stefania, monaca di San Silvestro in Capite. Testo critico, introduzione, traduzione italiana a fronte, da un manoscritto latino del XIV secolo*, ed. Celeste Fornari and Luigi Borzi (Palestrina, 2010), 185–87.

12. A good introduction to this church's history is Eileen Kane, *The Church of San Silvestro in Capite in Rome* (Genoa: Edizioni d'Arte Marconi, 2005). A brief treatment of the Colonna relationship to the house can be found in J. S. Gaynor and I. Toesca, *S. Silvestro in Capite* (Rome: Marietti, 1963); a more wide-ranging analysis is in Brentano, *Rome before Avignon*, 230–47.

13. The chronological division laid out in this section reflects the period when Rome was dominated by an aristocratic elite, generally referred to as barons (*baroni*), distinguished from an earlier communal stage that overlapped with the influence of

These families did not constitute a clearly defined aristocracy reflected in noble titles; rather, they were dynastic lordships whose power came from their land holdings and their ability to control Rome's civic and ecclesiastical offices.[14] They were the senators, consuls, and magistrates of the Eternal City. They also represented a good portion of the cardinalate, so it is not surprising that most of the thirteenth century's popes came from Rome's great families. Mutually reinforcing power flowed between secular and religious institutions. For example, when Giacomo Savelli became Pope Honorius IV in 1285, he named his brother Pandulfo a senator, while a nephew became both papal marshal and rector of the papal lands in Tuscany. This sort of nepotism was in fact a common state of affairs.[15]

To some degree, these great family names represented distinct lineages. Along with the Colonna and Orsini, who might be described as the two first families of thirteenth-century Rome, were also the Savelli, Conti, Poli, and Annibaldi.[16] But intermarriage regularly served to build alliances, as the evidence of Margherita's parents and siblings discussed

---

the reforming papacy, as well as a later period from the fourteenth century when the popes were resident in Avignon and when Cola di Rienzo (d. 1354) briefly led a revival of the commune. For a useful overview of later medieval Rome, see Sandro Carocci and Marco Venditelli, "Società ed economia (1050–1420)," in *Roma medievale*, ed. André Vauchez (Rome: Laterza, 2006), 71–116. Brentano's *Rome before Avignon* remains the best survey in English of these families, while Carocci's *Baroni di Roma* is an excellent overview of their origins, with brief notes on individual members. An important new study of the development of Roman political power is Chris Wickham, *Medieval Rome: Stability and Crisis of a City, 900–1150* (Oxford: Oxford University Press, 2014). See also his *Sleepwalking into a New World: The Emergence of Italian City Communes in the Twelfth Century* (Princeton, NJ: Princeton University Press, 2014).

14. For a recent overview of the way the Colonna family amassed power over specific parts of the city of Rome and the Campagna, see Keyvanian, *Hospitals and Urbanism*, 262–87, and helpful maps at 156–57.

15. On the ways in which families used the papal office to extend their own territorial holdings and political authority, Daniel Waley, *The Papal State in the Thirteenth Century* (New York: St Martin's Press, 1961), remains useful.

16. See Wickham, *Medieval Rome*, map 6, for these families' areas of influence.

above demonstrates. Such marital ties also influenced patronage. It is no coincidence that Giovanni Colonna was made senator and Giacomo Colonna elevated to the cardinalate during the pontificate of their mother's nephew, Nicholas III (Giangaetano Orsini).[17] Still, dynastic interests were most often explicitly patriarchal, with families working to protect their own patrimonies and advance their onomastic interests. Thus it is necessary to recognize that Margherita Colonna's *vitae* testify to Colonna status in Roman society, as much as to her individual holiness.

The Colonna first had come to power in the middle of the twelfth century as counts of Tusculum. From there, they gained other lordships in the hills to the east and southeast of Rome, including Palestrina, Capranica, Zagarolo, and Colonna, from which presumably the family took its name. They also added properties within Rome itself, coming to dominate the area of the city from the Mausoleum of Augustus to the Quirinale Hill and surrounding neighborhoods. In both city and countryside, they erected towers and fortified palaces. In Rome, they had built a major residence on the site of the Baths of Constantine by the middle of the thirteenth century and still others in the ancient Field of Mars.[18] They also owned houses that they rented out to tenants and shopkeepers. Most of these buildings were destroyed at the end of the thirteenth century during the conflict between the Colonna and Pope Boniface VIII (discussed below). A description stemming from that conflict, however, suggests how effectively the Colonna used material space to assert their wealth and power.

Cardinal Pietro Colonna, Margherita's nephew, wrote to the recently elected pope Clement V in 1305 seeking restitution for the family's lost

---

17. The Franciscan chronicler Salimbene, writing in the 1280s, specifically referred to this relationship in hinting that Nicholas III appointed Giacomo Colonna to the cardinalate as part of a pattern of nepotism. Joseph L. Baird, Giuseppe Baglivi, and John Robert Kane, trans., *The Chronicle of Salimbene de Adam* (Binghamton, NY: Medieval and Renaissance Texts and Studies, 1986), 160.

18. Frederick Gregorovius, *History of the City of Rome in the Middle Ages* (1894–1902; repr., New York: Italica Press, 2000), vol. 5, pt. 1, 214–16.

Map 1. Thirteenth-century Rome. The Colonna dominated the neighborhoods around San Silvestro in Capite. Map by Cartography and GIS Center,
University of Wisconsin-Milwaukee. © Lezlie S. Knox and Sean L. Field.

properties.[19] His lengthy descriptions may be exaggerated, since they
portray all the lost structures as *nobilissimi, antiquissimi, pulcherrimi*—
most noble, most ancient, intensely beautiful—and to such a degree that
they could never be rebuilt satisfactorily. Nonetheless, Pietro provided a
clear sense of how the Colonna hoped to impress and intimidate visitors to their massive palace in Palestrina. Its grand staircase had over
one hundred steps and was wide enough for a horse to ascend. A visitor

19. The document is transcribed in Ludwig Mohler, *Die Kardinäle Jakob und
Peter Colonna: Ein Beitrag zur Geschichte des Zeitalters Bonifaz' VIII* (Paderborn:
Schöningh, 1913), 215–18; see 216 for Palestrina and Mount Prenestino.

would arrive in an area shaped like a half circle or a letter C, which Pietro explained reflected the fact that the property had once been owned by the Roman emperor Julius Caesar. This visitor also could see a family chapel modeled after the Pantheon. In sum, the Palestrina of the Colonna was meant to be understood as a microcosm of imperial Rome. Such residences represent the places in which Margherita grew up before she left with her companions for the complex of houses the family owned on Mount Prenestino (which Boniface's troops also destroyed, as Pietro noted in the same document).

Although those buildings are gone, visual evidence of Colonna influence survives in many of Rome's major churches. The patronage of elite families enhanced the spiritual prestige of these institutions, even as family chapels, altars, and tombs promoted family interests with their ostentatious displays of heraldic devices.[20] By the second half of the thirteenth century, the Capitoline Hill, which included both the Senate and the Franciscan Church of Santa Maria in Aracoeli, served as a focus for many Roman elites.[21] The Orsini family crest appears on the exterior of the adjacent senatorial palace, while the Savelli's heraldry is on the Aracoeli itself directly outside one of their family chapels. Claudia Bolgia suggests that the height and perhaps the number of these chapels represented a competition similar to the contest to build higher towers attached to their family palaces. The Colonna seem to have regularly attended Mass at the Aracoeli and had several family chapels within the

---

20. This patronage has received significant attention from art historians. Julian Gardner, *The Roman Crucible: The Artistic Patronage of the Papacy, 1198–1304* (Chicago: University of Chicago Press, 2013), provides an excellent introduction to elite patronage in Rome and the surrounding countryside, as well as references to other studies, including Richard Krautheimer's classic *Rome: Profile of a City* (Princeton, NJ: Princeton University Press, 1980).

21. See Claudia Bolgia, "Ostentation, Power, and Family Competition in Late-Medieval Rome: The Earliest Chapels at S. Maria in Aracoeli," in *Aspects of Power and Authority in the Middle Ages*, ed. Brenda Bolton and Christine Meek (Turnhout: Brepols, 2007), 73–105. The Friars took over the Aracoeli in 1250 when they needed a larger (and more prominently located) site in Rome. Previously it had housed a community of Benedictine monks.

church.[22] Their decoration appears to have been a particular interest of Giovanni Colonna's. Dressed as a Roman magistrate, he appears in one mosaic with the Virgin and Child, John the Baptist, and St. Francis. Both family crest and inscription identify him.[23] He presumably appears in another donor portrait with the same saintly group in a chapel located to the right of the high altar.[24] This figure kneels in his senatorial robes (blue with a red mantle, topped with a collar and hat made from vair, a kind of variegated squirrel fur) in front of Francis, who presents him to the Madonna. The Aracoeli thus offered the Colonna a prominent location to demonstrate their influence on Rome's secular and spiritual institutions.

Certainly, the Colonna patronized other Roman churches as well.[25] In their own neighborhood, San Silvestro in Capite had both Colonna

---

22. Lady Altruda also attended masses there, which may be how Margherita came to know her. See *Vita I*, ch. 10.

23. "D[omi]N[u]S IOH[annes] DE COLU[m]PNA." See Bolgia, "Ostentation, Power," 77–79. This mosaic was removed from the church in the seventeenth century (when an inscription was added incorrectly dating it to 1228). Its original location is not clear, although Bolgia argues it was probably not the chapel on the left, where it was traditionally presumed to have been located. Donal Cooper and Janet Robson describe it as a retable, a framed piece that would have been above the altar table. See their *The Making of Assisi: The Pope, the Franciscans, and the Painting of the Basilica* (New Haven, CT: Yale University Press, 2013), 21.

24. There is no inscription on this mosaic, and we lack documentation to confirm his identity. Its dating and the donor's clothing effectively confirm that it represented Giovanni and not a member of the Capocci family who were later associated with this chapel. See Bolgia, "Ostentation, Power," 98–99. Giovanni also was buried in the Aracoeli after his death in 1292 or 1293, although his tomb is no longer extant.

25. Paul Binski provides a useful itinerary to Colonna symbols appearing throughout Rome in "Art Historical Reflections on the Fall of the Colonna, 1297," in *Rome across Time and Space: Cultural Transmission and the Exchange of Ideas, c. 500–1400*, ed. Claudia Bolgia, Rosamond McKitterick, and John Osborne (Cambridge: Cambridge University Press, 2011), 278–90; see also John Osborne, "A Possible Colonna Family Stemma in the Church of Santa Prassede in Rome," in *A Wider Trecento: Studies in Thirteenth- and Fourteenth-Century Art Presented to Julian Gardner*, ed. Louise Bordua and Robert Gibbs (Leiden: Brill, 2012), 21–31; and Serena Romano, "I Colonna a Roma: 1288–1297," in *La nobiltà romana nel medioevo:*

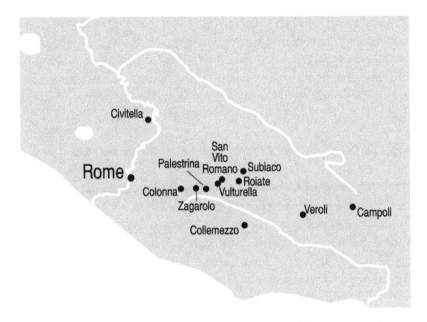

Map 2. Rome and its environs. The Colonna dominated the area around Palestrina. Map by Cartography and GIS Center, University of Wisconsin-Milwaukee. © Lezlie S. Knox and Sean L. Field.

and Orsini coats of arms on the transept, as well as family tombs that lined the walls.[26] But the most famous surviving example of Colonna patronage appears in the decoration of the important papal Church of Santa Maria Maggiore, whose refurbishment was begun by Pope Nicholas IV and continued by the Colonna cardinals after his death in

---

Atti del Convegno organizzato dall'École française de Rome e dall'Università degli studi di Roma "Tor Vergata" (Roma, 20–22 novembre 2003), ed. Sandro Carocci (Rome: École française de Rome 2006), 291–312. Outside of Rome, recent attention has focused on Colonna influence in the Basilica of Saint Francis in Assisi. See Rosalind Brooke, *The Image of Saint Francis: Responses to Sainthood in the Thirteenth Century* (Cambridge: Cambridge University Press, 2006), and Cooper and Robson, *Making of Assisi.*

26. These tombs have not survived, although the family heraldry is still present on the walls of the church. An early description regrettably only notes that numerous members of the family were entombed there. See Giuseppe Carletti,

1292.[27] Giacomo still appears with Nicholas IV on the apse mosaic, and both he and Pietro were on the now-lost facade mosaic.[28] While many of these projects began after her death, it is nevertheless important to imagine Margherita Colonna moving through a Rome whose monuments often displayed literal signs of her family's prominence and power.

FEMALE FRANCISCANS AND ROMAN RELIGIOUS WOMEN

This discussion of Colonna patronage has already demonstrated the family's interest in promoting and associating itself with the Franciscan order. Colonna ties to the Franciscans were deep and lasting. Margherita Orsini (mother of Margherita Colonna) could herself have known Francis of Assisi,[29] and her children evinced a deep attachment to the *Poverello*. Beyond spiritual affinities, this attachment translated into practical and public support for the order. For instance, the contemporary Franciscan chronicler Salimbene praised Giacomo Colonna as a committed

---

Memorie istorico-critiche della Chiesa e Monastero di S. Silvestro in Capite di Roma (Rome: Nella Stamperia Pilucchi Cracas, 1795), 99. This work was based on Carletti's visits to the church and to its archives, which he described as disorganized and sparse (ix), as well as on some earlier antiquarian accounts (again dismissed as confusing and poorly done).

27. In addition to Brooke, *Image of Saint Francis*, Cooper and Robson, *Making of Assisi*, and Gardner, *Roman Crucible*, see Gardner's early essay "Pope Nicholas IV and the Decoration of Santa Maria Maggiore," *Zeitschrift für Kunstgeschichte* 36 (1973): 1–50, which characterized Santa Maria Maggiore as a "Colonna church" because of both its location and the family's patronage. The Lateran similarly has been so characterized, particularly during the tenure of Pietro Colonna. The younger cardinal appeared in the apse mosaic (only a nineteenth-century copy survives), but prior to their conflict with Boniface VIII both Colonna cardinals supported Nicholas's renovations of the church. For the explicit Franciscanism of Nicholas's artistic program, see Cooper and Robson, *Making of Assisi*, 27–32.

28. A seventeenth-century sketch preserves a record of this design. See a reproduction of it in Cooper and Robson, *Making of Assisi*, 33.

29. *DV*, 101, citing ties between Senator Matteo Rosso Orsini and Francis. Echoed by Brentano, *Rome before Avignon*, 183.

friend of the order, recognizing his advocacy on its behalf.[30] Ample evidence from our texts indicates that Margherita's spirituality was strongly influenced by Franciscan models as well. One might therefore expect that both she and her family could have wished to see her become a formal member of a Franciscan community. By the early 1270s, as Margherita was rejecting the marriage Giovanni had planned for her, the landscape of "female Franciscanism" presented several possible paths for an aristocratic Italian woman.

Francis of Assisi's band of *Fratres minores* (Lesser Brothers or Friars Minor) had received papal approval for their new, apostolic life of wandering, poverty, and preaching before Francis's death in 1226 and canonization in 1228.[31] Women were as keen as men to follow the mendicant way of life. Some specifically identified or at least were labeled as *Sorores minores* (Lesser Sisters or Sisters Minor), spiritual sisters to the *Fratres minores*, raising questions for the church about whether women would be allowed to live the kind of active life among the poor that Francis's early followers had embodied.[32] Among the most ardent of Francis's early

---

30. The Latin is "Totaliter est amicus ordinis Fratrum Minorum." See Salimbene de Adam, *Cronica*, ed. Giuseppe Scalia (Turnhout: Brepols, 1999), 1:258; trans. Baird, Baglivi, and Kane, *Chronicle*, 160. Salimbene knew Giacomo during his student days at Bologna and even guided him on pilgrimage one May to Ravenna. Evidence for Giacomo's support for the more radical "Spiritual" wing of the Franciscan order is discussed below.

31. Most recent accounts of the Franciscan movement nuance rather than fundamentally shift the basic narrative outlined by John H. Moorman's *The History of the Franciscan Order from Its Origin to the Year 1517* (Oxford: Clarendon Press, 1968). Two recent biographical studies of Francis notably engage the problematic sources for early Franciscanism: Augustine Thompson, *Francis of Assisi: A New Biography* (Ithaca, NY: Cornell University Press, 2012), and André Vauchez, *Francis of Assisi: The Life and Afterlife of a Medieval Saint*, trans. Michael F. Cusato (New Haven, CT: Yale University Press, 2012). A more substantial challenge is posed by Amanda Power, "Reframing the Friars Minor: From Old Origins to New Beginnings," unpublished paper given at the Leeds International Medieval Congress, 2015.

32. The best-known description of the *Sorores minores* comes from a 1216 letter by Cardinal Jacques de Vitry. An English translation appears in Regis Armstrong, *The Lady: Clare of Assisi, Early Documents* (New York: New City Press, 2006),

followers was Clare, founder of a female community at San Damiano (outside Assisi) living an enclosed life but dedicated to absolute poverty. By the 1230s, Pope Gregory IX had tied Clare's community to a number of other houses as the Order of San Damiano.[33] But questions about enclosure, the women's relationship to the male Franciscans, and the role poverty should play in female Franciscan life caused controversy for decades. Clare died in 1253 and was quickly canonized in 1255 as the papacy sought to mold her image into that of a more traditional enclosed nun. This process culminated in Pope Urban IV's creation of the Order of St. Clare in 1263. The cardinal protector for the Franciscans at this point was in fact none other than Giangaetano Orsini (future pope Nicholas III), nephew of Margherita Orsini and cousin to Margherita Colonna. The rule that he helped craft for the Order of St. Clare insisted on enclosure but did not embrace the kind of poverty for which Clare had fought. After 1263 (when Margherita Colonna would have been about eight years old), the Order of St. Clare thus represented the papally sponsored mainstream of female Franciscan life.[34]

427–28. For a discussion of what this letter does and does not tell us about early Franciscanism, see Catherine M. Mooney, "The 'Lesser Sisters' in Jacques de Vitry's 1216 Letter," *Franciscan Studies* 69 (2011): 1–29.

33. This "order" came into existence through the efforts of the papal curia, and especially Cardinal Hugolino dei Segni (who would become Pope Gregory IX). Only some of the female communities had an affiliation with the Franciscan Friars, and few of them saw Clare's foundation at San Damiano as their model. See Catherine M. Mooney, *Clare of Assisi and the Thirteenth-Century Church: Religious Women, Rules, and Resistance* (Philadelphia: University of Pennsylvania Press, 2016); Maria Pia Alberzoni, *Clare of Assisi and the Poor Sisters in the Thirteenth Century* (St. Bonaventure: Franciscan Institute Publications, 2004); Maria Pia Alberzoni, *La nascita di un'istituzione: L'Ordine di S. Damiano nel XIII secolo* (Milan: Edizioni CUSL, 1996); and Lezlie S. Knox, *Creating Clare of Assisi: Female Franciscan Identities in Later Medieval Italy* (Leiden: Brill, 2008), 19–55.

34. In addition to the studies cited in the previous note, see Lezlie Knox, "The *Form of Life* of the Poor Ladies," in *The Writings of Clare of Assisi: Letters, Form of Life, Testament and Blessing*, ed. Michael W. Blastic, Jay M. Hammond, and J. A. Wayne Hellmann (St. Bonaventure, NY: Franciscan Institute Publications, 2011), 59–104 (with references to other studies of the Sisters' forms of life).

There were still, however, other options for Franciscan-inspired religious women. For one thing, just before her death Clare herself had obtained approval for her own "form of life," which insisted on absolute poverty for San Damiano. But very few other houses were granted permission to follow it, and scant evidence survives to suggest that many others sought to do so.[35] Even the Sisters of San Damiano abandoned it when they moved inside the city walls of Assisi and occupied the new Basilica of Santa Chiara. A further option was the Order and Rule of the *Sorores minores inclusae*. This rule (as already noted) had been created by Isabelle of France, sister of King Louis IX of France, together with a team of Franciscan masters of theology at the University of Paris, and had been granted final approval in 1263. It avoided the issue of poverty, focusing instead on the ideal of humility and an institutional identity grounded in the name *Sorores minores*, with tighter ties forged between male and female Franciscans (this was the rule that San Silvestro in Capite would eventually profess).[36] Finally, and most critically for understanding Margherita Colonna's vocation, all over Europe, but particularly in Italy, various Franciscan-inspired holy women lived outside any formal order or rule at all.[37] These penitents might be pious single women or widows living in family homes; powerful patronesses (such as

---

35. Clare of Assisi and Agnes of Prague seem to have been exceptional figures in their emphasis on poverty as the central question for female monasticism, but for a perspective centered on their priorities see Joan Mueller, *The Privilege of Poverty: Clare of Assisi, Agnes of Prague, and the Struggle for a Franciscan Rule for Women* (University Park: Pennsylvania State University Press, 2006).

36. For Isabelle of France in a Franciscan context, see Sean L. Field, *Isabelle of France: Capetian Sanctity and Franciscan Identity in the Thirteenth Century* (Notre Dame, IN: University of Notre Dame Press, 2006); on her rules specifically, see Sean L. Field, *The Rules of Isabelle of France: An English Translation with Introductory Study* (St. Bonaventure, NY: Franciscan Institute Publications, 2014), as well as Jacques Dalarun, Sean L. Field, Jean-Baptiste Lebigue, and Anne-Françoise Leurquin-Labie, eds., *Isabelle de France, soeur de Saint Louis: Une princesse mineure* (Paris: Éditions franciscaines, 2014).

37. See Darleen Pryds, *Women of the Streets: Early Franciscan Women and Their Mendicant Vocation* (St. Bonaventure, NY: Franciscan Institute, 2010); and Luigi Pellegrini, "Female Religious Experience and Society in Thirteenth-Century Italy," in *Monks and Nuns, Saints and Outcasts: Religion in Medieval Society. Essays in Honor*

Isabelle of France) who lived at or near their foundations without taking canonical vows; or small groups living under the spiritual care of sympathetic Friars. Some of these lay religious women were even venerated as saints, albeit informally and in local contexts.[38]

Within this range of options, Margherita's brothers apparently wanted to place her in an existing Franciscan nunnery or to establish a new one for her. The idea of having Margherita enter the best-known female Franciscan community in Italy, Santa Chiara in Assisi, clearly appealed to the family.[39] Had Margherita gone down this path, the Colonna could have devoted well-publicized patronage to the Basilica of Santa Chiara, as they did for the Basilica of San Francesco. When it became clear that this possibility would not materialize, perhaps the next best option was to keep Margherita closer at hand, in the Eternal City itself. In that case, the Colonna could have tried to place her at the existing female Franciscan community in Rome, San Cosimato in Trastevere, which had been founded in 1233. But there is no evidence that they seriously considered this idea, perhaps because San Cosimato lay outside of the Colonna neighborhoods of the city and would have presented problems as an effective site for family patronage.[40] Instead, the Colonna

---

of Lester K. Little, ed. Sharon Farmer and Barbara H. Rosenwein (Ithaca, NY: Cornell University Press, 2000), 97–122.

38. The best-known examples of these women in the Italian context and Franciscan orbit include Umiliana Cerchi (d. 1246), Rose of Viterbo (d. 1253), and Margherita of Cortona (d. 1297). Of the three, only Rose had a canonization process during the thirteenth century, and it was abandoned after the death of Clare of Assisi. The bibliography on each woman is fairly extensive, but two good article-length introductions are Bernard Schlager, "Foundresses of Franciscan Life: Umiliana Cerchi and Margaret of Cortona," *Viator* 29 (1998): 141–66, and André Vauchez, "Female Sanctity and the Franciscan Movement," in *The Laity in the Middle Ages: Religious Beliefs and Devotional Practices*, ed. Daniel E. Bornstein (Notre Dame, IN: University of Notre Dame Press, 1993), 171–84.

39. Keyvanian, *Hospitals and Urbanism*, 266, asserts that Margherita's brothers wanted her to enter San Silvestro in Capite. But in fact San Silvestro was a male Benedictine monastery until after Margherita's death.

40. *BF*, 1:112; Brentano, *Rome before Avignon*, 247 and following. We know of no evidence for patronage of this house by the Colonna, who directed their support to San Silvestro in Capite and a later daughter community, San Lorenzo in

seem to have envisioned sponsoring a new Roman foundation, which could have furthered their sister's religious vocation while providing a freshly visible demonstration of the family's support for the Franciscan order. Indeed, the family did develop exactly this kind of relationship to San Silvestro in Capite once Margherita's followers eventually moved there in 1285.[41] But this move occurred only after Margherita's death. Why did she not enter or found a Franciscan nunnery herself?

In fact, the texts strongly suggest that Margherita identified with the more active life of charity and service to the poor represented by Francis and his early followers, rather than with the enclosed life of the Sisters of the Order of St. Clare. In all likelihood, Margherita never became a Franciscan nun because that was simply not the life she sought. Perhaps her family encouraged the possible move to Santa Chiara, and Margherita decided against it. It was probably her brothers who assumed that in that case a more formal monastery should be constructed on her behalf—hence Giovanni's expression of personal and family shame at having to admit that this had never been accomplished (*Vita I*, ch. 9). Margherita herself sought out situations, first at Vulturella, next with Lady Altruda of the Poor in Rome, and finally with her followers on Mount Prenestino, where an unenclosed life outside the formal church

---

Panisperna (discussed below), on the Quirinale Hill. Other Clarissan houses—i.e., houses that professed the 1263 Rule of St. Clare—existed throughout the countryside outside Rome. See Mariano d'Alatri, "Gli insediamenti Francescani del Duecento nella custodia di Campagna," *Collectanea Franciscana* 47 (1977): 297–316 (although he considered Margherita's community as more formally constituted than it was during her lifetime).

41. See Giulia Barone, "Margherita Colonna e le Clarisse di S. Silvestro in Capite," in *Roma Anno 1300: Atti della IV Settimana di Studi di storia dell'arte medievale dell'Università di Roma "La Sapienza" (19–24 maggio 1980)*, ed. Angiola Maria Romanini (Rome: L'Erma di Bretschneider, 1983), 799–805. Many of the house's fourteenth-century abbesses were surnamed Colonna. Of course, intermarriage presents the possibility that those named Conti or Annibaldi were also relatives. Of the two abbesses identified by geographical names, it seems noteworthy that they came from the Colonna patrimony. See the list in Étienne Hubert, "Économie de la propriété immobilière: Les établissements religieux et leurs patrimoines aux XIVe siècle," in *Rome aux XIIIe et XIVe siècles: Cinq études*, ed. Étienne Hubert (Rome: École française de Rome 1993), 177–229, at 188n34.

hierarchy allowed her to use family resources to aid the poor. In the end, her family must have been persuaded to follow her wishes.

It is thus historically inaccurate to represent Margherita Colonna as a Franciscan nun, even though this identification has persisted since the end of the Middle Ages.[42] Instead, her status as an unenclosed, charismatic holy woman leading a spiritual group in contact with the world needs to be recognized as representative of a particular interpretation of Franciscan life. Indeed, Brother Bartholomeo of Gallicano's vision in *Vita II* (ch. 17), in which Margherita appears with Clare of Assisi and Filippa Mareri, another noncloistered holy woman whose small community was affiliated with the Franciscans, serves as a reminder that an insistence on distinguishing between professed nuns and unenclosed holy women can obscure contemporary spiritual affinities.

Margherita Colonna's semireligious way of life also reflected Rome's long local tradition of independent female religious institutions. In the early thirteenth century, there were only seven formal convents in Rome. Brenda Bolton, who has studied these foundations, describes them generally as independent, uncloistered, and fairly small.[43] They were much like the semireligious beguines that Jacques de Vitry had admired in northern Europe and whose way of life he recognized in other small and semireligious communities throughout central Italy. In Rome, these penitents were often called *bizoke* or *pinzochere*. Some might live as enclosed urban recluses,[44] but many, such as Lady Altruda, whose household plays a key role in *Vita I*, were active in the bustling streets of Rome.

---

42. For example, Mariano of Florence's 1519 history described her as a "sora di sancta Chiara" (Sister of Saint Clare). On Mariano, see Knox, *Creating Clare of Assisi*, esp. 144–55, and the discussion at the end of this introduction.

43. Brenda Bolton, "Daughters of Rome: All One in Christ Jesus," *Studies in Church History* 27 (1992): 117–30.

44. For example, Prassede, a Roman recluse who entered a cell in Rome in the first years of the thirteenth century, knew Francis of Assisi personally, had ties to important churchmen, and then benefited from the saint's miraculous cure after his death. The earliest version of this miracle story has recently been recovered. See Jacques Dalarun, *The Rediscovered Life of St. Francis of Assisi, [by] Thomas of Celano*, trans. Timothy J. Johnson (St. Bonaventure, NY: Franciscan Institute Publications,

Unlike some other Italian female penitents, these Roman women often seem to have been less motivated by extreme asceticism or the personal embrace of apostolic poverty than by a desire to serve Christ through helping the poor. Nonetheless, their extracommunitarial status did make the institutional church uncomfortable. Early in the thirteenth century, first St. Dominic and then Pope Innocent III attempted to regularize Rome's female houses. Innocent, in fact, made plans for the Dominican foundation of San Sisto to serve as a sort of giant convent (with sixty or more nuns, whereas most Roman nunneries had fewer than ten women), which would be strictly enclosed.[45] But even as San Sisto's prestige grew, these independent, open communities persisted. The spiritual landscape of Margherita's Rome was notably receptive to informal female religious life.[46]

In sum, Margherita's family clearly admired her Franciscan-inspired religious vocation but ultimately allowed her to realize it outside the walls of any formal convent. After her death, her brothers also seem to have recognized a new opportunity to shape her memory and promote her as a saint. They did this first and foremost by writing and sponsoring the two extant hagiographies.

2016), 51. Prassede's name and the fact that she lived in Rome are supplied only in the more developed version included later in Celano's *Treatise on Miracles* (ca. 1250), #181.

45. San Sisto has received significant attention from scholars (thanks in part to numerous surviving documents, a chronicle, and other writings). A good orientation to that community and relevant bibliography is Anne L. Clark, "Under Whose Care? The Madonna of San Sisto and Women's Monastic Life in Twelfth- and Thirteenth-Century Rome," in *Medieval Constructions in Gender and Identity: Essays in Honor of Joan M. Ferrante*, ed. Teodolinda Barolini (Tempe: Arizona Center for Medieval and Renaissance Studies, 2005), 29–42.

46. This openness continued into the fourteenth and fifteen centuries, as recent research by James Palmer is demonstrating. He presented "Women, Religion, and Community in Late Medieval Rome" at the 2016 New College Conference on Medieval and Renaissance Studies. This research builds on his work in "Gold, Grain, and Grace: Piety and Community in Late Medieval Rome" (PhD diss., Washington University, 2015).

THE TWO "LIVES" OF MARGHERITA COLONNA: DATING, AUTHORSHIP, AND COMPOSITION

The *Life of the Blessed Virgin Margherita, of the Family Name Colonna* (referred to here as *Vita I* for the sake of convenience) evidently was written after Margherita Colonna's death and before the formal organization of San Silvestro in Capite, hence between early 1281 and fall 1285. Because the final two miracles (chs. 17 and 18) give the impression of some stretch of time having elapsed since Margherita's burial, the text's editor, Livarius Oliger, suggested that a date around 1282–83 seemed most likely. This reasoning was sensible, but it is also distinctly possible that the work could have been begun almost immediately in 1281, with the final miracles being added slightly later.

Oliger was also the first to arrive at the surprising conclusion that the author of *Vita I* was none other than Senator Giovanni Colonna. Far more expected would be a life written by a Franciscan confessor. If a member of Margherita's own family were going to compose a *vita*, certainly her spiritual adviser Cardinal Giacomo would have been the obvious candidate. But in fact, Oliger's identification of Giovanni Colonna as the author of *Vita I* is correct beyond any reasonable doubt. The dedicatory letter to *Vita II* actually provides some of the clearest evidence for this assertion, since it is evidently addressed to Cardinal Giacomo Colonna and states specifically that his older brother Giovanni has already written a life of Margherita. The possibility that the life referred to there might not be identical with the surviving *Vita I* is negated by a number of passages in the latter that equate Giovanni with the first-person author of the text.[47]

Given that *Vita I* was composed by Margherita's own brother, it is worth noting that Giovanni was writing in the immediate aftermath of one of the peaks of Colonna power. During the reign of their cousin Pope Nicholas III (1277–80) Giacomo had been made a cardinal (1278) and Giovanni had served as senator of Rome (1279/1280), but Nicholas

---

47. See particularly chapters 9, 15, and 16, where our notes draw attention to this evidence.

had died a few months before Margherita. Giovanni may have begun writing in the uncertain interim before the election of the (French) pope Martin IV in February 1281, and he surely completed his text before Martin's death (March 1285). The 1281–85 window for the text's composition thus coincided with a reshuffling of the Roman political cards that momentarily left Giovanni somewhat removed from the center of power.[48]

Giovanni Colonna based a large portion of his text on his own observations and recollections, sometimes explicitly noting his eyewitness status. Very likely Giacomo provided his firsthand perspective as well. Giovanni was not an experienced author, and sometimes his text threatens to escape his control as he veers back and forth across the chronological course of events to include anecdotes as they occur to him. Moreover, the work at times has a distinctly unfinished feel. This quality is most obvious in chapter 6, where a note concerning two accidentally omitted miracles indicates an unrealized intention to revise. Nor is the author's Latin a model of elegance or economy, to put it charitably. And yet the text is not merely a preliminary or haphazard collection of memories. Giovanni, for example, frequently shapes his narrative by including chapter endings that point back to the moral of the preceding material and chapter introductions that point forward to the contents to come.

Giovanni Colonna's text is loaded with biblical and liturgical allusions, which may seem surprising for a layman. But—beyond the possibility of some "ghostwriting" by Cardinal Giacomo or another clerical associate—most of these passages would have been known to a pious, literate Christian from breviary readings, Marian hymns, offices for popular early martyr-saints (such as Cecilia, Margaret, Agnes, and Catherine), and the liturgies and legends of the more recent saints Clare and Francis of Assisi. Giovanni also employs a number of Latin maxims that are quoted by earlier church authors such as St. Ambrose, but these may

---

48. Keyvanian, *Hospitals and Urbanism*, 267, makes the interesting suggestion that *Vita I* was written specifically to convince Honorius IV to hand over San Silvestro in Capite to the Colonna (she actually alludes to both *vitae* and to Biblioteca Casanatense ms. 104, though *Vita II* was not yet written and the manuscript dates from the fourteenth century).

well have been known to him at second hand rather than as a result of deep reading in the church fathers.

The narrative of *Vita I* is at heart propelled by a series of interlocking visions experienced by Margherita, Giacomo, Giovanni, and others. Indeed, one might think of the text as essentially a compilation of visions strung together by Giovanni Colonna's commentary. The very first vision (ch. 2) was in fact experienced (and presumably reported) by Giacomo Colonna, as he saw Margherita carried through the air by two angels. And Margherita's decision to embrace a life of chastity (ch. 3) was confirmed when the Virgin Mary appeared to her in a chariot as she slept. After Margherita had left Giovanni's home and begun her informal community at the family compound on Mount Prenestino (ch. 6), one of her brothers came to try to convince her to return home and marry, in accordance with her station. But this brother had a dream in which he was threatened with death if he attempted to carry out his intention. These examples demonstrate the ways visions are often as much about interactions between the Colonna siblings as a group as they are uniquely about Margherita.

The visions could thus sometimes serve as textual reinforcements of family solidarity. For example, when Margherita went to Vulturella to try to dedicate herself as an oblate (ch. 9), Giacomo sought her return. When Margherita refused, it was Giovanni who next set out to retrieve her. But the Virgin then appeared to Margherita and advised her to depart, thus putting her in accord with her two brothers' desires. Visions serve other functions in the text as well, for instance helping to establish Margherita's Franciscan identity, as when Margherita saw a "certain preacher" whom she identified as St. Francis and adopted as her spiritual model (ch. 6). Or they underscore Margherita's authority to pronounce on religious questions, as when a vision (ch. 8) settled a question she and Giacomo had been debating concerning Doubting Thomas and the wounds of Christ.

The long chapter 12 stands as in some ways the center of the text, bringing together multiple visions by several actors (in a fashion that is sometimes rather challenging to follow). It provides a good example for the way dreams and apparitions circle and swirl around each other in this work. Giovanni's main source for this series of visions is clearly Margherita's group of female followers, and one woman in particular who is described as having taken leadership of the community after Margherita's death—quite possibly Stefania (author of *Vita II*, see below). At the Feast of St. John in the last year of Margherita's life (24 June 1280), this Sister witnessed a pilgrim with a fiery face, who came begging alms. This vision caused Margherita herself to recall an earlier vision in which Giacomo had beseeched Christ for mercy, which led her to realize that this pilgrim similarly could be identified as Christ. Giacomo was not present for these events, yet when he heard this story he upbraided the Sisters for not showing sufficient honor to Christ. The first Sister then experienced another supernatural visit from the pilgrim, and Margherita miraculously knew of it even though the Sister had not wanted to admit it. The pilgrim next appeared to Giacomo, who failed to recognize the divine visitor and so did not honor Him as he should have. Margherita's brother hence learned his lesson about criticizing the Sisters. And all this was confirmed by another vision in which the first Sister saw Giacomo and the pilgrim locked bodily together. The figure of the pilgrim (Christ) thus becomes a focal point upon which these varying figures pin their spiritual and practical desires.

As Margherita neared the end of her life in December 1280, the time of her death was miraculously revealed to her (ch. 14), and she experienced a series of visions of Mary and the Magi on Christmas Day. Giovanni, with Giacomo and other members of the family, was at her deathbed and then her burial at the Church of San Pietro on Mount Prenestino (ch. 15). Indeed, Giovanni Colonna describes himself as feeling his sins roll off of him at that moment because of his sister's intervention. And one evening shortly thereafter Giacomo had a vision of his sister in glory with a group of saints.

Giovanni concludes his text with a small group of miracles (chs. 16–18). The first actually concerns himself, as he begins to tell of a vision involving a king. Unfortunately, there is a lacuna in the text here. It is unclear not only exactly what point Giovanni wishes to relate with this vision, but also how much other material might now be lost. When the text resumes, it recounts three miracles told by an older, married man. One concerns a vision at the Church of San Pietro on Mount Prenestino; the other two are healing miracles concerning himself and his wife.

In sum, Giovanni Colonna wrote to offer a case for his sister's sanctity. He portrayed her as a visionary whose actions were miraculously approved by the Virgin and by Christ. He emphasized her charitable work in the world and her intention to join or found a more stable monastic community. On this last point, however, one suspects that Giovanni purposely glossed over Margherita's own perspective on her unenclosed religious life. As discussed above, the evidence suggests that Margherita herself did not desire the life of an enclosed nun. The basic trajectory of her religious development moves from rejection of marriage to a pious life with like-minded women based on Mount Prenestino and solidified by the adoption of a Franciscan-inspired form of dress but without a formal religious profession. Her own choices veered always toward an active religious life in the world. Giovanni's strategy may have been to acknowledge that fact while framing it as a result of the insurmountable obstacles that kept her from adopting a more traditional religious role in a nunnery.

A second hagiographic narrative was composed a few years later. Since it refers to Pietro Colonna (Giovanni's son; Margherita's nephew) as cardinal, it must have been composed, or at least completed, after Pietro was named to that office in May 1288. And because Giovanni himself is referred to as though he is still alive, the text must date from before about April 1292 (certainly before the end of 1294). The dedicatory letter shows that the text was commissioned by Cardinal Giacomo Colonna, and it reveals the author's name as "Stefania." Although this woman's precise identity remains uncertain, the outlines of her relationship to Margherita and the Colonna family seem clear.

In her dedicatory letter, Stefania describes herself as "presiding over our... band of Sisters, and the whole gathering entrusted to me." Assuming that the dating given above is correct, the phrasing would suggest that Stefania must have held a leadership role at San Silvestro in Capite, the formal Franciscan community founded at Rome by Margherita's followers in 1285. And indeed Stefania presents herself at several points in her own text as Margherita's successor to leadership of the band of women gathered around her.[49]

---

49. For example, chapters 3 and 7.

One might therefore assume that Stefania was abbess of San Silvestro. But no "Stefania" appears in any capacity in the published registers for San Silvestro up to 1300.[50] The only abbess of San Silvestro known between 1285 and 1293 is "Herminia," who appears in that role in documents from 1285 to July 1288, and again in 1293.[51] Oliger suggested that this difficulty might be gotten around if "Stefania" and "Herminia" were actually one and the same person; but because there is no evidence that the nuns of San Silvestro adopted new "religious" names upon their professions, we regard this hypothesis as unlikely.[52] Oliger also suggested that Stefania might have held the office of "president" at San Silvestro, on the basis of the use of the Latin word *praesidens* in her self-description ("presiding over our ... band of Sisters," as referred to above). "President" was an office unique to the Rule of the *Sorores minores*, providing a "second in command" who could step in if an abbess was unable to carry out her duties. But because Stefania's language here is actually taken directly from an earlier source (discussed below) written centuries before the Rule of the *Sorores minores* came into existence, the appearance of the Latin word *praesidens* in her text probably cannot be taken to refer to that specific office.[53]

What, then, was Stefania's likely role at San Silvestro? One possibility is that she was indeed abbess, serving a term sometime between 1288 and 1292, since this is the interval when no documentary evidence

---

50. Oliger further indicated he had searched the unpublished records in the Archivio di Stato at Rome up to 1330 and could find no record of her.

51. Vincenzo Federici, "Regesto del monastero di S. Silvestro de Capite," *Archivio della Società romana di storia patria* 22 (1899): 418–23. For a partial list of abbesses up to 1400, see Hubert, "Économie," 188n36. On the history of the archives of San Silvestro, see Antonio Montefusco, "Secondo: Non conservare. Per una ricostruzione dell'archivio del monastero di San Silvestro in Capite a Roma," *Archivio della Società Romana di Storia Patria* 135 (2012): 5–29.

52. For instance, Margherita's nieces Barbara and Giovanna retained their given names in documents that referred to them after they professed at San Silvestro in Capite.

53. It is true that Stefania could, conceivably, have chosen the passage precisely because it did contain vocabulary that by chance reflected her status as president. This possibility, however, seems remote.

reveals the name of the abbess and coincidentally also exactly the window for the text's composition. Another might be that Stefania's text began earlier than is usually supposed, before 1285, with the section that mentions Cardinal Pietro Colonna being added after 1288. In that case she could have written her dedicatory letter while exercising informal leadership of Margherita's followers at Mount Prenestino, before Herminia's election as first abbess of San Silvestro in 1285. Some support for that idea might be found in the fact that chapter 12 of *Vita I* draws its evidence from a Sister who is said to be leading the surviving band of Margherita's followers. The description, which must predate 1285, is similar to the way Stefania refers to herself in her dedicatory letter.

Perhaps Stefania held no formal office at all, but as a senior figure among the Sisters at San Silvestro, and as a woman who had been close to Margherita Colonna, she felt comfortable describing herself as entrusted with some kind of responsibility for the wider group. Reinforcing this interpretation is Oliger's further suggestion that Stefania was likely related to Margherita Colonna. Not only were a number of the early nuns of San Silvestro from the Colonna family, but the name Stefano was common for males in several branches of the family (one of Senator Giovanni Colonna's sons, for example, was named Stefano). It would not be unexpected to encounter the female analogue, just as Giovanni/Giovanna and Giacomo/Giacoma were used by the Colonna across several generations. Moreover, numerous episodes in her text reveal Stefania's privileged access not only to Margherita but to her brothers.[54] Thus it is reasonable to picture Stefania as the cousin, the niece, or even just possibly the sister of her subject.[55] If so, a status as senior member of

---

54. Perhaps the strongest example is in chapter 28, where Stefania personally convinces Giacomo Colonna to rest after three days of vigil at his sister's sickbed.

55. Stefania has Margherita addressing her as "dearest sister" in chapter 3; but because her followers were referred to as Sisters, this cannot be taken as certain evidence of a biological relationship. Stefania also several times has Margherita referring to "our brothers" (e.g., ch. 7) in a fashion that should be grammatically distinct in the Latin from "my brothers" and thus could be taken to include Stefania in the sibling relationship; again one should be cautious because of Stefania's rather imprecise Latin. No genealogical source lists a "Stefania" among Margherita's siblings, or

the Colonna family at San Silvestro might have been enough to lend her an air of authority, whether or not she held any formal office.

If Stefania was in fact the Sister who had provided Giovanni Colonna with much of his information for the long chapter 12 in *Vita I*, then it might have made particular sense for Giacomo Colonna to turn to his (possible) kinswoman for further evidence about his sister's sanctity. Moreover, the timing here may not be coincidental. As the Colonna sought to promote Margherita's cult, the reign of their close ally Pope Nicholas IV (Jerome of Ascoli) from 1288 to 1292 offered the opportunity to solicit support at the highest levels of the church. But if the family was feeling some urgency, why did Giacomo himself not write about the sister with whom he had such close personal and spiritual ties? Perhaps his ecclesiastical responsibilities occupied him, but it seems equally possible that he was confident in Stefania's ability to represent his sister's holiness. Indeed, her text was probably meant to gather more material in preparation for a serious attempt at canonization hearings. Stefania in fact presented her work in just this way, as something added to (and certainly not superseding) Giovanni's *Vita I*.

As Oliger noted long ago, Stefania's Latin is very uneven, and the text was evidently put together in several sections and stages. But what neither Oliger nor any other previous scholar has realized is that the unevenness and the apparent *verbosità* of some chapters result not from floundering attempts at a flowery Latin style but from Stefania's wholesale textual borrowings from multiple sources.[56] Most notably, she adapts entire sections from Gregory IX's canonization bulls for two of the thirteenth century's emblematic saints, Elizabeth of Hungary and Francis of

---

anywhere on the Colonna family tree. Because daughters were not always well documented, the lack of evidence does not preclude the idea that Stefania was related to some branch of the Colonna, and the possibility of a sibling relationship to Margherita does not seem completely out of the question.

56. These borrowings receive a full textual demonstration in Sean L. Field, "The Sources and Significance of Stefania's *New Statement on Margherita Colonna*," forthcoming in *The Sacred and the Sinister*, ed. David J. Collins.

Assisi.[57] She also draws extensively on the popular *Collationes* of John Cassian (d. ca. 430),[58] on a twelfth-century letter falsely attributed to Odo of Cluny,[59] on a prayer more persuasively credited to Odilon of Cluny,[60] and on a letter to a nun written by the twelfth-century bishop Arnulf of Lisieux.[61]

Once these borrowings are recognized, Stefania's actual composition process comes into focus. Her first two chapters are prefatory material. Chapter 1 is simply the dedicatory letter to Giacomo Colonna. Here, searching for appropriately impressive language, Stefania first draws on

---

57. For Elizabeth of Hungary's canonization bull, see Leo Santifaller, "Zur Originalüberlieferung der Heiligsprechungsurkunde der Landgräfin Elisabeth von Thüringen vom Jahre 1235," in *Acht Jahrhunderte Deutscher Orden in Einzeldarstellungen: Festschrift zu Ehren Sr. Exzellenz P. Dr. Marian Tumler O.T. anlässlich seines 80. Geburtstages,* ed. Klemens Wieser (Bad Godesberg: Verlag Wissenschaftliches Archiv, 1967), 73–85; English translation in Nesta de Robeck, *Saint Elizabeth of Hungary: A Story of Twenty-Four Years* (Milwaukee, WI: Bruce, 1954), 200–203. For Francis's canonization bull, see *BF*, 1:42–44; English translation in Regis J. Armstrong, J. A. Wayne Hellmann, and William J. Short, *Francis of Assisi: Early Documents* (New York: New City Press, 1999), 1:565.

58. John Cassian, *Collationes XXIIII,* ed. Gottfried Kreuz and Michael Petschenig, 2nd ed. (Vienna: Verlag der Österreichischen Akademie der Wissenschaften, 2004), Corpus scriptorum ecclesiasticorum Latinorum 13 (Conlationum pars secunda, sive conlationes XI–XVII: Praefatio), 311–12; English translation in John Cassian, *The Conferences,* trans. Boniface Ramsey (New York: Newman Press, 1997), 399.

59. Second dedicatory letter to the *De reversione beati Martini a Burgundia,* falsely attributed to Abbot Odo of Cluny but actually written in the mid-twelfth century. Edited by André Salmon, "De reversione beati Martini a Burgundia tractatus," in *Supplément au chroniques de Touraine* (Tours, 1856), xi–xxviii, 14–34, at 16–17.

60. "Un opuscule inédit de saint Odilon de Cluny," *Revue bénédictine* 16 (1899): 477–78 (the article is unsigned).

61. Frank Barlow, ed., *The Letters of Arnulf of Lisieux* (London: Royal Historical Society, 1939), 7–9 (letter "Ad G. monialem"); English translation in Carolyn Poling Schriber, *The Letter Collections of Arnulf of Lisieux* (Lewiston, NY: Edwin Mellen, 1997), 27–30. On this letter, and Stefania's use of it, see Anne L. Clark, "From Anonymity to a New Identity: A Twelfth-Century Letter to a Nun and Its Hagiographic Afterlife," paper given at the International Medieval Congress at Leeds, 2016.

John Cassian but then mainly adapts pseudo-Odo of Cluny's dedicatory letter, which was supposedly written to Fulk the Good, Count of Anjou, concerning the translation of St. Martin of Tours. Then, to lead into her main text, her second chapter uses nearly word-for-word quotations from Elizabeth of Hungary's canonization bull. In a sense, Stefania is boldly "precanonizing" Margherita by lending her St. Elizabeth's attributes. Chapter 2 does make brief reference to Giovanni Colonna's early attempts to find a husband for Margherita but embeds them in further wholesale borrowing, primarily from Arnulf of Lisieux's letter to a nun.

As Stefania turns to her own recollections, an initial section (chs. 3–5) concerns Margherita's teachings to her followers and a vision in the days leading up to Christmas 1280. Stefania punctuates this first cluster of recollections with a chapter (6) that simply—and audaciously!—replaces Francis of Assisi with Margherita in Francis's canonization bull. Making only small changes of gender and circumstance as necessary, Stefania again tacitly declares Margherita's sanctity and even hints at her apocalyptic significance by putting her in Francis's place amid the laudatory rhetoric of Gregory IX's praise for the founder of the *Fratres minores*. A second narrative sequence (chs. 7–8) focuses on Margherita's final illness. It is then likewise brought home with a chapter (9) that again puts Margherita in place of Elizabeth of Hungary in Elizabeth's canonization bull. This chapter ends with the statement that the author will now turn to some of Margherita's miracles, adding an "Amen" to give a sense of closure. There follow six brief miracles (chs. 10–15) witnessed by people from the surrounding area. Thus it seems likely that this opening "death and miracles" sequence (chs. 3–15) formed a discrete stage of composition.[62]

Next come three visions concerning Margherita (chs. 16–19). The first was experienced (on 7 January 1281) by Stefania herself; the second by a Franciscan brother, Bartholomeo; and the third by Margherita's unnamed older sister. These visions are followed (chs. 19–20) by a

---

62. The layout of the unique manuscript supports this interpretation, since four blank lines are left at the end of the page following the "Amen." In "From Anonymity," Clark suggested that perhaps *Vita II* was intended to provide readings for a liturgical office dedicated to Margherita.

summation and by Stefania's prayer to Margherita, the latter adapted from Odilon of Cluny. Again, quoting from an earlier, authoritative text marks a closing point.

The rest of the *vita* seems to suddenly restore Margherita to life. A story dated April 1280 may well have been told to Stefania by Giovanni or Giacomo Colonna (ch. 21), and a brief vision experienced by Margherita does not indicate a source (ch. 22). At last the final chapters (chs. 23–31) retell the story of Margherita's death from Stefania's eyewitness perspective, except that she unexpectedly inserts another posthumous miracle (ch. 25). Thus it would seem that after completing a first pass through Margherita's "life and miracles" (chs. 1–15) Stefania decided that a more detailed version of some of these events was still necessary, and so added her additional visions and deathbed recollections as a second stage of composition (chs. 16–31).[63]

The text as it is transmitted in the unique manuscript is not complete, breaking off in midsentence. It is possible that very little of the original text has been lost. But there are also some remarkable omissions in the text. Since Stefania completed her text after 1288, it is quite notable that no mention is made of the foundation of San Silvestro in 1285, and nothing is said of Margherita's remains being translated there at that time. Thus a substantial last section of the original work could be lost.[64]

Stefania clearly had access to *Vita I*, but she never quotes from it or (after the introductory "Letter") refers to it directly. In part, Stefania evidently saw her new work as complementing Giovanni's, adding memories where she, her Sisters, and others had fresh material to contribute. Yet she just as surely had her own, more ambitious agenda. For example, her use of the canonization bulls for Elizabeth and Francis lends Margherita's life a much larger importance, placing Margherita in

---

63. This interpretation could lend weight to any possible hypothesis that might date the dedicatory letter to before 1288 (since the reference to Pietro Colonna achieving the cardinalate comes only in the second section).

64. Or perhaps the story of her translation and miracles associated with her Roman tomb were recorded in a separate document that was lost and never brought together with these two independent texts.

the context of God's overarching plan for humanity. Moreover, Stefania's portrait centers more on Margherita's relationship to her spiritual Sisters and less on her biological brothers. Above all, Stefania's own closeness to the saint shines through, highlighting her own active role in questioning and interpreting Margherita. In this text, Margherita does not just report visions; she "unlocks" them to Stefania, who describes herself as "joined to her by the bond of overflowing love" (ch. 4). Moreover, Margherita's visions sometimes predict Stefania's future role as leader of the community (ch. 7).

Indeed, in a number of places, Stefania seems to tacitly contradict Giovanni's earlier account. At no point does she specifically state that *Vita I* had something wrong. But since she clearly had access to the earlier *vita*, she must have been conscious of offering somewhat different versions of events. Perhaps the best example is Giovanni's rather tepid reference to Margherita's vision of three roads (*Vita I*, ch. 11). Stefania not only gives this vision far more weight but puts Margherita on the third (most arduous) path, not the middle path of the three. Implicit in this new narrative is the sense that Stefania, not Giovanni, really understood the vision's content and meaning. In this light, it is notable that one of the stories related by Stefania (ch. 16) has Margherita warning her brothers not to "overstep" themselves. Although the passage is not explained, Stefania may have wished to warn the Colonna brothers about being too heavy-handed with the new community of San Silvestro. In any case, her text claims a greater importance for Margherita's band of female followers than Giovanni's narrative does. If it was indeed Stefania who provided material for Giovanni Colonna's chapter 12 (concerning the visit of the "pilgrim"), then the way Cardinal Giacomo Colonna is implicitly chastised there for criticizing the nuns' comportment may fit into this pattern as well.

THE IMPORTANCE AND INTEREST OF THE TEXTS

The two hagiographic lives of Margherita Colonna open up new perspectives on numerous historical questions. Here we limit ourselves to suggesting what they might reveal about the impact of authorial gender and status on hagiographic perspective; about the fluid nature of female

Franciscan identity in the years after the creation of the Order of St. Clare; about the experience and influence of female visionaries; and about the process of saint making at the heart of an aristocratic Roman family.

These two lives offer new insight into the ways gender and status could affect the production of hagiographic texts. In recent decades, scholars have explored the dynamics that shaped the way male church-men (often mendicant confessors) wrote about saintly medieval women.[65] Even as men attempted to legitimate and promote the women about whom they wrote, they often focused attention on women's bodies as sites of holy suffering that manifested a mystical access to divine visions and voices. In these texts, male authors often retained a great deal of tex-tual and intellectual authority, while women's agency might be limited to acting as visionary conduits for God's messages and to exercising an as-cetic control over their own physicality. But men and women also col-laborated in complex ways—for example, when women dictated to male scribes, who then added their own voices and editorial filters.[66] This strand of scholarship has been fruitful not only in exposing the strategies of male hagiographers but also in attempting to get a little closer to the women's lived experience once the distorting effects of those strategies are stripped away.

But much less attention has been paid to women writing about other women as saints. Only a relatively small group of such texts is extant for the long thirteenth century. Female-authored texts about contemporary saintly women (that is, texts about women whom the author actually knew, rather than martyr-saints from the deep Christian past) include

---

65. The essential starting points for this bibliography are John W. Coakley, *Women, Men, and Spiritual Power: Female Saints and Their Male Collaborators* (New York: Columbia University Press, 2006), and the essays collected in Catherine M. Mooney, ed., *Gendered Voices: Medieval Saints and Their Interpreters* (Philadelphia: University of Pennsylvania Press, 1999). See also John W. Coakley, "Women's Tex-tual Authority and the Collaboration of Clerics," in *Medieval Holy Women in the Christian Tradition, c. 1100–c. 1500*, ed. Alastair J. Minnis and Rosalynn Voaden (Turnhout: Brepols, 2010), 83–104.

66. Kimberley M. Benedict, *Empowering Collaborations: Writing Partnerships between Religious Women and Scribes in the Middle Ages* (New York: Routledge, 2004).

the *Life of Isabelle of France* (ca. 1283), by the Franciscan abbess Agnes of Harcourt; the *Life of Douceline of Digne* (ca. 1297), by the Franciscan-inspired beguine prioress Felipa of Porcelet; the *Life of Beatrice of Ornacieux* (between 1303 and 1310), by the Carthusian prioress Marguerite of Oingt; and a life of Gertrude of Helfta, written by a fellow Benedictine nun (after 1302). The first three of these texts were written in French dialects, and the fourth is in Latin.[67]

Stefania's work was composed before all but Agnes of Harcourt's and thus is an important and early, though largely overlooked, element in this dossier. In fact, Stefania's authorial perspective matches very well with that of Agnes and Felipa. Like these authors, Stefania was writing about the charismatic founder of her community (even if San Silvestro did not formally come into existence until after Margherita's death). Her recollections center on anecdotes, visions, and miracles that demonstrate the community's spiritual and institutional legitimacy. Moreover, like Agnes of Harcourt with Isabelle, and Felipa of Porcelet with Douceline, Stefania saw herself as inheriting an element of Margherita's authority. She thus made certain to record statements from Margherita that would imply her support for that inheritance. Indeed, Stefania at first lived a life not dissimilar to Felipa's informal beguine existence but later must have vowed to follow the Rule of the *Sorores minores*, which was written

---

67. The first three of these texts are discussed in Sean L. Field, "Agnes of Harcourt, Felipa of Porcelet, and Marguerite of Oingt: Women Writing about Women at the End of the Thirteenth Century," *Church History* 76 (2007): 298–329. For an overview and further bibliography, see Renate Blumenfeld-Kosinski, "Holy Women in France: A Survey," in Minnis and Voaden, *Medieval Holy Women*, 241–65. For the texts in English, see Sean L. Field, *The Writings of Agnes of Harcourt: The Life of Isabelle of France and the Letter on Louis IX and Longchamp* (Notre Dame, IN: University of Notre Dame Press, 2003); Kathleen Garay and Madeleine Jeay, trans., *The Life of St. Douceline, a Beguine of Provence* (Cambridge: D. S. Brewer, 2001); Renate Blumenfeld-Kosinski, trans., *The Writings of Margaret of Oingt: Medieval Prioress and Mystic* (Newburyport, MA: Focus, 1990); and Alexandra Barratt, ed., *Gertrude the Great of Helfta: The Herald of God's Loving-Kindness: Books One and Two* (Kalamazoo, MI: Cistercian, 1991), 37–95. Gertrude's "Life" is actually inserted as book 1 of her *Legatus divinae pietatis*. See further Alexandra Barratt and Debra L. Stoudt, "Gertrude the Great of Helfta," in Minnis and Voaden, *Medieval Holy Women*, 453–73.

by Isabelle of France for Longchamp and was the same rule under which Agnes of Harcourt lived and wrote.

The lives of Gertrude of Helfta and Beatrice of Ornacieux emerged from slightly different contexts, but they too were written by fellow Sisters looking to highlight the merits of imposing figures in their order or community. Thus Stefania's account fits in well with the historical context that drove this larger group of women to write about other saintly women, and it can be mined for new evidence of how female hagiographers constructed images of saintly founders, what narrative strategies they employed, and what perspectives they chose to stress.

Similarly, laymen wrote very few saints' lives in this century. The most famous was surely Jean of Joinville's life of Louis IX (St. Louis), completed by 1308 but probably begun several decades earlier.[68] We are not aware, however, of any extant life of a female saintly figure written by a layman in the thirteenth century, and certainly not of such a life written by the woman's biological brother.[69] Giovanni Colonna's *Life of the*

---

68. Joinville, *Vie de saint Louis*, ed. Jacques Monfrin (Paris: Garnier, 1995); translated by Caroline Smith in *Chronicles of the Crusades* (New York: Penguin, 2008). For a review of the argument that the core of the text was probably begun in the 1270s or 1280s, see M. Cecilia Gaposchkin, *The Making of Saint Louis: Kingship, Sanctity, and Crusade in the Later Middle Ages* (Ithaca, NY: Cornell University Press, 2008), ch. 7.

69. There are a few contemporary cases of male clerics writing lives of their saintly sisters, for instance the fascinating life of Margaret of Jerusalem (d. ca. 1214, also known as Margaret of Beverly) by her brother, the Cistercian Thomas of Froidmont (d. 1225), recently discussed in Anne E. Lester, *Creating Cistercian Nuns: The Women's Religious Movement and Its Reform in Thirteenth-Century Champagne* (Ithaca, NY: Cornell University Press, 2011), 147–49. Similarly, an exciting new example of this dynamic is John of Morigny's treatment of his sister Bridget in his *Liber florum celestis doctrine*, edition and commentary by Claire Fanger and Nicholas Watson (Toronto: Pontifical Institute of Mediaeval Studies, 2015); an English translation by the same two scholars is forthcoming from Pennsylvania State University Press. Some texts written by laymen about women may have been lost. For example, Andrea Saramita apparently wrote a now-lost *vita* of the highly controversial holy woman Guglielma in the late thirteenth century. See Barbara Newman's brilliant studies "Agnes of Prague and Guglielma of Milan," in Minnis and Voaden, *Medieval Holy Women*, 557–79, and "The Heretic Saint: Guglielma of Bohemia, Milan, and Bru-

Blessed Virgin Margherita is truly an unusual text in this sense, allowing us to ask how a powerful male aristocrat and layman might go about portraying the sanctity of his sister.

Moreover, when these two already privileged perspectives are put together, something unique emerges. There are only a few examples in the entire thousand-year stretch of the Middle Ages in which a man and a woman both wrote extant lives of a contemporary holy woman. The two lives of St. Radegund (d. 587) by Venantius Fortunatus and Baudonivia seem to be the only instance before Margherita Colonna.[70] The next case from the later Middle Ages would be Colette of Corbie (d. 1447), with lives written by Pierre de Vaux and Perrine de la Roche.[71]

---

nate," *Church History* 74 (2005): 1–37. And generally on the importance of brother-sister relationships in religious life, see Fiona J. Griffiths, "Siblings and the Sexes within the Medieval Religious Life," *Church History* 77 (2008): 26–53 (thanks to Julia Bolton Holloway, Barbara Newman, and Anne Clark for bibliographic suggestions). But we have not been able to identify another text that exactly matches the authorial dynamic of the layman Giovanni Colonna's life of his sister for the thirteenth century.

70. Translations can be found in Jo Ann McNamara and John E. Halborg, *Sainted Women of the Dark Ages* (Durham, NC: Duke University Press, 1992), 70–105. Studies comparing the two authors' approaches include Jason Glenn, "Two Lives of Saint Radegund," in *The Middle Ages in Texts and Texture: Reflections on Medieval Sources*, ed. Jason Glenn (Toronto: University of Toronto Press, 2011), 57–70; Ruth Wehlau, "Literal and Symbolic: The Language of Asceticism in Two Lives of St Radegund," *Florilegium* 19 (2002): 75–89; Simon Coates, "Regendering Radegund? Fortunatus, Baudonivia, and the Problem of Female Sanctity in Merovingian Gaul," in *Gender and the Christian Religion*, ed. R. N. Swanson (Rochester, NY: Boydell, 1998), 37–50; John Kitchen, *Saints' Lives and the Rhetoric of Gender* (Oxford: Oxford University Press, 1998), 115–53; and Lynda L. Coon, *Sacred Fictions: Holy Women and Hagiography in Late Antiquity* (Philadelphia: University of Pennsylvania Press, 1997), 126–35.

71. Texts in Ubald d'Alençon, ed., *Les vies de sainte Colette Boylet de Corbie, réformatrice des Frères mineurs et des clarisses (1381–1447), écrites par ses contemporains le P. Pierre de Reims dit de Vaux et sœur Perrine de la Roche et de Baume* (Paris: Picard, 1911). Renate Blumenfeld-Kosinski is currently preparing the first English translation of these texts. For analysis, see Elisabeth Lopez, *Colette of Corbie (1381–1447): Learning and Holiness*, trans. Joanna Waller (St. Bonaventure, NY: Franciscan Institute Publications, 2011); Joan Mueller and Nancy Bradley Warren, eds.,

In all three cases, a learned male wrote the first life and a woman the second, adding her personal observations to the male hagiographer's more abstract perspective. Yet the female author offered more than simply a coda to the original *vita*. As a member of the subject's community or band of followers, she was able to give an "inside" look at the saint with notably different emphases from those of the male author. A rather extraordinary contextual continuity thus seems to link these three examples across eight centuries. For Radegund and Colette, however, the male hagiographer was a churchman or confessor—Venantius Fortunatus was a noted poet as well as bishop of Poitiers, while Pierre de Vaux was a Franciscan and ardent reformer as well as Colette's confessor. Thus Margherita's *vitae* provide the opportunity to analyze not only gendered perspectives but also the differences between clerical and secular viewpoints.[72]

One representative example is the two authors' treatment of Margherita's "three roads" vision. As already noted, their two accounts differ sharply. Giovanni (*Vita I*, ch. 11) places this vision firmly in the context of physical suffering, connecting it to the onset of the painful ulcer in Margherita's leg, which he describes as an imitation of Christ's suffering. After graphically depicting the flow of blood and pus from the ulcer "which broke her flesh and skin and took root in her bones," he briefly mentions that "three paths were shown to her." She chose the middle one, meaning "she would have to go through blood," which turned out to be true, since "she crossed through blood, for such was her suffering." For Stefania (*Vita II*, ch. 5), by contrast, the "three roads" vision has nothing to do with physical suffering. It rather concerns the wide road of seductive pleasures, the middle road of frightful thorns through which only a few may pass, and the third path, chosen by Margherita, who "would fly like a supremely pure dove to those lands which Christ, the

---

A Companion to Colette of Corbie (Leiden: Brill, 2016); and *Sainte Colette et sa posterité*, preface by André Vauchez (Paris: Éditions franciscaines, 2016).

72. The importance of this kind of comparison was suggested by Giulia Barone, "Le due vite di Margherita Colonna," in Modica, *Esperienza religiosa*, 25–32; and by Bianca Lopez, "Between Court and Cloister: The Life and Lives of Margherita Colonna," *Church History* 82 (2013): 554–75.

Sun of Justice, looks upon and illuminates." Thus, although elsewhere Stefania certainly does detail the suffering caused by Margherita's ulcer, in this case the male author transforms a vision into an emblem of a bleeding female body, whereas the female author understands the vision to have a metaphoric, rather than somatic, message.[73]

It is also useful to juxtapose Margherita's *vitae* with the lives of other holy women affiliated with the Franciscans. These hagiographic legends, and in some cases artistic representations, allow explorations of what is sometimes called female Franciscanism.[74] Some scholars have approached this category from an institutional perspective, examining the relationship between female communities and the Friars Minor, while others have focused on women's embrace of typically Franciscan spiritual themes, such as devotion to the humanity of Christ and His passion, an embrace of apostolic poverty, and an orientation toward humility, asceticism, and caring for others.[75] Margherita's two *vitae* provide a new vantage point on the multifaceted nature of female Franciscan identity, both institutionally and spiritually, during the 1270s.

For example, Margherita avoided professing any religious vow, even while adopting a habit just like that worn by the Sisters in Assisi. Notably this habit is one of the few references to Clare of Assisi or institutional forms of female Franciscan life in her *vitae*. Giovanni Colonna described how Margherita donned a habit made out of cheap cloth just

---

73. On male churchmen transforming bodily metaphors into literal descriptions of suffering female bodies, see Amy Hollywood, *The Soul as Virgin Wife: Mechthild of Magdeburg, Marguerite Porete, and Meister Eckhart* (Notre Dame, IN: University of Notre Dame Press, 1995), esp. 26–56.

74. A particularly useful comparison for Margherita Colonna might be with the *vita* of her contemporary Margherita of Cortona (the similarity of names has caused the two women to be all too easily confused!), written by the Franciscan Giunta Benegnati around 1308 and recently translated by Thomas Renna as *The Life and Miracles of Saint Margaret of Cortona (1247–1297)*, ed. Shannon Larson (St. Bonaventure, NY: Franciscan Institute Publications, 2012).

75. However, Sarah McNamer has correctly challenged the assumption that these behaviors are always markers of Franciscan affiliation. See her *Affective Meditation and the Invention of Medieval Compassion* (Philadelphia: University of Pennsylvania Press, 2010), esp. ch. 4.

like the Sisters', accompanied by a rough hair cloak (*Vita I*, ch. 6). Stefania adds that Margherita wore "the religious habit of the most blessed Clare" through the rest of her life (*Vita II*, ch. 9). At the same time, Margherita had shorn her hair, making her rejection of her secular state clear by dropping her long curls into the privy (*Vita II*, ch. 10). Analogous tonsures figure in the lives of many holy women as a sign that they had moved away from their secular lives. In fact, a similar scene happens in Clare's own legend, though neither Giovanni nor Stefania makes direct reference to it.[76] Indeed, Giovanni follows his description of Margherita's religious dress with an account of a mystical experience that makes clearer her spiritual orientation. In this vision, a preacher urged her and a female companion to adopt this habit. Margherita quickly recognized the preacher as St. Francis from a portrait she had seen of him, perhaps at the monastery of Subiaco. As she knelt before him to receive his blessing, Francis gave Margherita a red gem in the shape of a cross, which was then absorbed into her body as a sign of her intention to follow Christ.[77] Or rather, Giovanni admits that ultimately his sister's intention was to follow Francis in his embrace of Christ's suffering and poverty: "Conforming to the habit of the most holy Father Francis in this way, she took up the cross from him which he bore and preached. For, just as he left everything behind, she made herself poor, and what she had begun did not fall from her heart. And she, the very least of the *minores*, served the

---

76. See the English translation in Armstrong, *Lady*, 286–87. The editor suggests that Thomas of Celano was probably not the author of Clare's *Legenda*, but more recent scholarship has demonstrated Celano's authorship. See Marco Guida, *Una leggenda in cerca d'autore: La Vita di santa Chiara d'Assisi. Studio delle fonti e sinossi intertestuale* (Brussels: Société des Bolladistes, 2010).

77. A slightly later visionary, Clare of Montefalco, also had a cross implanted in her heart by Christ during a vision that occurred in 1294. She lived in a convent that was governed by the Augustinian rule but where the Sisters' confessors were Franciscans, a situation that points to problems linking institutional and spiritual affiliations. Her ties to Giacomo Colonna are briefly discussed below. A solid introduction to the extensive literature on Clare of Montefalco remains Enrico Menestò, "The Apostolic Canonization Proceedings of Clare of Montefalco, 1318–1319," in *Women and Religion in Medieval and Renaissance Italy*, ed. Daniel E. Bornstein and Roberto Rusconi (Chicago: University of Chicago Press, 1996), 104–29.

poor of Christ and the servants of Christ just as he did" (*Vita* I, ch. 6). This passage provides an explicit statement that Margherita—the very least (*minima*)—was too a Franciscan (one of the *minores*).

Margherita's Franciscan identity was also expressed through the active life of her religious community on Mount Prenestino. The Sisters spent most of their time caring for the local poor, using the Colonna wealth to sustain them, much as Margherita had done with her dowry in Rome. As Bianca Lopez has argued, Margherita's charity differs from the ideals of Clare of Assisi, whose own embrace of poverty was so absolute that she rejected any guaranteed means of support for her community.[78] Margherita and her Sisters even opened up their house to a group of poor women and children who would live with them. Margherita's asceticism was also less institutional than personal. The *vitae* provide details about her ascetic practices, from refusing to sleep in a bed at night, to fasting regularly, to practicing bodily mortifications. It is possible to connect some of these practices to her own *imitatio Francisci*, but they generally fit into a much wider pattern of ascetic behavior found in lives of female penitents and other saintly figures.

Particular elements of the cult of saints as it developed in Italian cities also offer an interesting framework for examining Margherita's holiness. There are numerous examples of thirteenth-century holy men and women whose presence enhanced the spiritual prestige of a given town or whose actions fulfilled key civic roles, including charity and peacemaking.[79] Most of these urban saints were laity rather than bishops or professed religious. They often desired to live humbly and to commit themselves to prayer, while also expressing their devotion actively by

---

78. Lopez, "Between Court and Cloister."

79. For an overview of medieval Italian urban saints' cults, see Diana Webb, *Patrons and Defenders: The Saints in the Italian City-States* (New York: St. Martin's Press, 1996), as well as her collection of translated *vitae*, *Saints and Cities in Medieval Italy* (New York: St. Martin's Press, 2007). Webb's studies focus on urban sanctity in the twelfth and thirteenth centuries (the examples given in this paragraph all are included in this work with the exception of Rose of Viterbo). For the development of *sante vive*, female living saints often associated with the princely cities of the fifteenth and sixteenth centuries, see Gabriella Zarri, *Le sante vive: Profezie di corte e devozione femminile tra '400 e '500* (Turin: Rosenberg e Sellier, 1990).

providing for the urban poor. For example, Homobonus (Omobuono) of Cremona (d. 1197) was a wealthy merchant who gave alms regularly and spent much of his time praying in his local parish church.[80] Peter Pettinaio of Siena (d. 1289) similarly cared for the sick in a local hospice and sought to live simply, although he flourished in his trade.[81] Umiliana Cerchi (d. 1246) used family wealth to support Florence's needy.[82] Other urban saints, however, had much humbler origins or fewer resources. In addition to Rose of Viterbo (d. 1251), whose lack of family wealth or connections was one obstacle to entering a Franciscan convent, Zita of Lucca (d. 1272) was a maidservant whose piety inspired her employers to a deeper faith.[83] And of course, in many ways, Francis of Assisi was an urban saint—arguably the most successful one. Kenneth Baxter Wolf has emphasized the importance of a "burgher culture" in Francis's rejections of wealth. He has argued provocatively that Francis's embrace of poverty was not about assisting the urban poor and should be understood as fulfilling the needs of medieval bourgeois culture.[84]

---

80. While Pope Innocent III canonized Homobonus in 1202, his cult remained mostly local and did not grow to prominence until the end of the thirteenth century. See André Vauchez, *Sainthood in the Later Middle Ages*, trans. Jean Birrell (Cambridge: Cambridge University Press, 1997), 129–31; and Vauchez, *Omobono di Cremona (d. 1197): Laico e Santo. Profilo storico* (Cremona: Edizioni Nuova Editrice Cremonese, 2001).

81. Marita von Weissenberg, "'What Man Are You?' Piety and Masculinity in the *Vitae* of a Sienese Craftsman and a Provençal Nobleman," in *Religious Men and Masculine Identity in the Middle Ages*, ed. P. H. Cullum and Katherine J. Lewis (New York: Boydell Press, 2013), 112–25.

82. In addition to the Schlager article cited above, see Anne M. Schuchmann's discussion of her urban piety in "The Lives of Umiliana de' Cerchi: Representations of Female Sainthood in Thirteenth-Century Florence," *Essays in Medieval Studies* 14 (1997): 15–28.

83. See Pryds, *Women of the Streets*, on Rose (whose own vocation did not necessarily lead her to want to enter a convent). Zita of Lucca, like the other figures, is mentioned briefly in Vauchez's *Sainthood*, although her Italian cult has received less attention than that of some of the other figures.

84. Kenneth Baxter Wolf, *The Poverty of Riches: St. Francis of Assisi Reconsidered* (Oxford: Oxford University Press, 2003), esp. 77–89. For medieval discomfort with the rise of commercial society, see the classic study by Lester Little, *Religious*

These texts also add rich new texture to our overall picture of medieval visionary culture. Medieval saints' lives are often filled with visions, revelations, and apparitions. Scholars have devoted a great deal of attention to female visionaries and their ability to wield political and spiritual power.[85] The nature of such visions could vary widely, though appearances of the Virgin, the Christ Child, and the adult Christ were common staples. Some women, such as the thirteenth-century beguine author Hadewijch, reported visions tinged with erotic union with Christ;[86] others, like Beatrice of Ornacieux, seemed to have centered a visionary life on the Eucharist; and still others, such as the somewhat later Ermine of Reims, even fought dreamlike visionary battles with demons.[87]

A few of Margherita Colonna's visions have a hint of "bridal mysticism," as in *Vita I*, chapter 6, where Christ places a ring on her finger that is then overgrown with flesh. Certainly Giovanni Colonna uses the common "bride" or "betrothed of Christ" trope throughout his text.[88] Stefania similarly sees Margherita in a vision (ch. 16) disappearing into

---

Poverty and the Profit Economy in Medieval Europe (Ithaca, NY: Cornell University Press, 1978).

85. A good overview is Barbara Newman, "The Visionary Texts and Visual Worlds of Religious Women," in *Crown and Veil: Female Monasticism from the Fifth to the Fifteenth Centuries*, ed. Jeffrey F. Hamburger and Susan Marti, trans. Dietlinde Hamburger (New York: Columbia University Press, 2008), 151–71; for a more detailed study with bibliography on historical, literary, anthropological, and art historical perspectives, see Barbara Newman, "What Did It Mean to Say 'I Saw'? The Clash between Theory and Practice in Medieval Visionary Culture," *Speculum* 80 (2005): 1–43; on visions and political influence, see Renate Blumenfeld-Kosinski, *Poets, Saints, and Visionaries of the Great Schism, 1378–1417* (University Park: Pennsylvania State University Press, 2006).

86. A solid introduction can be found in Bernard McGinn, *The Flowering of Mysticism: Men and Women in the New Mysticism—1200–1350* (New York: Crossroad, 1998), 200–222.

87. Renate Blumenfeld-Kosinski, *The Strange Case of Ermine de Reims: A Medieval Woman between Demons and Saints* (Philadelphia: University of Pennsylvania Press, 2015).

88. On the shifting resonance of this label, see Dyan Elliott, *The Bride of Christ Goes to Hell: Metaphor and Embodiment in the Lives of Pious Women, 200–1500* (Philadelphia: University of Pennsylvania Press, 2012).

"the bedchamber of her Husband." By and large, however, Margherita's is not a "love mysticism" or *mystique courtoise*.[89] Far more central to her spirituality are her visions of the Virgin Mary. It should be noted that these visions are all reported by Giovanni Colonna and so may reflect a male sense that identification with the Virgin is most appropriate for a female would-be saint, as well as the larger Marian devotion evidenced by the Colonna family in this generation.[90] It is also notable that Eucharistic piety is only a very minor element in Margherita's visions.[91]

In any case, some of the most striking visual images in *Vita I* occur as Giovanni attempts to describe his sister's encounters with the Virgin. For instance, in chapter 3 Mary arrives at Margherita's bedside in a "chariot,"[92] seeming to circle her bed as Margherita attempts to turn away from the blinding light. The fact that Giovanni had to try to explain (somewhat awkwardly) why it was legitimate for Margherita to turn away in the face of the Virgin's splendor strongly indicates that he was indeed relating and interpreting what Margherita had described to him. Moreover (as noted), Margherita is not the only visionary in these texts. She herself appears *in* visions experienced by her brothers, an unidentified sister, Stefania, several local Franciscans, and others. Visionary

---

89. Barbara Newman, *"La mystique courtoise*: Thirteenth-Century Beguines and the Art of Love,"* in *From Virile Woman to WomanChrist: Studies in Medieval Religion and Literature* (Philadelphia: University of Pennsylvania Press, 1995), 137–67.

90. On the role of the Virgin in Giovanni's text, see the perceptive remarks in Daniele Solvi, "Maria nell'agiografia femminile di area minoritica: Da Chiara d'Assisi a Margherita da Cortona," *Theotokos* 19 (2011): 329–54, at 342–46. The Colonna family's art patronage reflected a clear Marian focus, as seen in the apse mosaic at Santa Maria Maggiore (the coronation of the Virgin), the donor mosaics of Giovanni Colonna in the Araceoli, and the family chapel attached to their palace in Palestrina (which Pietro Colonna described as dedicated to the Virgin). Giacomo Colonna's seal also featured the Virgin. See Julian Gardner, "Some Cardinals' Seals of the Thirteenth Century," *Journal of the Warburg and Courtauld Institutes* 38 (1975): 72–96.

91. There is a brief reference in *Vita I*, ch. 4, to Margherita seeing a dove above a priest when he holds up the body of Christ.

92. The Latin word is *currus*, perhaps echoing the "fiery chariot" in which Francis of Assisi appeared, according to Thomas of Celano (in turn linking Francis to the prophet Elias in 4 Kings 2:11).

culture in fact saturates these texts, providing new opportunity to assess some of the ways in which visions could function in women's religious experience as well as in textual representations of sanctity.

Finally, another key comparative framework for Margherita is her status as a family saint. Ample evidence suggests that even before her death the Colonna promoted Margherita's saintly reputation. This promotion of a family member as a living "saint" seems to be nearly unique for an elite Roman family of the time, in a context where the *baroni* were far more likely to pursue authority through ecclesiastical offices in the papal curia.[93] Cardinal Giacomo Colonna would seem to have been the initial force in shaping family support for Margherita's endeavors. It was he who first urged her to reject marriage and follow a path of holy celibacy, and it was he who acted as her main confidant and spiritual adviser. Yet Senator Giovanni Colonna's role should not be underestimated. As secular head of the family, he must have approved the use of the family estate on Mount Prenestino as the ultimate site for Margherita's followers to congregate in the informal community. And while Giovanni gives credit to his brother the cardinal for participating in Margherita's active charitable work, again the eldest brother must have offered some level of support for these endeavors as well, since they involved dispensing Colonna resources. Moreover, surely Margherita's brothers could have prevented her from going to Vulturella had they

---

93. Compare Aviad M. Kleinberg, *Prophets in Their Own Country: Living Saints and the Making of Sainthood in the Later Middle Ages* (Chicago: University of Chicago Press, 1992). While there absolutely were Roman women and men who had saintly reputations, it is notable that no canonization process for a local saint was launched prior to Francesca Romana's, which began shortly after her death in 1440. (Certainly both Catherine of Siena and Bridget of Sweden were prominent in fourteenth-century Rome, but both women were considered foreigners.) In many ways Francesca's sanctity may seem to parallel Margherita's. She was a laywoman who used family wealth to practice charity, and she founded a religious community. For a good English-language introduction to Francesca Romana, see Anna Esposito, "St. Francesca and the Female Religious Communities of Fifteenth-Century Rome," in Rusconi and Bornstein, *Women and Religion*, 197–218.

really wished to do so. Giovanni (by his own later account) seems to have purposely decided to let Margherita stay—at least for a short while—with Lady Altruda of the Poor in Rome. By the last years of her life, Margherita was evidently occupying a well-established place in the local landscape of the region around Palestrina as a known source of pious charity for the poor and as a woman with a reputation for visionary access to the divine. Whatever their earlier reluctance might have been, her brothers had, in the end, provided the practical support necessary to carve out this position. The community on Mount Prenestino may not have been a formal institution, but it was unquestionably a Colonna one.

Thus Margherita's deathbed became a site for family solidarity that celebrated her life while looking to future rewards—not only hers in heaven but the wider family's on earth. Her nephew Pietro, the future cardinal, was brought to her bedside for a blessing, as were nieces who would ultimately help form the core of San Silvestro in Capite. Margherita even used the moment, according to Stefania (*Vita II*, ch. 29), to offer an enigmatic hint that Cardinal Giacomo could expect to be elevated to the papacy! Giovanni immediately started collecting miracles from the moment of her death (indeed, the text contains suggestions that he was gathering notes for a *vita* even while his sister lived). For instance, Giovanni was notified when a local man and his wife reported miraculous visions and cures (*Vita I*, chs. 16–18), and these witnesses were rushed off to give sworn testimony to Franciscans, who then called the surrounding townspeople together to hear these stories.

The Colonna and the local Franciscans quickly began promoting Margherita's tomb as a site for potential miracles. Indeed, in one of the most intriguing episodes anywhere in the two *vitae*, Stefania notes (*Vita II*, ch. 25) that a local man was disgusted at the way "the lords of Colonna are scurrying around trying to force their sister into the chorus of the saints!" A miraculous cure taught this skeptic the error of his ways, yet Stefania's inclusion of the episode shows just how publicly the Colonna were working to build momentum for belief in their sister's sanctity. This process had begun while she was still alive, as the family searched for a way to accommodate and profit from her vocation as an unenclosed holy woman; it continued through her death and into the next decades in more concerted efforts to achieve formal recognition of her cult.

THE AFTERLIFE OF MARGHERITA COLONNA

In 1285, Margherita's surviving followers moved from Mount Prenestino to the heart of Rome. At the same time, they exchanged their informal religious way of life for incorporation as an enclosed community of Franciscan nuns. The steps in this process were laid out in a bull issued by Pope Honorius IV that September.

According to Honorius, after Margherita's death her longtime followers had worn religious habits but without vowing any specific rule. They now approached the pope with a request to be permitted to adopt the Rule of the *Sorores minores inclusae*. As already noted, this rule and order had been created by Isabelle of France, sister of King Louis IX of France, with final papal approval coming in 1263. Although Honorius did not comment on it, he would have been well aware that this choice was novel for Italy. The Order of *Sorores minores* was enjoying moderate success in France as an alternative to the Order of St. Clare (and would shortly begin to do so in England), but no Italian community had yet followed this path. It is not clear exactly who made this choice or why. There is no reason to believe that Margherita Colonna herself ever expressed a particular interest in the *Sorores minores*. But some Italian Franciscan women had evinced a desire to adopt this rule as early as the 1260s,[94] and the wishes of the new abbess "Herminia" and her Sisters may well have been a factor. Pope Honorius had also directed Cardinal Jerome of Ascoli, bishop of Palestrina, to receive these women's professions and affirm their choice of abbess, which was accomplished while the band of Sisters was still residing on Mount Prenestino. As former minister general of the Franciscans, Cardinal Jerome would certainly have known something of the Order of *Sorores minores'* history and status and must have at least approved of this choice. But it is also notable that Cardinal Giacomo Colonna's name was written on the back of Honorius's

---

94. See Lezlie S. Knox, "Audacious Nuns: Institutionalizing the Franciscan Order of Saint Clare," *Church History* 69 (2000): 41–62.

bull.[95] It was surely Giacomo who had ensured papal acquiescence, and it may well have been he who first suggested the choice of this specific branch of the female Franciscan family, perhaps for its association with the Capetian court and as a way of making the new community unique in the Italian scene.[96]

In any case, to provide a physical location for the new community, Honorius expelled the last Benedictine monks from San Silvestro in Capite and turned over this ancient house to the new, Colonna-sponsored community of *Sorores minores*. His bull *Ascendit fumus aromatum* of 24 September 1285 then ratified and formalized these actions and ordered that at least four male Franciscans be assigned by their order to reside there to provide pastoral care. Two subsequent bulls provided the text of the rule and stipulated that Franciscans would have to supply even more Friars for the new community when events required their presence.[97] The house was thus definitely "Franciscan" in its institutional ties as well as its spirituality. It was just as surely "Colonna" in its peopling and patronage, with the family undoubtedly eager to extend its control over the monastery's vast holdings.[98] A later papal bull even referred to the community as having been founded for Giovanni Colonna's daughters, Giacomo Colonna's nieces, and "other women of their lineage."[99] Giacomo Colonna was appointed protector by 1288 and actually authored a set of additional constitutions to augment the Rule of the *Sorores minores*. A number of women from the family entered the com-

---

95. This indicates that the bull was sent to his attention, even though the greeting of the text itself addresses the abbess and Sisters. The endorsement is noted by Brentano, *Rome before Avignon*, 241.

96. It is interesting to note another connection to the Capetians, in that San Silvestro in Capite was thought to house among its relics some of the bones of St. Denis, patron saint of the French monarchs. See Rigord's *Histoire de Philippe Auguste*, ed. and trans. Élisabeth Carpentier, Georges Pon, and Yves Chauvin (Paris: CNRS Éditions, 2006), 209n2012.

97. See the translations of Honorius's three bulls in this volume.

98. A point emphasized by Keyvanian, *Hospitals and Urbanism*, 267.

99. *BF*, 5:156; *DV*, 31–32. In this bull John XXII recalled San Silvestro as being founded by Giacomo and Giovanni Colonna "pro filiabus dicti Ioannis ac neptibus ipsorum cardinalis et Ioannis aliisque mulieribus de ipsorum genere."

munity and served as abbesses over the next decades, while surviving testaments demonstrate continuing material support from the Colonna as well.[100]

By 1285 the time therefore may have seemed right for the Colonna to consider moving forward on Margherita's possible canonization. The first step in such a move was to demonstrate that miracles were occurring and that local veneration was accruing. The authoring of a *vita* would both record and promote such a burgeoning reputation for sanctity. Thus Giovanni Colonna had been collecting testimonials to miracles associated with Margherita and had completed a draft of *Vita I* by this point. His brother Giacomo would shortly ask Stefania to begin work on *Vita II* as well, if he had not done so already.

A second public gesture toward possible canonization was to engineer a "translation" of the would-be saint's body. The rituals that marked the moving of a saintly figure's earthly remains, or relics, allowed supporters a chance to demonstrate devotion and perhaps to experience, record, and promote new miracles. The move to San Silvestro provided the perfect opportunity for such a translation, as Margherita's tomb at San Pietro on Mount Prenestino could be opened and her remains publicly marched down to Rome in a formal procession and reinterred at the new foundation, where she would fulfill the role of founder and eventually (ideally) patron saint.

Unfortunately, the earliest surviving account of this translation comes only from Mariano of Florence's early sixteenth-century history of the Order of St. Clare.[101] He based his account on documents kept at San Silvestro in Capite (including the *vitae*), and perhaps also on the Sisters' oral traditions. His narrative thus may be based on now-lost evidence but also must reflect local memories of the event. Mariano explained that as the procession reached the Colonna section of Rome, San Silvestro's bells began to ring spontaneously, seemingly pulled by angelic hands. He claimed that this sign of Margherita's heavenly status impressed both the papal court and the Roman people. In any case, with

---

100. See Graham, "Patronage," 225; and Brentano, *Rome before Avignon*, 245–47.

101. See the translation in this volume; and on Mariano, see below.

Margherita's tomb transferred to San Silvestro, the Colonna now would have been well positioned to ask the papal court to consider formal recognition of her cult.

After Pope Honorius IV's death in April 1287, there was a clear opportunity to advance Colonna interests. The cardinals meeting in Rome that summer could not agree on a new pope. The heat was intense, and malarial fevers raged. Six of the cardinals died, and most of the others fled the city for the cooler hill towns surrounding Rome. The exception was Cardinal Jerome of Ascoli, who was by now a firm ally—if not an outright client—of the Colonna.[102] Jerome had entered the Franciscan order as a young man and had studied in Paris. By his forties, he was a provincial minister. In 1274 he was elected minister general, an office in which he continued until 1278, when he was named a cardinal together with Giacomo Colonna. He also began acting as a papal diplomat, including participating in a mission to Constantinople that sought to reunite the Latin and Greek churches, and it was probably Colonna influence that had contributed to his appointment as bishop of Palestrina in 1281. Now, in 1287, he alone of the cardinals remained in the city. When the cardinals reconvened in February 1288, they unanimously selected Cardinal Jerome as Pope Nicholas IV, impressed with his courage and sense of responsibility.

This choice can only have delighted the Colonna, who were rewarded with the appointment of a second family cardinal, Giovanni's son Pietro, in May. The alliance between Nicholas and the Colonna was widely commented upon in contemporary Rome.[103] For instance, a visiting Florentine cleric described Giacomo Colonna as "the other pope," while a contemporary satirical image showed Nicholas IV trapped in a column with only his mitered head poking out and two other col-

---

102. Gardner provides a useful summary of his career in *Roman Crucible*, 23–25. The most in-depth biography remains Antonino Franchi, *Nicolaus Papa IV, 1288–1292 (Girolamo d'Ascoli)* (Ascoli Piceno: Cassa di Risparmio di Ascoli Piceno, 1990); see also the essays collected in Enrico Menestò, ed., *Niccolò IV: Un pontificato tra oriente ed occidente* (Spoleto: Centro Italiano di Studi sull'alto Medioevo, 1991).

103. See examples in Brooke, *Image of Saint Francis*, 441–42, as well as Gardner, *Roman Crucible*, 23–25.

umns squeezing him on both sides. This was a visual pun invoking the family name and coat of arms, since the Colonna stemma showed a single column (*columna* in Italian), referring simultaneously to their toponym and to a famous relic—a piece of the column against which Christ was scourged—that an earlier Colonna had brought back from the Crusades.[104]

In addition to being a Colonna ally and an able administrator, Nicholas IV was a Franciscan pope who saw his new office as a way to assert his order's prominence in the church. For example, Donal Cooper and Janet Robson recently have considered how he used his patronage of projects in Assisi and Rome to assert that the Friars Minor were leading the church into a new age.[105] The Colonna supported these projects as well, ensuring their completion after Nicholas's death (as discussed above).

It is thus tempting to speculate that Nicholas might have wished to open a canonization process for Margherita, which would have benefited both the Colonna family and the Franciscan order. Certainly Nicholas IV must have been aware of Margherita's life and reputation. Although it seems unlikely that the two ever met (surely one of the *vitae* would have commented on such an encounter), the then cardinal would have heard about her piety and activities from his friend Giacomo Colonna. Moreover, as Jerome of Ascoli, Nicholas was probably the minister

---

104. The caricature no longer exists, and scholars rely on the description from the nineteenth-century historian of medieval Rome, Frederick Gregorovius. See *History of the City*, vol. 5, pt. 2, 514–15. The relic remains on display in the chapel of San Zeno in the ninth-century Church of Santa Prassede. This church also had strong Colonna connections because of its location near Santa Maria Maggiore and because the first Colonna cardinal, Giovanni Colonna, had been named cardinal-priest of Santa Prassede in 1217, the same year he left with an army for the newly established Latin Empire of Constantinople. He may have donated the relic on his return in 1222. The family stemma still appears on tomb frontals, now removed and displayed in a small chapel inside the church's side door.

105. An inscription marking the new apse mosaic for the Lateran Church explicitly argues that his elevation as the first Franciscan pope represents the culmination of this age. See Cooper and Robson, *Making of Assisi*, 17–33 (including a translation and picture of the inscription at 26–27), and Brooke, *Image of Saint Francis*, 439–53. Both books contain useful bibliographic references to earlier studies.

general who had given Margherita permission to enter Santa Chiara in Assisi. This permission could have come about only through specific family intervention and would necessarily have reflected some indications from the Colonna about their sister's virtues. Finally, as bishop of Palestrina from 1281, Jerome would have been responsible in some sense for the Sisters who were still living in Colonna houses on Mount Prenestino at that point, and it was he who first received their professions as they moved to join the Order of *Sorores minores*. With all of these points of contact, Nicholas IV must have heard about the miracles associated with Margherita's tomb in his diocese.

Yet there is no direct evidence that overt papal support for Margherita's canonization ever materialized. Had Nicholas sought to open canonization hearings, he would have had to follow well-established procedures. Even if strong evidence existed for a local cult, formal investigation (the canonization process) was still required before recognition as a saint by the Roman Church.[106] André Vauchez has shown that the growing legalization of the process and the lengthening time it took to secure proper documents and testimonies contributed to a decline in the number of processes after 1267.[107] That year saw the canonization of Hedwig of Silesia (ca. 1175–1243), a Polish princess whose sainthood furthered family interests,[108] but the cults of other royal holy women found considerably less official enthusiasm. For instance, initial attempts to spark a canonization process for Isabelle of France (d. 1270), founder of the *Sorores minores*, went nowhere.[109] And while a process for another

---

106. The best introduction to medieval canonization processes is Vauchez, *Sainthood*.

107. Between 1198 and 1267 there were forty-seven processes resulting in twenty-three canonizations. Ibid., esp. 61–62.

108. On Hedwig and the cults of other "saintly princesses," see Gábor Klaniczay, *Holy Rulers and Blessed Princesses: Dynastic Cults in Medieval Central Europe*, trans. Éva Pálmae (Cambridge: Cambridge University Press, 2002), ch. 5.

109. The nuns of Longchamp finally received permission to celebrate Isabelle's cult locally in 1521, at the same moment that Mariano of Florence was renewing interest in Margherita Colonna. See Sean L. Field, "Paris to Rome and Back Again: The Nuns of Longchamp and Leo X's 1521 Bull *Piis omnium*," *Studies in Medieval and Renaissance History*, 3rd ser., 11 (2014): 155–223.

royal woman, Margaret of Hungary, was begun after her death in 1270, it fizzled to a close and did not result in canonization until 1943.[110] In fact, no canonizations were proclaimed between 1267 and 1297. The only ongoing process across that period concerned King Louis IX of France. Pope Gregory X had begun tentative moves toward his canonization in 1272, and the French pope Martin IV had instigated formal hearings in 1282–83. Nicholas IV continued the process, but it would not be completed until 1297 under Boniface VIII.[111] Thus the saintly king of France, with all the backing of the Capetian crown, still required three decades of well-funded political pressure to achieve sainthood. This was not an auspicious era in which to attempt the creation of a new saint.

As for the religious order that might have promoted Margherita's canonization, there is no evidence for any larger Franciscan effort. At the risk of overgeneralization, the Franciscans simply did not need Margherita. Francis of Assisi unquestionably remained the focus of the order's hagiographical celebrations, but by the 1280s three other Franciscan saints had liturgical feasts that were celebrated throughout the order and regularly commemorated in artistic programs in its main churches. These were Anthony of Padua (canonized in 1232), Elizabeth of Hungary (1235), and Clare of Assisi (1255), who in some sense represented the three main branches of the order—the Friars, lay penitents, and enclosed nuns.[112] Certainly others were honored, such as the Friars

---

110. Viktória Hedvig Deák, *La légende de sainte Marguerite de Hongrie et l'hagiographie dominicaine*, trans. Alexis Léonas, preface by André Vauchez (Paris: Éditions du Cerf, 2013).

111. See Gaposchkin, *Making of Saint Louis*, ch. 1.

112. This is not to suggest that these three were perfect representatives of these institutions—especially the women. Elizabeth was never a professed tertiary and could not have been one, since there was no formalized third order at this time. Clare's official hagiographical legend also dilutes her Franciscanism (e.g., her insistence on apostolic poverty). The idea of Francis as the founder of three orders was certainly common by the 1240s, but it represented an idealized interpretation of events as much as a historical fact.

martyred in Morocco in 1220,[113] but their cults were less developed. Franciscan holy men and women whose reputations were firmly rooted in their local context generally gained little traction.[114] While such individuals could add to the Franciscan order's reputation, the time and effort required to prove their holiness prevented serious interest in pursuing canonization.

With little support from the papacy or the Franciscans, the Colonna themselves were unquestionably the greatest promoters of Margherita's cult. Thus the dramatic (if temporary) reversal of the family's fortunes in the 1290s explains why any preliminary moves toward possible canonization came to a sudden halt. Initially, the deaths of Giovanni Colonna and Nicholas IV in 1292 must have slowed whatever momentum existed. But Nicholas IV's death led to a more ominous string of events. After a two-year interregnum during which the Colonna and Orsini battled to influence the other cardinals, and the brief reign of Celestine V (July–December 1294), Cardinal Benedetto Caetani assumed the papal throne as Pope Boniface VIII.[115] Within just a few years of his election, the Colonna faced exile, loss of office, and the destruction of their properties.

Tension had been rising between the Colonna and Caetani since the 1280s as the Caetani were expanding their holdings and political influence in areas abutting the Colonna patrimony.[116] These simmering re-

---

113. Isabelle Heullant-Donat, "La perception des premiers martyrs franciscains à l'intérieur de l'ordre au XIIIe siècle," in *Religion et mentalités au Moyen Age: Mélanges en l'honneur d'Hervé Martin*, ed. Sophie Cassagnes-Brouquet et al. (Rennes: Presses Universitaires de Rennes, 2003), 211–20. Christopher H. MacEvitt's monograph on Franciscan narratives of martyrdom at Muslim hands is forthcoming.

114. Filippa Mareri, who appears in *Vita II*, ch. 17, is an example of a Franciscan-affiliated holy woman who had a local reputation for piety and miracle working but whose cult did not extend far beyond her native Rieti.

115. The most accessible biographical study in English remains T. S. R. Boase, *Boniface VIII* (New York: Constable, 1933). For a more scholarly and current view, see Agostino Paravicini Bagliani, *Boniface VIII* (Turin: Einaudi, 2003).

116. Paravicini Bagliani, *Boniface VIII*, provides a strong narrative. For overviews in English (in addition to Boase), see Peter Partner, *The Lands of St. Peter: The Papal State in the Middle Ages and the Early Renaissance* (Berkeley: University of California Press, 1972); and Waley, *Papal State*. Much of the documentary evidence is

sentments erupted on 3 May 1297 when Stefano Colonna (the late senator Giovanni's son) ambushed a papal mule train as it neared Rome along the Appian Way and seized 200,000 florins that were intended to purchase the town of Sermoneta from the Annibaldi. The Colonna soon agreed to return this money but refused to make additional restitution or punish Stefano. Matters quickly escalated. From their castle at Longhezza, Cardinals Giacomo and Pietro Colonna published a brief on 9 May denouncing Boniface's tyranny and calling for a council to investigate his legitimacy as pope.[117] On 10 May Boniface declared Giacomo and Pietro Colonna rebels against the church and the city of Rome and stripped them of all ecclesiastical authority, including their status as cardinals. The next day, in a second manifesto, the Colonna accused Boniface of having murdered his predecessor. On 23 May the Colonna were excommunicated and all their goods and properties confiscated.

Both sides soon had armies in the field, with Boniface calling on troops from the Papal States and offering other communes new privileges for fighting against the Colonna heretics. The Colonna cast about desperately for allies, unsuccessfully appealing for help to Philip IV of France (Boniface VIII's canonization of Louis IX in August 1297 may have helped sway Philip). In response, on 14 December Boniface announced a formal crusade against the Colonna and succeeded in whipping up substantial support in the Papal States.[118] Zagarolo was burned,

---

compiled in Jean Coste, *Boniface VIII en process: Articles d'accusation et dépositions des témoins (1303–1311)* (Rome: L'Erma di Bretschneider, 1995).

117. Boase, *Boniface VIII*, 176. However, for a broader perspective on the Colonna's conflict with Boniface VIII as an example of ritual violence connected with an illegitimate papacy or *sede vacante* (i.e., the interregnum between papal elections), see Joëlle Rollo-Koster, "The Politics of Transition: Pillaging and the 1527 Sack of Rome," in *Aspects of Violence in Renaissance Europe*, ed. Jonathan Davies (New York: Routledge, 2013), 41–60.

118. On the declaration of crusade, see Pierre-Yves Le Pogam, "La lutte entre Boniface VIII et les Colonna par les armes symboliques," *Rivista di storia della chiesa in Italia* 61 (2007): 47–66. Oddly, the 14 December 1297 bull declaring a crusade against the Colonna has never been edited, though the substance was repeated in the bull *Olim Jacobum de* of 30 December and edited in *BF*, 4:457. But Le Pogam's article now has printed a newly discovered letter from Cardinal Mathew of Acquasparta, dated 11 January 1298, that contains the text of the first bull of 14 December.

the castle at Colonna fell to mines and catapults, and Colonna homes in Rome were destroyed. Dante would comment that, rather than fighting Saracens or Jews, Boniface had now declared war on the Lateran.[119]

San Silvestro in Capite was caught up in this war. On 11 December 1297, just three days before Boniface formally launched the crusade against the Colonna, Giacomo Colonna was officially replaced as protector (a deposition already implied in the earlier stripping of all church office), and Giovanni Colonna's daughter Giovanna was removed as abbess.[120] In April 1298 the pope stripped San Silvestro of its distinctive status as a house of the Order of *Sorores minores* and subsequently excommunicated the community and seized some of its properties in punishment for its resistance.

By autumn 1298, Palestrina had surrendered after a siege, and the Colonna were forced to submit. In October the two Colonna cardinals waited barefoot and with ropes around their necks for the pope at Rieti and then were confined at Tivoli. In spite of this submission, Boniface ordered that the Colonna palace and houses at Palestrina and Mount Prenestino be razed and the grounds sewn with salt, much as the Romans had done to Carthage. A by-product of this destruction was thus to erase the site of Margherita Colonna's original, informal community.[121] In the face of this implacable hostility, Giacomo and Pietro fled from Tivoli in June 1299 and remained in hiding for the next four years.

The Colonna would have their revenge in 1303. King Philip IV of France was locked in his own battles with Boniface VIII and sent agents to arrest the pope at his summer palace in Anagni in September. The armed force for this coup, however, was provided by Sciarra Colonna, another son of Senator Giovanni. These forces held Boniface captive in harsh conditions for two days while they plundered his treasury. With

---

119. Dante, *Inferno* 8.85–111; from this perspective, the Lateran was a "Colonna church." In this canto, Dante imagines the pope meeting with Guido da Montefeltro, who advises on how to trick the Colonna into surrendering.

120. See translations in this volume.

121. Thus causing Robert Brentano to accuse Boniface of "tamper[ing] with the cult of their saintly virgin Margherita"; see *Rome before Avignon*, 181. Yet in spite of all the rhetoric, it seems clear that Palestrina was not in fact entirely destroyed. See the judicious comments in Le Pogam, "Lutte," 58.

the help of the townspeople of Anagni, Boniface managed to escape and return to Rome, but the aged pope never recovered and died a month later. The formal status of the deposed Colonna cardinals remained in limbo during the short pontificate of Benedict XI (October 1303–July 1304), though Benedict did lift San Silvestro's excommunication, order its possessions returned, and grant permission for the community to return to the Order of *Sorores minores*.[122] Giacomo and Pietro were at last reinstated as cardinals by Clement V (r. 1305–14) in 1306. But by 1309 Clement's ongoing problems with Philip IV of France and preparations for the upcoming Council of Vienne caused him to settle the curia in Avignon, where the Colonna cardinals were obliged to spend much of their time. In sum, even after having been restored to papal good graces, the Colonna had challenges enough simply reconstituting their holdings and authority. San Silvestro in Capite continued to be a key site of Colonna patronage, but Margherita's memory may have begun to fade, with her supporters in the College of Cardinals across the Alps.

The Colonna cardinals, in fact, had begun to broaden and shift their patronage. Several figures who now received their support were female mystics who may in some ways have reminded them of Margherita, or even taken her place.[123] Giacomo had been in contact with Angela of Foligno (d. 1309) and Clare of Montefalco (d. 1308) even before the shattering events of 1297. He had offered an approval of Angela's *Memorial*,[124] and Clare was even said to have predicted the Colonna's fall from power.[125] Pietro Colonna also displayed devotion to Clare and corresponded with her, and since he had served as *podestà* of Foligno he likely had some knowledge of Angela's career.[126] About the time that

---

122. See the translation in this volume.

123. Graham, "Patronage," ch. 5, makes this suggestion.

124. For the text, see Angela of Foligno, *Complete Works*, trans. Paul Lachance (New York: Paulist Press, 1993), 123; for analysis, see Maria Pia Alberzoni, "L'*approbatio*': Curia romana, ordine minoritico e *Liber*," in *Angèle de Foligno: Le dossier*, ed. Giulia Barone and Jacques Dalarun (Rome: École française de Rome, 1999), 293–318.

125. Graham, "Patronage," 229.

126. Neither woman was a member of the Order of St. Clare. Angela was a widowed laywoman who may have been a Franciscan tertiary and certainly was

Angela and Clare died, Giacomo Colonna also helped to found a second house of *Sorores minores* in Rome at San Lorenzo in Panisperna.[127] Though this community was never quite so closely tied to the Colonna as was San Silvestro, it still may have helped divert the cardinal's interest for a time.[128]

---

closely tied to the Franciscans, while Clare was leader of a community that followed the Augustinian Rule but relied on Franciscans for its pastoral care. But for assessment of the ties between these female mystics and Spiritual Franciscan circles, see David Burr, *The Spiritual Franciscans: From Protest to Persecution in the Century after Saint Francis* (University Park: Pennsylvania State University Press, 2001), 315–46, as well as Graham, "Patronage," ch. 5.

127. The exact date of this foundation is unclear, but Giacomo's involvement must have come after his reinstatement in 1306 and well before the first papal mention of his patronage in John XXII's bull of 1 August 1318. See *BF*, 5:155 (#322). The summary there does not reveal what rule the community was following, but certainly it was part of the Order of *Sorores minores* in 1370, when Urban V fulfilled the community's request to have a new copy of the rule (as it had been issued to San Silvestro in Capite) sent to it. See *BF*, 6:446 (#1101). It seems virtually certain that Giacomo Colonna had arranged for this community to adopt the same rule as that followed at San Silvestro, perhaps around 1308. A superficial treatment of the house's history can be found in Patrizia De Crescenzo and Antonio Scaramella, *La chiesa di San Lorenzo in Panisperna sul colle Viminale* (Rome: Istituto Poligrafico dello Stato, 1998). Emily Graham presented new research in "Foundation and Reform: The Colonna and Female Franciscans in Medieval Rome," at the 2015 International Medieval Congress at Leeds.

128. Two contemporary chronicles claim that Pietro Colonna was married at the time of his appointment to the cardinalate in 1288 and that his discarded (and unnamed) wife entered a convent (the Florentine Giovanni Villani wrote, "Fece fare monaca" [She was made a nun]). Many historians have doubted this claim, but Keyvanian, *Hospitals and Urbanism*, 273–75, accepts it, suggests that the wife approved, and speculates that the Colonna built for her the monastery of San Giacomo al Colosseo and that the community would have followed the Rule of the *Sorores minores*. We are aware of no evidence that San Giacomo al Colosseo was ever a house of *Sorores minores*, and we generally agree with scholars who find Pietro's marriage unlikely, since Boniface VIII would surely have used that fact to slander him had it been true. The seventeenth-century sources that explicitly link the discarded wife to this church appear to conflate three different strands of San Giacomo's history, according to recent research by Pasquale Iacobone. In brief, Cardinal Giovanni Colonna (d. 1245) was the founder of several hospitals near the Lateran, which—

Moreover, Angela of Foligno and Clare of Montefalco were at least loosely tied to the controversial wing of the Franciscans known as the Spirituals, radicals convinced of the apocalyptic significance of their rigorous interpretation of apostolic poverty.[129] Giacomo Colonna increasingly adopted a politically fraught stance as patron of key figures within this movement, as Emily Graham's work has recently emphasized. Giacomo's support for his sister's life of poverty may be evidence for his early inclination in this direction, and Salimbene reports him calling "his very close friend" John of Parma, the former minister general and an inspirational figure for the Spirituals, to Rome in 1284.[130] But the contest with Boniface VIII must have solidified this alliance with the Spirituals, who hated Boniface almost as much as did the Colonna. Most directly, one of the great Spiritual leaders of this generation, Angelo Clareno, was a member of Giacomo's household in the last decade of the cardinal's life, and Giacomo also wrote an extant letter in support of the

---

almost a century later—his descendant Pietro Colonna "refounded" through his patronage. A list of Roman churches dating from circa 1230 makes clear that the Church of San Giacomo already was extant, but its earliest documentation comes only from 1386, when it served as a pilgrims' hospital supported by a confraternity. By the middle of the fifteenth century, texts describe *case sante* adjacent to the hospital. *Case sante* could refer to communities of *bizzoche*, pious lay women who could follow one of the mendicant rules, but in this case there is no reference to a particular order. While there are certainly significant gaps in the historical records allowing for the Colonna to have placed a daughter-in-law in a convent in 1288, it seems more likely to us that the combination of Colonna patronage of hospitals and churches in the Lateran neighborhood, combined with a later history of religious women supporting this hospital, contributed to this antiquarian claim. See Pasquale Iacobone, "Gli affreschi jacopei della distrutta Chiesa di San Giacomo al Colosseo in Roma," *Compostellanum* 49 (2004): 421–54, esp. 425–32. Iacobone transcribes the anonymous seventeenth-century manuscript, which explicitly ties Pietro, acting at the recommendation of his uncle Giacomo, to the establishment of a convent, whose order and rule are never named (Biblioteca Apostolica Vaticana Vat. Lat. 8039 B, cc. 25–26), in ibid., 428n28. For a brief overview of the no-longer extant church, see Rosa Vásquez Santos, "Saint James in Rome: The Vanished Churches," *La Corónica* 36 (2008): 75–98, at 76–79.

129. The best overview is Burr, *Spiritual Franciscans*.

130. Baird, Baglivi, and Kane, *Chronicle*, 558.

Spirituals of Provence (28 February 1316), shortly before John XXII began his infamous crackdown.[131] Thus, as John turned sharply against these "renegade" Franciscans, Giacomo's ability to influence events may have waned. For instance, it may not be a coincidence that in the earliest known manuscript of Angela of Foligno's book the opening reference to Giacomo's approbation appears to have been scratched out, perhaps showing that his support was perceived as a liability.[132] Moreover, Giacomo was in declining health well before his death in 1318. With his demise, Pietro Colonna was named his successor as protector of San Silvestro, before his own death in 1326.[133] Thus by the 1330s the generation of Margherita's nieces and nephews who had actually known her passed from the scene, and her memory was largely eclipsed for the better part of two centuries.

A Colonna did, however, eventually become pope. In 1417, as Pope Martin V, Oddo Colonna became the first pope to return to Rome after the Great Schism. Whether or not there was family interest in reviving Margherita's cult—and it seems likely there was not—it was clear that the new pope's priorities needed to focus on reestablishing the papacy in Rome and restoring its sacred places.[134] He canonized only one saint, an obscure eleventh-century German hermit.[135]

---

131. Livarius Oliger, "Fr. Bertrandi de Turre processus contra spirituales aquitaniae (1315) et card. Iacobi de Columna litterae defensoriae spiritualium provinciae (1316)," *AFH* 16 (1923): 322–55, at 350–55. A vivid study of John XXII's campaign against supporters of the Spirituals is Louisa A. Burnham, *So Great a Light, So Great a Smoke: The Beguin Heretics of Languedoc* (Ithaca, NY: Cornell University Press, 2008).

132. Biblioteca Comunale di Assisi ms. 342.

133. *DV*, 31–32; *BF*, 5:156.

134. See Elizabeth McCahill, *Reviving the Eternal City: Rome and the Papal Court, 1420–1447* (Cambridge, MA: Harvard University Press, 2013).

135. A process for Sebald of Nuremburg began in 1418 at the request of his native town and resulted in his canonization in 1425. This pontificate also witnessed processes for three Swedish figures (approved at the Council of Constance), as well as Catherine of Siena's continuing process. For these cases, which Vauchez considers the end of the medieval tradition, see his *Sainthood*.

Indeed, there is scarce evidence for an active cult dedicated to Margherita Colonna in the later Middle Ages.[136] Both halves of the unique, composite manuscript that today contains both *Vita I* and *Vita II* were copied at San Silvestro in the fourteenth century, but we are aware of no additional fourteenth-century sources indicating devotional interest in her.[137] The published registers from San Silvestro in Capite record donations to the convent and confirm continued Colonna support for the community but provide no specific evidence of pilgrims visiting Margherita's tomb there or efforts to promote her cult to a wider audience.[138] These registers do identify a reliquary designed to hold her cranium, which received brief attention in a history of Roman churches that was composed during Martin V's reign and referred to Margherita as "saint."[139] However, the fact that Mariano of Florence (who, recall, in 1519 had provided the earliest surviving account of the translation of her relics into Rome) added no new miracle stories to those in *Vita I* and

---

136. The miracles recorded in the two *vitae* demonstrate interest in Palestrina and the surrounding communities, but any local cult seems to have been dislocated by her tomb's translation to Rome and the subsequent conflict between the Colonna and Boniface VIII.

137. In a footnote to his 2007 article "La lutte entre Boniface VIII et les Colonna," Le Pogam indicated that frescoes depicting the life of Margherita Colonna recently had been discovered in the Aracoeli. This seems to have been a misunderstanding. Not only was Lezlie Knox unable to identify these frescoes during visits to the Aracoeli or through consultations with its sacristan, but personal communication with Claudia Bolgia, the art historical expert on this church, confirms that there is no known cycle dedicated to Margherita Colonna. We thank Claudia Bolgia for this information and for her suggestion that there may be some confusion with a contemporary fresco cycle uncovered behind Baroque "remodeling" that Tommaso Strinati has identified as painted by Pietro Cavallini in the 1280s or 1290s. See his catalogue, *Aracoeli: Gli affreschi ritrovati* (Milan: Skira, 2004), as well as Claudia Bolgia, *Reclaiming the Roman Capitol: Santa Maria in Aracoeli from the Altar of Augustus to the Franciscans, c. 500–1450* (New York: Routledge, 2017).

138. Federici, "Regesto."

139. This work remains unpublished; see *DV*, 85–86, as well as a description of the reliquary in Carletti's *Memorie istorico-critiche*, 138. The current location of this reliquary is unknown; it may be lost unless it is in the possession of the Colonna family.

Vita II hardly suggests a flourishing cult.[140] Rather, it was Mariano himself whose historical writings brought Margherita Colonna's saintliness to wider attention in the early modern period.

This Tuscan Friar may have first learned about Margherita when he visited Rome around 1516 and prepared a pilgrim's guidebook to the city.[141] His description of San Silvestro in Capite there focused mostly on the antiquity of the church and its ownership of the relics of John the Baptist's head and the Holy Face.[142] His guidebook mentioned Margherita's tomb but gave no details about the reliquary or her life, simply repeating what earlier authors had written.[143] But at some point Mariano did visit San Silvestro, where presumably he consulted the unique manuscript containing *Vita I* and *Vita II*. On the basis of these sources, he included a new retelling of Margherita's life in his vernacular history of the Order of Saint Clare, the *Libro delle Povere Donne* (1519).[144] This work became enormously influential for subsequent representations of Mar-

---

140. *DV*, 41. On the promotion of Italian saints in this period, see Alison K. Frazier, ed., *The Saint between Manuscript and Print: Italy, 1400–1600* (Toronto: CRRS Publications, 2015).

141. In just two decades he wrote fifteen different historical and devotional works. Lezlie Knox is currently working on a study of Mariano's biography and milieu.

142. Mariano of Florence, *Itinerarium urbis Romae*, ed. Enrico Bulletti (Rome: Pontificio Instituto di Archeologia Cristiana, 1931), 215–16. On these relics, see Kane, *Church of San Silvestro*, 16–26.

143. This "lacuna" may seem surprising, but Mariano's descriptions of other churches in this work similarly demonstrate a lack of interest or firsthand knowledge. For example, he incorrectly describes the location of papal tombs in Old Saint Peter's and does not mention the already famous Pinturicchio frescoes of the recently canonized Bernardino of Siena (painted 1484–86) that were located in a chapel just to the right of the main entrance in the Aracoeli. See Carol M. Richardson, *Reclaiming Rome: Cardinals in the Fifteenth Century* (Leiden: Brill, 2009). A close reading of his text reveals that Mariano based his accounts of various sites on earlier guidebooks, particularly Francesco Albertini's *Opusculum de mirabilibus novae et veteris urbis Romae* (see Peter Murray, ed., *Five Early Guides to Rome and Florence* [Farnsborough: Gregg, 1972]).

144. See above, note 11.

gherita's life. One example of this influence is visual. The earliest surviving depiction of Margherita Colonna is a watercolor that represents her among all the saintly female followers of Francis and Clare, which Sister Dorothea Broccardi included in one of the manuscripts of the *Libro delle Povere Donne*.[145] Mariano also referred to Margherita briefly in his *Compendium* (ca. 1522), an abridgement of a longer Latin chronicle known as the *Fasciculus*, which apparently contained a longer Latin version of Margherita's *vita*.[146]

Later Franciscan historians such as Marco of Lisbon (d. 1591) learned about Margherita from Mariano's work, as did the prolific Counter-Reformation author Antonio Gallonio.[147] His 1591 *Historia delle Sante Vergini Romane* featured Margherita's life along with a woodcut of her kneeling quietly in humble prayer before a crucifix. But Gallonio also consulted the two *vitae* preserved in manuscript at San Silvestro and thus is the most important early modern biographer of Margherita Colonna after Mariano of Florence.[148] Between 1600 and 1800, at least fifteen more authors wrote on Margherita, generally in various hagiographic publications and local histories of Roman churches.[149] But as these early modern treatments moved farther and farther from the original sources, they tended to create a bland "saint" Margherita whose

---

145. Volterra, Biblioteca Guarnacci, ms. 6146, fol. 1v. This image has been published by Ilaria Bianchi, "La gloria della serafica Chiara e del suo ordine: Suor Dorothea Broccardi copista e miniatrice nel convento di San Lino a Volterra," in *Vita artistica nel monastero femminile: Exempla*, ed. Vera Fortunati (Bologna: Editrice Compositore, 2002), 106–13, image at 111. This "Clarissan tree" was unknown to Oliger, but see his survey of Margherita's later iconography in *DV*, 88–93.

146. This *fasciculus* has been lost since 1769, when the unique manuscript was sent from Florence to the Congregazione dei Riti, the predecessor of the contemporary Vatican office that handles canonizations.

147. For an overview of his writings, see Jetze Touber, *Law, Medicine, and Engineering in the Cult of Saints in Counter-Reformation Rome* (Leiden: Brill, 2014).

148. See Oliger's analysis in *DV*, 44–49.

149. Surveyed by Oliger in *DV*, 49–64. Many of these authors were Franciscans, including such well-known names as Luke Wadding.

humble piety obscured the memory of the unenclosed, active, and intensely visionary historical woman.[150]

In 1847, Pope Pius IX conferred formal beatification on Margherita Colonna. This step may have been taken primarily at the urging of the modern Colonna family (Marcantonio Colonna served in the Vatican under Pius).[151] *Vita I* and *Vita II* were evidently completely unknown at the curia, and the decree of beatification made no attempt to describe new miracles or an influx of pious pilgrims.[152] But if Margherita's beatification sparked any modest rise in pilgrimage at San Silvestro, it would have been interrupted in 1875, when the Italian state suppressed most religious communities. The Sisters moved from San Silvestro to a Benedictine convent in Trastevere, taking with them Margherita's relics. The Franciscan Attilio Cadderi, the most prolific promoter of a new effort toward canonization for Margherita, recently has written of visiting her shrine while on pastoral visits to the Sisters in the 1960s and 1970s. Intriguingly, he has also reported that during that period some of Margherita's relics suddenly disappeared and then remained missing for several decades until (with the exception of the bust holding her cranium) they reappeared in 1992 in a church in Paliano, a small town near Palestrina.[153] In Rome, the chapel in the Galleria Colonna (attached to the family palazzo) today displays a nineteenth-century stained-glass window representing Margherita's translation to Rome.[154] This private room (it normally has a rope preventing Saturday morning tourists from entering) is the only surviving marker of Margherita in the city. In fact, her modern cult is now centered back where it began, on Mount Prenestino, in the modern town of Castel San Pietro. A small chapel dedicated

---

150. Cadderi includes useful bibliographic lists that expand on Oliger's earlier discussion; see his *Beata Margherita Colonna*, esp. 182–84 and 187–89.

151. Prospero Colonna, *The Colonna Family: A Short Selective History* (Rome: Campisano, 2010), provides a good overview of his family's long history.

152. This decree is printed in *DV*, 223–26, and is reprinted in Cadderi, *Beata Margherita Colonna*, 179–81.

153. Cadderi, *Beata Margherita Colonna*, 185–86.

154. This scene is not historical. It shows the woman reclining on a funeral bier held aloft by four Friars, accompanied by another Friar wearing a cardinal's robes over his habit. This chapel also contains one of the Aracoeli mosaics.

to her memory stands on the site of the houses in which she lived with her companions. More dramatically, at the Church of San Pietro Apostolo, dedicatory plaques on the porch draw attention to her, and visitors can actually view her bones in a glass casket beneath the high altar. Thus in the twenty-first century, much as when Giovanni Colonna and Stefania were writing, Margherita's cult is supported by family, local Friars, and pious inhabitants of the hills around Palestrina.

ONE

The Life of the Blessed Virgin Margherita of the Family Name Colonna, by Giovanni Colonna

The first "life" of Margherita Colonna was composed by her older brother, the Roman senator Giovanni Colonna. It was begun shortly after her death on 30 December 1280 and was completed before 1285.

Our translation is based on the text edited in *DV*, 111–88, compared with Rome, Biblioteca Casanatense ms. 104, folios 1–26.[1] We have found very few errors in Oliger's edition, and we have accepted the vast majority of his emendations where passages seem to have been miscopied by the scribe or corrupted at an earlier stage of transmission. Chapter numbers follow those established by Oliger, but for paragraph breaks within chapters we have sometimes deviated from his editorial decisions.

---

1. For *Vita I* and *Vita II*, we have had the benefit of the Italian translation recently published in Attilio Cadderi (P. Carlo, O.F.M.), *Beata Margherita Colonna (1255–1280): Le due vite scritte dal fratello Giovanni, senatore di Roma e da Stefania, monaca di San Silvestro in Capite*, ed. Celeste Fornari and Luigi Borzi (Palestrina, 2010). We have generally preferred a style of translation that stays closer to the Latin, but Cadderi's Italian has been helpful in considering possible interpretations of difficult passages.

CHAPTER I. HERE BEGINS THE LIFE OF THE BLESSED VIRGIN
MARGHERITA, OF THE FAMILY NAME COLONNA[2]

Margherita was born of a noble line of Romans.[3] While she remained
"in her family household,"[4] not yet having left the secular world but
having lost her more worthy parent,[5] she came under the tutelage of her
mother and her brothers.[6] Then, while she was still a very young girl,
her mother died.[7] But although she was released from a mother's [over-
sight],[8] she did not misuse the freedom granted her to do as she pleased;
rather, she willingly placed herself under the control and direction of the
[elder][9] of her brothers so that she might live with him in a more modest
fashion. Yet [later,] when she had set out in the service of Christ, she
instead stayed under the power and guardianship of her more worthy
brother [Giacomo], who had inspired her toward a holy manner of life.[10]
This [brother, Giacomo], because of both the holy esteem in which he
was held and his accumulated accomplishments, was raised to the ser-

---

2. "Incipit vita beate Margarite virginis cognomine de columpna" is in red as
an overall title, while also taking the place usually allotted to chapter titles in the
manuscript. Oliger added in brackets his own chapter title, "De ortu et prima eius
iuventute."

3. Margherita's birth can be placed ca. 1254–55.

4. Cf. Antiphon 3, I Vespers, *Officium rhythmicum in festo s. Clarae*, in Giovanni
Boccali, "Testi liturgici antichi per la festa di santa Chiara (sec. XIII–XV)," *AFH* 100
(2007): 150, and in *AH*, vol. 5, no. 54, p. 157.

5. That is, her father, Oddone Colonna, who died in 1256 or 1257.

6. Her mother was Margherita Orsini. Her brothers Giovanni and Giacomo
are featured prominently in this text; she also had three other brothers named
Oddone, Matteo, and Landolfo.

7. Margherita Orisini died ca. 1265–66, according to *DV*, 80.

8. This is our conjecture where a word is missing (with space left) in the
manuscript.

9. A word is again missing from the manuscript (with space left), and Oliger's
conjecture of *senioris* seems sound. The passage would thus refer to Giovanni
Colonna.

10. The sentence foreshadows her later decision to turn away from the secular
world and Giovanni Colonna's household.

vice of the universal church and now occupies the most worthy office of cardinal.[11]

While dwelling in the world, *she* therefore *kept herself unsullied by it*.[12] For chastity had been inborn in her mind, and it *grew* with her *from infancy*.[13] As the unsteady years of blooming girlhood approached, she became increasingly modest, ever more sure in her progress, bearing a heart wise in age while still tender in years. Just as in all her deeds and acts there was nothing worthy of reproach, so there was no one who would speak *ill of her*,[14] for the Lord was always watching over her.[15]

CHAPTER II. ON HER VIRGINITY, AND THE VISION BETWEEN THE ANGELS[16]

Indeed, she was a wise virgin,[17] so chaste and modest, just as widespread reputation and the judge of truth proclaimed her to be. Thus many noblemen longed for her hand in marriage, inspired more by the firmest belief in her goodness than enticed by an ample dowry or her high birth. Indeed, in their quest for marriage some preferred her to her older sister

---

11. Giacomo was named cardinal deacon of Santa Maria in Via Lata by Nicholas III (who as Giangaetano Orsini was first cousin to Margherita Colonna and her brothers) on 12 March 1278.

12. Cf. James 1:27.

13. Job 31:18.

14. Cf. Judith 8:8.

15. This is the first example of the author's recurring habit of drawing a moral at the end of each chapter.

16. This chapter title was never copied into the space left for it. Instead it is found only in a highly abbreviated cursive hand in the margin. Generally, chapter numbers (but not titles) were noted in a faint contemporary hand in the margin; this is the only case where a title is thus noted. Oliger assumed it could be treated as the author's original intention, and we have followed him by including it here.

17. Cf. Matthew 25:1–4; and *Officium rhythmicum in festo s. Clarae*, ed. Giovanni Boccali, "Testi liturgici antichi per la festa di santa Chiara," 155; also first Antiphon for Matins in *AH*, vol. 5, no. 54, p. 158.

of marriageable age.[18] But, by God's will, obstacles stood in the way while the wise virgin's decision still remained unknown.

During this time,[19] while her older brother [Giovanni], with whom she was then living, was busy finding her an earthly husband, her more worthy brother [Giacomo], the one just mentioned, in a more worthy fashion tried to betroth her in a more worthy marriage. He had been educated in goodness from the cradle itself, and, having come into the lot of Aaron[20] while studying in Bologna,[21] he was advanced into the *blessing of sweetness*[22] and became that *merchant* of the heavenly *pearl*,[23] *who when he had found it* gave up all his possessions in order to obtain it.[24]

Thus it came to pass that [Giacomo] had to return home to arrange his father's financial obligations, according to God's will.[25] Then he preached the pearl[26] [of wisdom] hidden in his heart to his Margherita; and like an envoy [of God] he endeavored to consecrate this virgin to the Son of the Virgin.[27] He explained that in earthly marriages happiness is

---

18. *Vita I*, ch. 6, states that Margherita actually had two older sisters of marriageable age still at home. In fact, Margherita is known to have had at least two older sisters. Giacoma married Pietro Conti, and a sister of unknown name married Oddone di Sant'Eustachio. An older sister with six children is mentioned in *Vita II*, ch. 18, who may or may not have been identical with one of the two previously mentioned.

19. *DV*, 80–81, plausibly puts these events ca. 1272.

20. Aaron (older brother of Moses) was the first high priest of the Israelites. But Giacomo Colonna was never ordained as a priest, so the passage probably refers to his assuming the title of deacon.

21. On Giacomo's student stay in Bologna, see Tilmann Schmidt, "Eine Studentenhause in Bologna zwischen Bonifaz VIII. und den Colonna," *Quellen und Forschungen aus italienischen Bibliotheken und Archiven* 67 (1987): 108–41.

22. Psalm 20:3.

23. The Latin "Margarite celestis" is a play on Margherita's name (*margarita* means "pearl" in Latin), and on the biblical comparison of the kingdom of heaven to a priceless pearl.

24. Cf. Matthew 13:45–46. Oliger points out that Bonaventure's *Legenda maior* 1.4 plays on the same biblical passage.

25. Oddone Colonna had been dead for some fifteen years at this point, so these were long-lasting testamentary questions.

26. *Margaritam*, again the common play on words.

27. Cf. 2 Corinthians 11:2.

fleeting and ends in grief after many woes and sorrows.[28] But, by contrast, in never-ending marriages where bodily integrity remains, the soul is betrothed to a heavenly spouse. For in these [eternal marriages], if there is some initial weariness, it lasts only a little while or disappears quickly, because of the *comforts* that *according to the multitude of sorrows give joy to the soul.*[29] Instead, the soul rejoices without end when it is finally brought to the marriage chamber of the longed-for spouse. Often and more often again he repeated these points and others like them to his listener. In divinely eloquent words, and seizing every opportunity of time and place, he beat upon the ears of this virgin. And the virgin willingly heard his words, and now sought times at which she would be free to listen secretly.[30] Her soul was transfixed by the piercing *sword* of the word *of God,*[31] and at that moment she first resolved to preserve her virginity from then on, dedicating it to God in all humility. Moreover, her brother's preaching could *not* have been *in vain.*[32] For he advised, as was his practice, that one begin a conversation with a prayer that one not speak *in vain.* For a *seed sown upon good ground yields fruit a hundred fold.*[33]

Of the two brothers who were working at cross purposes as to the place in life that the virgin should occupy, the efforts of one [brother, Giovanni], came to nothing, and his concern was in vain. For after complicated negotiations, he promised this virgin, without her knowledge, to

---

28. The text actually moves into the present tense here to give Giacomo's exhortation an air of urgency. We nevertheless translate in the historical past.

29. Psalm 93:19.

30. As Oliger noted, there may be an echo here of Thomas of Celano's *Legenda S. Clarae* 3.5–6, though there is no verbal match. See Giovanni Boccali, *Legenda latina sanctae Clarae virginis assisiensis* (Santa Maria degli Angeli: Edizioni Porziuncola, 2001), 100; and Regis J. Armstrong, *The Lady: Clare of Assisi, Early Documents* (New York: New City, 2006), 284.

31. Cf. Ephesians 6:17.

32. Cf. 1 Corinthians 15:10.

33. Luke 8:5–8. This praise of Giacomo Colonna's prayer and preaching is a good first indication of the text's desire to laud the larger Colonna family generally as well as Margherita Colonna specifically.

a suitor whose noble birth and wealth were not unequal to her own.[34] When [Margherita] heard what had been done, she was not at all pleased; yet the wise girl kept this to herself until the appropriate moment. The efforts of the other [brother, Giacomo], however, were not in vain. For he debated many issues with his brother, even if he did not then disclose the as yet unripe decision of the virgin concerning those matters about which he had been so persuasive, because the virgin wanted her hand in deeds to precede her tongue in words, and her promise to be given by its execution. The wise man nevertheless discerned what she would do at the right moment, bending her soul to his holy advice.

Before the more worthy brother [Giacomo] was given final confirmation in a letter from the virgin (for he had left his home and his other brother), God showed him a lofty indication of his sister's future status with a wondrous prophetic sign.[35] He was praying ceaselessly for his sister, beseeching the poor and the friends of God whom he knew to be worthy, obtaining their consent to pray for her, adding devotion upon devotion, asking help from the flocks of saints—especially from the holy virgins by whose example he was praying that she would be instructed and consecrated—that they would intercede with the Son of the Virgin so that his sister's "heart" would be made "immaculate and her body" not be corrupted.[36]

Therefore, upon the arrival of the Feast of the Blessed Virgin Margherita, who has been listed in the catalogue of saints for many years, he was filled with greater devotion to her on behalf of his sister who

---

34. *Vita II*, ch. 2, calls this potential husband a "proconsul."

35. Giacomo had presumably returned to Bologna at this point. It is worth noting that the first vision in the text is experienced not by Margherita but by Giacomo.

36. The phrase "ut *cor* sororis *immaculatum* fieret ne confuderetur *et corpus*" strongly echoes an Antiphon for the feast of Saint Cecilia (November 22). Cantus ID, 2863; Stephen Joseph Van Dijk, *Sources of the Modern Roman Liturgy: The Ordinals by Haymo of Faversham and Related Documents (1243–1307)*, Studia et documenta Franciscana 1–2 (Leiden: E. J. Brill, 1963), 2:171.

shared the same name of Margherita.[37] That day he dined with the Friars[38] and saw to it that they solemnly celebrated Mass in honor of the virgin whose feast it was. And wholeheartedly committing himself to that same devotion, he fed pilgrims and *the harborless in* his own lodgings.[39] And when everything had been solemnly carried out as it should, in the middle of the day when everyone else in the house had retired for their midday nap, he remained alone in the garden, in back where there is a meadow, and devoted himself completely to reading the legend of the most blessed virgin whose feast he was celebrating. And as he came to the passage where it reads, "Margherita, virgin, come to the repose of your Christ!"[40] he was immediately transformed. And, as though led to a performance, he saw his sister between two guardian angels, carried through the air by their efforts. He saw this and marveled and watched intently for as long as he was able; and the whole time he was able to recognize his sister.[41] After an hour the vision began to shift, so that the house now blocked his sight. Then he ran, and racing through the house he came outside to the square in front of the house where the miraculous vision was being directed. Once again he beheld her just as he had seen

---

37. According to popular belief the early virgin saint Margaret/Margherita was martyred under Diocletian after refusing to give up her faith. Her feast day is 20 July, and although the year in question here is not entirely certain, 20 July 1272 seems likely.

38. The Latin *fratres* (when not used in a biological sense) can generally be taken to refer to Franciscans in this text; the passage therefore indicates the Franciscans of Bologna. The earliest permanent Franciscan community in that city was founded in 1219, presumably as a house of study. It grew rapidly and seems to have served as a host for Giacomo Colonna during his own time studying in Bologna. For Franciscan education, see Neslihan Şenocak, *The Poor and the Perfect: The Rise of Learning in the Franciscan Order, 1209–1310* (Ithaca, NY: Cornell University Press, 2012).

39. Cf. Isaiah 58:7.

40. "Passio sanctae Margaritae virginis et martyris," in Boninus Mombritius, *Sanctuarium seu vitae sanctorum, novum hunc editionem*, vol. 2 (Paris: Fontemoing, 1910), 194.

41. One suspects a scribal error or omission in the Latin, which reads, "et perspexit quam diu potuit et potuit usquequo sororem agnovit."

her, in the middle between the two [angels]. And just as he had known her and known whom she was with before, so here he recognized her again, until the vision took itself up on high and flew off, away from the sight of his steady gaze.

Of course from such a vision he concluded that he was seeing that she had been *brought out of prison to praise the name of the Lord.*[42] But, in fact, it was not so! In truth it signified the passage *out of Egypt* of the daughter *of Israel.*[43] Her brother [Giacomo] had not yet heard of this change, though it had clearly occurred. But a short while later, through a certain written prophecy,[44] the virgin let him know that she had left her house and her brother [Giovanni], going to reside at Mount [Prenestino], until she should arrive "at the Mount which is Christ."[45]

We have seen that this did indeed come to pass.[46] For although she had longed to build her own monastery where she could enclose herself with her followers, vowing service to the Lord, and though she had decided to go to the monastery at Assisi,[47] she was able to do neither of these things. She was prevented, until—after extreme self-deprivation, innumerable expenses, the endurance of great sickness, *in all patience,*[48] as the story of her life will show—she "might shatter the alabaster bottle

---

42. Psalms 121:4; 141:8. That is, Giacomo interpreted this vision at first as meaning that his sister had died.

43. Cf. Numbers 33:38; Deuteronomy 4:46; etc. That is, Margherita's passage out of "bondage" from the secular world.

44. The Latin is "sub quodam vaticinio per transcriptum." The use of the word *vaticinio* is interesting, indicating a prophecy or prediction about the future, not just a report of Margherita's current resolve. This would seem to be the same "letter" referred to several paragraphs previously.

45. The phrase "ad montem, qui Christus est" is from a collect for the Mass of St. Catherine. *CO*, no. 1521; Van Dijk, *Sources*, 2:305; Robert Lippe, ed., *Missale Romanum Mediolani, 1474* (London: Harrison and Sons, 1899), 402.

46. The rest of this paragraph foreshadows Margherita's later story.

47. That is, to join the community originally founded by Clare of Assisi at San Damiano, which had moved within the city walls of Assisi in 1260.

48. 2 Timothy 4:2.

of her body"[49] in the houses of the aforesaid Mount [Prenestino],[50] and the church in the nearby region might breathe with the fragrance of her good fame, and she might move on to Christ.

CHAPTER III. ON THE BLESSED VIRGIN'S SPEECH TO HER AND THE INSPIRATION GIVEN TO HER

For good reason I have briefly wandered from the direct narrative of her life, but I will now return to it. The *day comes* and *the time is fulfilled*[51] when it was incumbent upon the brother [Giovanni] who had arranged her betrothal to now plan the virgin's trousseau, for he was still unaware of her determined resolution. When he sent her older sister[52] to ask her what she would like to have prepared in the way of costly garments, [Margherita] listened with disdain; and if colorful or[53] luxurious items were proposed, she laughed all the more scornfully. From this response her brother concluded that she was not happy with the husband to whom she had been promised. But it was not, as her brother supposed, because she sought a man of another social status, but because she was saving herself for Christ, to whom she afterward vowed herself. When he asked her some days later whether the proposed husband was pleasing to her, or whether someone else should be sought,[54] she told him plainly that if she had been intending to take any man for a husband she

---

49. Cf. Thomas of Celano, *Legenda S. Clarae* 5.16, in Boccoli, *Legenda*, 112, and Armstrong, *Lady*, 288 (cf. also Mark 14:3).

50. It is noteworthy that the plural ("in domibus Montis") is always used to refer to "houses" of the compound at Mount Prenestino that Margherita and her followers inhabited.

51. Cf. Jeremiah 50:27; Mark 1:15; Genesis 29:21; etc.

52. On the ambiguous references to Margherita's sisters, see note 18 above.

53. Oliger read "varia a preciosa" and emended to "varia aut preciosa"; in fact, the manuscript reads "aut."

54. Giovanni Colonna's apparent willingness (in his own recounting) to consider Margherita's wishes is notable and perhaps helps to explain the flexibility with which her particular religious vocation found expression with family support.

would have been content to leave the selection entirely to her brother; but she had now vowed her body and soul to Christ in pursuit of chastity.

This questioning took place after she had made her vow, but let the events that had happened to her before that time be narrated here.[55] The prudent virgin, giving thought to the situation, since she was no longer able to hide her decision to preserve her virginity, understood very well that revealing it would upset her brother [Giovanni], who loved her dearly; yet she chose to upset her brother and suffer the consequences rather than to retreat from her sacred undertaking. So she turned once more to Mary, the Mother of God, for whose Son she had started down this path, and poured herself entirely into praying that [Mary], the very lily of virginity, would guide her with advice and help, strengthen and support her, and preserve the person who was preserving herself unspoiled for her Son. After this earnest prayer, she went to bed the following night and allowed no other thought to enter her mind.

And as she slept, in the quiet of midnight,[56] the glorious Mother of God, the Virgin Mary, who has never failed when called upon, who had been most devoutly appealed to by the virgin girl, appeared to her. [The Virgin Mary], in whom the remedy of the salvation of the entire world is placed, deigned to come herself in person, as the bearer of tidings of deliverance. She came riding upon a certain chariot, preceded by great flashes of light and by a shining too great for the human eye to bear, like shining rays flashing from the rising sun, *and a light shined in the room*.[57] The chariot came right up to the bed where [Margherita] lay. And standing before her, the blessed Virgin said to her, "*Your prayer has been heard*,[58] and I have come here to fulfill it." *The soul* of the virgin girl *melted* after the Mother of Joy *spoke* to her.[59] And feeling deeply the inexpressible sweetness of this speech, [Margherita] poured forth an as-

---

55. This is the first example of the author's penchant for storytelling in the form of flashbacks. The vision preceded Margherita's formal refusal of marriage and her flight to Mount Prenestino.

56. The phrase echoes an Antiphon for the season of Nativity and Epiphany. Cantus ID, 2461; Van Dijk, *Sources*, 2:38, 214, 216. Cf. Wisdom 18:14–15.

57. Acts 12:7.

58. Luke 1:13.

59. Canticles 5:6.

tonishing shower of tears, so that afterwards she found her pillowcase soaked as though it had been submerged in a running stream. Thus, touched by the spirit of God, she answered the Virgin, "I give thanks to that spring from which all grace flows, our salvation, whom you, a virgin, bore in your womb; and I know well it will be fulfilled." Then, not being strong enough to endure the brilliance of such a light any longer, she turned over on her other side. Then the chariot went forward along that side of the bed to which the girl had turned. And once more the Virgin Mother of God stood right before her and added these words to what she had already said: "*I will not leave you.*"[60] With this said, the chariot began to move and to recede with its splendor. But before it was gone, the sleeping virgin awoke; and rising up she saw the chariot and its undercarriage with the vanishing vision of light. At once, "because the grace of the Holy Spirit knows no slow undertakings,"[61] even before she left her bed or did anything else, this daughter *vowed a vow of Jacob* to her Christ,[62] where she consecrated her soul and flesh more firmly to Him. She later gave an unheard-of report about this matter: that no hesitation ever tantalized her mind concerning what she had sworn, because the Mother of Truth, who had declared that her prayer had been heard, was incapable of speaking anything but the truth.

Great is the Lord and exceedingly to be praised in the city of our God, in the virgin Margherita, *His holy mountain,*[63] where He has shown forth so kindly! *Let us raise our eyes* to her, and let us learn from the passion of her devotion, so that help may come to us[64] as it came to her when she opened wide the mouth of her desire to receive grace, and the Lord filled it; for it is written: *Open your mouth wide and I will fill it.*[65] For Truth says in the Gospel: *Ask and you shall receive, seek and you shall find, knock and*

---

60. Hebrews 13:5.

61. *Sancti Ambrosii mediolanensis opera, pars IV, Expositio evangelii secundum Lucum, fragmenta in Esaiam*, ed. M. Adriaen (Turnhout: Brepols, 1957), 39 (2.19).

62. Psalm 131:2.

63. Psalm 47:2.

64. Based on Psalm 120:2, the phrase echoes a collect used for feasts of the Virgin and other female saints. *CO*, 2507; Van Dijk, *Sources*, 2:122, 182, 187–89, 272, 316; Lippe, *Missale Romanum Mediolani*, 304, 442.

65. Psalm 80:11.

it shall be opened to you.[66] Because she asked, she received; because she sought, she found; because she knocked, it was opened to her. But woe to us! Because we do not have such desires, grace does not come. For again *the Lord is rich to all that call upon Him.*[67] And there is no difference between people of today and those of long ago, but He *is near to all that call upon Him in truth,*[68] just as in our time He was nearby in aid of the virgin Margherita, [and remains so] right up to now.[69]

Therefore let us not wonder when we hear that she turned to the other side because of the beating brilliance of the light, for one must believe that the virgin did nothing other than what was pleasing to God; her *soul, melted* by these addresses and tasting the spirit,[70] was unable to wish or to do anything else. But let us say that it was fittingly done as ordained by God, as when human weakness finds itself in the face of divine discourse, as it is written of Moses, *Moses hid his face for he dared not look at God.*[71]

CHAPTER IV. ON THE CHANGE MADE IN HER BY THE SPEECH OF THE MOTHER OF GOD

Inexpressible is the *sweetness* of the Lord! The Prophet marvels at *how great* it is, and gives name to the *multitude* of its immensity, and so I will not attempt to describe *how* after those addresses he *hid* [this sweetness] in His virgin *fearing* him,[72] and how He brought everything around to

---

66. Matthew 7:7.

67. Romans 10:12.

68. Psalm 144:18.

69. Oliger emended "proximus diebus nostris virginis Margarite" to "proximis diebus nostris virgini Margarite." We have preferred to follow the manuscript reading. The last two words *usque huc* were added in the margin, but apparently by the original scribal hand.

70. Canticles 5:6.

71. Exodus 3:6. It is notable that Giovanni must try to interpret Margherita's idiosyncratic vision in a way that points toward a moral lesson, thus indicating that he really was reporting what his sister had related, with all its quirks.

72. Cf. Psalm 30:20.

her hopes. Let those who have *tasted and seen* His *sweetness*[73] themselves delight in hearing that the virgin was drunk with the temperance of the spirit. We, who have not tasted in this way, let us long for this and believe it; and let us tell, insofar as we have seen it and known it, what kind of person the Holy Spirit taught her to become in her outward visible deeds.

Right away after she had made her vow, she entered the chapel located below the area of the hall and sang the Hours of the Blessed Virgin with great devotion and thanksgiving, even though at that time she had not yet learned the daily Hours, which she later pursued with great diligence and understanding.[74] One must believe that her innermost heart was inspired in this way, suffused with angelic passion and consumed in a raging fire of divine love. Now she groaned; now she sighed; now she *minded the things that are above*,[75] because [the Virgin Mary], who is mistress of all spirits above, had deigned to visit this world below on her account, in order to make her long for things above.[76] Now [Margherita] repeated the Hours that she had said, and now she multiplied the angelic greetings of the Virgin.[77] Now she poured forth the tears that mark the true depth of prayer beyond mere words. Nothing else pleased her but to groan, to weep, to sigh, to praise; and so she spent the entire night in this way. Nor was she afraid to be all alone, because she, who desired nothing but Christ, disregarded everything but him, for all her faith was in the Lord alone.

At dawn she went *into the hill country* where her more worthy brother [Giacomo] was staying.[78] She placed before him all that she had seen, not remaining silent about what she had known and suggesting that her mind had been completely renewed. She offered herself to him

---

73. Cf. Psalm 33:9.

74. It would seem that Margherita was physically still at the residence of Giovanni Colonna.

75. Cf. Colossians 3:2.

76. Again Giovanni slips into a breathless historical present, but we have translated with a past tense.

77. The *Ave Maria*.

78. Luke 1:39. Presumably she was going up Mount Prenestino to the Colonna residence at which Giacomo was staying upon his return from Bologna.

now *with her loins girded,*[79] prepared to follow this Moses sent to her by God, with all thought of Egypt behind her, now a daughter of Israel.[80] As [Giacomo] listened, his spirit was overcome with inexpressible joy. And *lifting up his eyes* to heaven *he gave thanks,*[81] because Christ's esteem had truly united them now as brother and sister in His calling.[82] He worried no more about her secular status, but returned to where he later beheld the sign of her future holiness.[83] We have already described this vision, except those happenings of the soul that are beyond our knowledge and are known only to Him *who made the hearts of* men.[84]

Once the vision and speech of the Mother of God caused this renewal within her, the virgin discovered in her bodily senses that her vision was miraculously altered, for things did not appear to her as they had before. Houses and palaces seemed like mere huts and camp tents, their occupants of little significance or regard. People seemed to her like only passersby, or like noisy troops breaking camp. Indeed, what is more, in some cases one thing seemed quite another in her sight. It seemed to her as if the land itself were repelling her, throwing her out, turning her away as though she were foreign to it. And just as with her vision, a similar change occurred in her taste, so that for two days she tasted nothing, nor did she desire anything. Indeed, anything that was placed before her, if she had tasted it, was despicable to her. Every sound of words and any speaker's voice troubled her hearing. What more? All her senses were immune to the exterior world, since her thoughts were concentrated on interior things, or, to put it more truly, were drawn to higher matters.

---

79. Cf. Exodus 12:1.

80. Cf. *Vita II*, ch. 19.

81. Cf. John 11:41.

82. The phrase echoes a collect for the Mass of Saints John and Paul. *CO*, 4893; Van Dijk, *Sources*, 2:145, 287; Lippe, *Missale Romanum Mediolani*, 344.

83. That is, the author seems to have now worked his way back to the point in the narrative when Giacomo, in Bologna on the feast day of St. Margaret, sees the vision of his sister Margherita between two angels. The indications are not entirely clear, however, because in chapter 2 it seemed that he had this vision before being certain that his sister would choose a life of virginity. But since the author says he has already described this vision, no other possibility is evident.

84. Psalm 32:15.

During those two days she wanted only to be left alone, to see nothing, hear nothing, say nothing except praises to God, which flowed more from her heart than her tongue.

After these two days the virgin took heart, and because it would be contrary to God's command to allow her body to perish from fasting— and not because she was hungry!—she placed a single chestnut in her mouth and began to chew. And while she returned to the exterior world by slow degrees, the mighty change that had so shaken her gradually gave way. Nevertheless, ever afterward she engaged with the transitory things of this world only in a transitory way, and *where* the *treasure* of her hope was, *there* her spirit was found, in eternal things.[85]

Because such things are great and very rare, the human mind would scarcely believe them if the spirit and the lessons of the comportment of the teacher to the gentiles did not convince us.[86] As is witnessed in the Acts of the Apostles, *When a light from heaven shined round about him, falling on the ground, he arose; and when his eyes were opened he saw nothing,* and his companions on the road, *leading him by the hands, brought him to Damascus. And he was there three days without sight: and he did neither eat nor drink.*[87] The following more wondrous things confirm the wondrous beginning of this virgin in God.

CHAPTER V. IN WHAT ENDEAVORS SHE ENGAGED, ONCE THIS *CHANGE OF THE RIGHT HAND OF THE MOST HIGH*[88] HAD BEEN BROUGHT ABOUT IN HER

And now I will relate the nature of this vessel that emerged from the furnace of divine love; how beautiful, how strong, how receptive to instruction, how full of grace in forethought, how fashioned for accomplishment!

---

85. Cf. Matthew 6:21. Oliger pointed to similarities in the way Francis of Assisi's vision was said to change in Thomas of Celano, *Vita prima di S. Francesco d'Assisi* 1.2, but there are no verbal matches between the two passages.

86. That is, St. Paul, in his conversion on the road to Damascus.

87. Acts 9:3–9.

88. Psalm 76:11.

She strove every day to be renewed in the very same emotions that she had tasted when suffused with *the blessings of sweetness.*[89] She sought them with many vigils, by extreme self-denial, by frequent and pure prayer, by bathing her mind's eye with tears. And thus remade in her renewed perception, she *proved what was the pleasing, perfect will of God,*[90] and strove for it with all her might, so that she would not fail, because indeed *deep calls on deep.*[91] Preserving intently the grace of God, she was acquiring other grace for herself.

Moreover, at that same hour at which the Mother of God had deigned to appear and to speak to her when she saw the vision, when the course of night was half run,[92] she would wake up and begin her nightly vigils; singing, praying, groaning, and crying, *according as* God *gave her to do.*[93] And she would stay continually awake and not go back to sleep. And if it happened that she did not rise at that hour, something wondrous to hear would occur; at the head of her bed there would be a certain sound, but not made by any of the women sleeping there, and she would wake up. And if she did not wake up, lest it be believed her ears were playing tricks, she would be shaken so that she would get up. Her Betrothed began to do these and other things with the virgin who was promised to Him, as preludes of holiness. And so this became her custom as long as she lived: she would rise at this hour, unsolicited, and consecrate the rest of the night in praise of God until morning, when she would hear Mass around the middle of Terce. And she would be so engrossed in prayer that, *praying the longer,*[94] she would lose track of time until, abruptly roused by one of the Sisters, as though woken from a deep slumber, she would return well after the time was past for singing the hours of Prime.[95]

---

89. Psalm 20:4.

90. Romans 12:2.

91. Psalm 41:8.

92. For liturgical echoes here, see note 56 above.

93. Cf. Acts 2:4.

94. Cf. Luke 22:43.

95. The temporal sequence implied here is confusing, since the author first refers to Margherita passing the night in prayer up until Terce (the "third hour" after dawn) but then has her Sisters rousing her after Prime (the "first hour").

While she was still living in the world in her brother [Giovanni]'s house, the austerity of her sleeping habits was not visible, because she practiced such things in secret. But later, in the houses at Mount [Prenestino], when she stayed with her household and the Sisters, there she was unable to hide these and other things from her household. She would have a bed splendidly made up for her in her little room, all piled up with blankets. This was fitting, since she was not yet a religious before she put on the habit that she adopted. But she would lie down on one blanket placed apart, sleeping and resting the brief time given to peaceful quiet. At dawn she would dishevel the bed herself, so that members of her household would think that she had slept in it.

No one who has not seen it would believe the flow of tears that she used to pour forth, and that I myself, the one who is writing this, have seen overflow. For the tears would flow as when a dam breaks after a stream of water has been dammed up in its course. The tears would fall from her eyes, not one by one, but in an uninterrupted flow, soaking the spots where they flowed to the ground to form the bed of a running stream. Members of her household used to discover that the numerous windowsills where she knelt in prayer would be drenched from her extensive crying. *Her heart* and her whole insides *would be* so *moved*[96] that we who were standing by would hear the commotion, and we would worry lest she pass away from its violence.

Once when she was weak and suffering night and day from a fever, I accompanied the brother [Giacomo] who managed the care of her body and soul when he came to see her. And when he had inquired how she was doing, after a while this brother, at her request, began to sing and recite with me the Hours of the Dead, because the virgin had not yet said them that day as was her daily custom. And then, though she was weak, she began to sing with us in a low voice. Right when we reached the psalm *To You, O God, I have lifted up my soul. In you, O God, I put my trust,* and so on,[97] what I have just written about happened to her,[98] which I

---

96. Cf. Genesis 43:30.
97. Psalm 24:1.
98. That is, Margherita began to cry profusely.

then myself noted down.[99] From the moment at which her *soul melted* at the speech of the Mother of God,[100] this very thing or something similar would happen to her; every day, at some hour of the day or night, she would pour forth such a shower of tears.

It was her custom that often when she was praying during the night or standing for the sacrifice at the altar, she could be seen genuflecting with such passion and reverence that her bones sounded as though they were breaking. She would remove her cloak and not put it back on until the sacrifice was finished, showing all reverence. And if in her presence it had. . . . [*Text is missing*][101] . . . Thus did something truly noteworthy happen to her: when in her devotion she beheld the Body of Christ that the priest was holding in his hand, she saw above him a pure white flying dove.

Reader! From this which you *read, understand.*[102] And you who are listening,[103] learn that the virgin was not averse to these inspirations and suffusing spiritual emotions—she who preserved with no respite the inspired goodness of vigils and tears, or, as I should more truly and humbly say, she to whom was granted the ceaseless performance of such things. For without doubt her flowing tears proved her deep emotions. Great indeed were her longings for Mary, the Mother of God, through whom she had realized the inexpressible goodness inspired in her. And thus [Mary] was always present to [Margherita] in spirit, so that very often she was worthy to behold things most marvelous and beautiful about her. Sometimes [Mary] appeared to her in order to fulfill her deep longing; sometimes in order to see that her will and God's will were known to [Margherita] about things she was to do. Hence the virgin was accustomed to say to her household, after it had begun to grow in the worship

---

99. This passage would seem to suggest that Giovanni Colonna was already making notes for a future *vita* during Margherita's lifetime.

100. Canticles 5:6.

101. As Oliger noted, text is evidently missing at this point. No blank space is left in the manuscript, however, and there is no sense that the scribe perceived a problem. Presumably a phrase was simply omitted in the process of copying.

102. Cf. Matthew 24:15; Mark 13:14.

103. It is interesting to note that Giovanni anticipates both readers and listeners of the text.

of God, "We have no abbess or superior to teach us the ways to maintain our religious way of life, so let us turn to our Lady, for she will be our teacher and she will guide us, her little flock, as it will seem pleasing and welcome to her Son and to herself!"[104] And without doubt she acted in this way so that in all matters she might turn to her own special refuge; and she advised and wished all others to be as earnest in devotion to Mary as she was herself. And if someone asked her for a prayer so that [Mary] might show her favor, [Margherita] would immediately enjoin that person, if literate, to recite the Song of the Virgin, *My soul does magnify the Lord*, and so on,[105] with the prayer "Grant, almighty God, what we your servants seek."[106] And for the illiterate she commanded the recitation of the greetings of the Virgin[107] with prayer and genuflection.

And since I have touched upon the topic of the greetings of the Virgin and genuflection, before proceeding to another vision that she had of the Virgin,[108] I will recall what occurred and comes to mind. When she had arisen at her regular hour, *before* she *came together*[109] with her companions to sing Matins—for this happened to her after she had gone up to stay at the houses on Mount [Prenestino]—and she was engaged in reciting the greetings of the Virgin and genuflecting, the enemy of mankind,[110] who intervenes to obstruct every good work, suddenly stood up before her, so that she was straightway struck with fear and halted in the good work she had begun. His frightening black form

---

104. The female noun *ministram* (translated here as "superior") is worth noting; the Latin for "teacher" here is *magistra*. The whole passage is an interesting commentary on the egalitarian nature of Margherita's early community.

105. The Magnificat, one of the oldest Marian hymns, often recited at Vespers; taken from Luke 1:46–55.

106. The Latin phrases "Concede quesumus omnipotens deus" and "nos famulos tuos" appear in numerous beseeching prayers. See for example *CO*, 1572, 707, 5307.

107. The *Ave Maria*.

108. Giovanni is again jumping out of the chronological order of his narrative, in this case to tell a related story that occurred later when Margherita's community on Mount Prenestino had taken shape.

109. Cf. Matthew 1:18.

110. That is, the devil.

revealed who he was. The virgin then crossed her heart, and because he did not vanish she realized that he had come to obstruct the good work she had begun. Then, rendered even more devout and earnest, she again repeated the greetings of the Virgin, just as she had already begun, genuflecting as she wished. And for every time she repeated it, the deceiver who had arrived took a step backward, until he totally disappeared, and with great spiritual consolation she finished the good works she had begun. Then at dawn she admonished her little flock to guard themselves against the *lying spirit*[111] who is always preparing traps to obstruct the good works of holy people. And if he should ever come to obstruct them in good works, she taught them that they should learn to say the greeting of the Virgin and to genuflect, as an impregnable shield against him, and she declared that he would immediately flee. Rejoicing in the power of the Virgin, she used to mock the fallible enemy about his failures and weakness.

Just a little later after the original vision,[112] Mary the Mother of God favored her virgin, who absolutely desired her and was devoted to her, with another most beautiful vision. Though [Margherita] had not as yet left the home of her brother [Giovanni] with whom she then lived, she nevertheless burned with longing. Therefore the blessed Virgin Mary, Mother of God, came to her, clothed in an ivory white gown. And standing aloft at a certain window, she offered herself to the view of the longing virgin. This virgin, sighing in admiration, exclaimed in joyful jubilation as is read in the Song of Love, *Who is she that comes forth as the morning rising?*[113] Because as she was speaking, from under the arms and breast [of the Virgin] she could see the morning rising. And as she recited further *fair as the moon*, the brilliance of the moon was coming forth from the face of Our Lady. And as she was finishing *bright as the sun*, she saw the flashing splendor of the sun come forth from the lap of

---

111. Cf. 2 Kings 22:22.

112. Giovanni is now once again describing the days after Margherita first experienced her transformative vision of Mary, when she was still living at his home before moving to Mount Prenestino.

113. Canticles 6:9. The following sentences continue to quote from this passage.

her blessed womb, a flash that illuminated the whole world and turned it into day, so that as she awoke she thought it was daytime. Then she beheld [the Virgin], by whom the virgin longed to be blessed, now extending her arm in benediction. And right away her wish was granted; she saw that above her was made the sign of the cross and benediction, so that just as she awoke she glimpsed the trace of the benediction while it was being performed. Thus was the Virgin able to lead the virgin to her Son the King, *as the eagle enticing her young to fly, hovering over them*;[114] thus was [the Virgin] soaring over the virgin daily and nurturing her in divine accomplishments.

CHAPTER VI. HOW SHE LEFT HER HOME AND WENT UP THE MOUNTAIN

And now, when the will to attend only to the praise of God had fully blossomed in the virgin, she found that[115] period of time of continued residence with her brother [Giovanni] to be barely tolerable, once she had been so inspired. So one morning, after the celebration of solemn Masses during which she completely dedicated herself to divine guidance, she said farewell to her brother and departed in the company of two respectable matrons, joyful in the paths of poverty and happy in the guidance of only her Betrothed. And she took herself to Mount Prenestino to dwell in those houses until God should dispose of her otherwise through the agency of her brother [Giacomo], who had encouraged her to live a celibate life and to whose tutelage she had given herself, although at that time he was away.[116] She did not request that anything be prepared, or ask for any help, believing that all things necessary would appear because she had resolved *to come to the service of God*.[117] Neither

---

114. Deuteronomy 32:11.

115. *Illud* is added in the margin by the original scribal hand.

116. Another reference to Giacomo's stay in Bologna. Margherita's decision was first alluded to at the end of chapter 2, and after several chapters that waver back and forth across this transformative moment, at last in chapter 6 the narrative moves forward to plans for her celibate future.

117. Ecclesiasticus 2:1.

her brother [Giovanni]'s tears nor leaving the family home with all its riches softened the virgin's spirit, since *leaving all things*,[118] having been sent *without purse and scrip*,[119] *denying herself and taking up her cross*,[120] she cheerfully flew to the poverty of Christ. Before entering these houses she sought out the church where Mass was being celebrated,[121] and the priest was then reciting that passage of the Gospel where Christ speaks, exalting that He comes from the Father, saying, *He that sent me, is with me, and He has not left me alone: for I do always the things that please Him.*[122] The virgin heard this as a great solace to her spirit; and knowing that this was spoken for her, she applied it to herself, because she would not be left alone by Christ if she always did what pleased Him, for whom she was forsaking all things.

She strongly undertook her service, when she weakened her body through many abstinences each day. Continuously, never letting up except when she was sick and obeying strict orders, she ate a fasting diet every day of the week except two; and on those two days she would eat in order to please her household more than to spare her hunger. On Fridays she was content with only bread and water. On days when she did not fast, it amounted to the same thing because of the paltry amount that she did eat; and, fasting or not, she took only enough to survive.[123] She shunned all the individual uniqueness that renders one despised by others, makes one the companion of vainglory, and turns all merit empty.

---

118. Luke 5:11; 5:28.

119. Luke 22:35.

120. Luke 9:23.

121. This is presumably the Church of San Pietro, at the Colonna stronghold of Castel San Pietro on Mount Prenestino, which was only a few minutes' walk from where the women would live.

122. John 8:29. Oliger pointed out that this reading is for the Mass for the Monday after the second Sunday of Lent. Since it is implied later in this chapter that Margherita spent seven years at Mount Prenestino before dying in December 1280, her arrival would seem to have been in 1273. This reasoning would date this passage to 6 March 1273, which seems to fit in well with the chronological progression of the narrative.

123. Compare the way Margherita's eating habits are described in *Vita II*, ch. 3.

Shunning only things that were specifically prohibited on days of fasting, she was nevertheless more abstinent in all things. And thus she reaped the greater reward of true self-denial, which is all the more worthy when hidden from human praise. She was rarely seen by her household and only for short periods of time when she came to them to revive herself in their company, and then she would listen to nothing but resounding praises of Christ and His mother.

There she more secretly maintained her celibate life, wearing a hair shirt next to her skin even though she had not yet put aside secular dress. And so she was subjected to much questioning and repeated reproaches from her brothers and those around them, blaming her because she had shunned a husband in marriage. And just as in this instance God sent down a contest for her to conquer, so she emerged victorious by repeatedly ignoring others' arguments. For instance, the mother of that nobleman to whom she had (without her knowledge) been betrothed sent two Dominicans[124] to convince her of the value of marriage and to say, among other things, that she was greatly undervaluing herself in devoting herself to poverty, and that this did not come from a noble heart. It is known that the virgin answered these words by saying that she had at home two older sisters who outshone all others in the nobility of their hearts.[125] Other women had provided barons and counts for themselves, but she had determined that she was to be betrothed to the Son of the only King. Those who had been sent to her departed because they did not believe that they could change her mind.[126]

Among her other brothers was one whose spirit was focused on the glory of this world,[127] who was indignant with his sister and blamed his

---

124. The Latin is *Fratres predicatores* (Preaching Brothers). It is interesting that Dominicans are sent to counter Margherita's Franciscan-leaning vocation.

125. In chapters 1 and 2 an older sister is mentioned; a sister also appears in *Vita II*, ch. 18. Here it is specified that Margherita has two older sisters (see note 18 above).

126. In the margin, "visio pulchra" is written in what appears to be the original scribal hand. It is then crossed out in red ink and enclosed in a red box.

127. This brother is obviously not Giacomo. Oliger thought it was unlikely to be Giovanni (the text's author) or Matteo (provost of St. Omer) and thus suggested that this brother must have been either Oddone or Landulfo (both laymen).

brothers in the strongest terms for taking the matter lightly. He thought that he could break the virgin's spirit and make her behave as he wished through weighty shouts and roaring threats, and he intended to recall her from her holy project by addressing her in the morning with a well-thought-out lecture. The night before his planned discussion, he saw in his sleep a strikingly beautiful palace that was said to belong to his virgin sister. The palace had seven balconies,[128] each adding to the special beauty of the palace. When he wished to enter, a certain old man armed with a club, who seemed to be the guardian of the place, appeared before him. Raising the club and threatening to strike, he said, "Are you the one who has come to shatter my treasure box? If you try this at any time or place, you will die!" This brother was so terrified by this vision that although his other brothers had not yet given up speaking [to their sister], he alone kept silent, insisting that he would never lecture her on this subject because he believed that her great desire in this matter had come from God.

The seven balconies of the palace could stand for the years during which she *brought forth fruits worthy of penance*[129] under a religious habit, which God decided to end at this number.[130] Each one ornamented the great structure of her spirit in its progress toward God. Her proposal of virginity she called her treasure, which she wished to have guarded and preserved through the efforts of the Mother [of God]. She persevered thereafter in silent opposition to men, dedicated only to the Virgin's Son to whom she had vowed herself, and who was often and more often bringing chaste caresses to His virgin, foreshadowing His love.

Once, while she was in prayer, it seemed to her that a crown of lilies was placed upon her head, arranged like a circle in a wreath around her entire head, and she was inhaling the scent of the blossoms, which smelled of fresh-cut lilies. I, the simple author, am a faithful witness to

---

The latter two are certainly viable candidates, but it also seems to us at least possible that Giovanni was here describing his own mystical vision, through which he came to realize his sister's destiny.

128. The Latin word is *solaria*, meaning literally "sun areas."

129. Cf. Luke 3:8.

130. That is, she lived for seven years after taking a religious habit.

these things, for I was there when she was breathing in these fragrances and I heard her marveling with me.

She received another presaging token from her Betrothed, which I also saw. While she was asleep it seemed to her that He was coming to her and offering a pledge by setting a ring upon her finger; and the ring was tightly squeezing her finger, binding so much that it reached down to the very bone. The flesh all around grew back over it and, because it was now ingrown, there appeared no possibility that the ring could be cut off. The marks of the ingrown ring remained in the virgin's flesh, which I myself saw as if it had been implanted in my presence and left that mark.

After she had put aside the secular clothes with which for some time she had concealed her holy calling, she clothed herself with cheap cloth, displaying an appearance to the outside world in accordance with the hair shirt she had worn beneath.[131] Her dress conformed in all regards to the habit of the Sisters of the Blessed Clare, except that she wore an exterior cloak of the same haircloth, or of a similarly cheap material, encircling her entire form, which she conceded for the greater preservation of her body.[132] She cut off her hair, by which she had caused defilement, so beautiful to behold was she, and she took this tonsure in the following manner. When, with high voice and deep emotion, genuflecting, she began to sing the hymn of the Virgin, *Hail, star of the sea*,[133] and when

---

131. Margherita's adoption of religious dress marked a more formal move away from the world; thus efforts to convince her to marry ceased at this point. In her own mind, adopting religious dress and cutting her hair clearly established an irrevocable commitment; it was not, however, a canonical vow equivalent to that of a nun. On religious vows in the thirteenth century, see Alain Boureau, *Le désir dicté: Histoire du vœu religieux dans l'Occident médiéval* (Paris: Les Belles Lettres, 2014).

132. This is the first specific statement in the text that Margherita took Clare of Assisi and the Sisters of the Order of St. Clare as models for her piety. For the Sisters' habit (which at the time had significant regional variations), see Cordelia Warr, *Dressing for Heaven: Religious Clothing in Italy, 1215–1545* (Manchester: Manchester University Press, 2010), 134–44.

133. *Ave maris stella*, the well-known Vespers hymn to Mary, sung during the Annunciation and other Marian Feasts. Cantus ID, 8272; *AH*, 2:39; Van Dijk, *Sources*, 2:127–29, 132–33, 155, 157, 160.

she came to the line *Show thyself a mother*, she chopped off her hair with the scissors she held in her hand. To show her greater scorn and contempt, she flung her tresses into the privy. Then, just as in her exterior habit, so too in her mind did she think herself low and humble. This is how she had always been on the inside, but now she showed it more clearly after putting on worthless clothing, not blushing in the service of the Lord.

And as to the habit that she adopted, she had been taught beforehand in a certain way by a vision that appeared to her. It seemed to her that she was listening to a certain preacher, and at the end of his sermon he was speaking that part of the Gospel, which she well remembered: *If any man will come after me, let him deny himself, and take up his cross, and follow me.*[134] She associated the one preaching this passage with the blessed Francis, [since] the image of the likeness of this father showed a similar habit.[135] She rose as this was spoken, as did another certain holy religious woman whose whole life was dedicated to the cross of Christ.[136] The virgin genuflected and asked for and received from that holy father a cross made of a certain red gem. Receiving it she said, "I do not wish, as others do, to put this on my shoulder, but in my breast, so that He for

---

134. Matthew 16:24; Luke 9: 23.

135. This may be a reference to the famous fresco of Francis painted in the Chapel of Saint Gregory in the Sacro Speco at Subiaco, a Benedictine monastery. The artist represented Francis standing barefoot in the Friars' habit with the knotted cord around his waist, but interestingly without the stigmata that would become an ubiquitous sign of his sanctity in medieval imagery. A brief text identifies him as *Frater Franciscus* (Brother Francis), which has led scholars to date the fresco to 1228 (after the chapel's consecration by Cardinal Hugolino and before Francis's canonization on 16 July). Subiaco is in Lazio, to the northeast of Palestrina and so also in lands under Colonna influence, which would have made a visit from Margherita entirely plausible. For further discussion of the Subiaco fresco, see Rosalind Brooke, *The Image of St. Francis: Responses to Sainthood in the Thirteenth Century* (Cambridge: Cambridge University Press, 2006), 160–64.

136. The text does not give any indication of who this "alia sancta mulier" might be, and Giovanni's circling narrative makes it difficult to date the vision. But presumably it occurred after Margherita had settled in the Colonna houses on Mount Prenestino, so this woman could be one of her companions and perhaps a Colonna relative given Giovanni's appreciative description of her.

whose love I bear it will never depart from my memory." While she was placing it about her heart, the cross was becoming fixed in her flesh. And having been fastened there, it was not falling away; the cross was trying to penetrate deeper within and was thus well fulfilled within her.

Conforming to the habit of the most holy Father Francis in this way, she took up from him the cross that he bore and preached. For, just as he[137] left everything behind, so did she make herself poor, and what she had begun did not fall from her heart.[138] And she, the very least of the *minores*, served the poor of Christ and the servants of Christ just as he had.[139]

¶Here or elsewhere, where it will seem [best] to the corrector, is lacking the vision that she saw about going up the mountain and about the triple crown placed on her head after she ascended.[140]

¶Another is missing too, about when she had a great thirst but was not troubled by it, and when she saw a big, beautiful full jug from which she wished to drink, but it was said to her that it was being saved because it was for the service of the other one,[141] and she was led to a rock from

---

137. The manuscript reads *ipsa*, which would indicate it was Margherita who left everything behind; Oliger emends to *ipse* to follow the apparent logic of the passage. We follow him while noting that the emendation is somewhat speculative.

138. Whereas the preceding paragraph indicated that Margherita necessarily modeled the specifics of her feminine dress on Clare and the Sisters of the Order of St. Clare, this vision strongly suggests that ultimately Margherita's goal was to show that she was following the model of Francis (in turn following Christ) and his adoption of poverty.

139. The final sentence here goes a step farther in defining Margherita's identity, insisting that she (feminine *minima*) was the least "of the Minors" (*minorum*): that is, a Franciscan.

140. These two notes that refer to missing visions are copied directly into the text by the scribe (that is, in this manuscript they are not marginal additions and were not added later). But they are underlined in red and are preceded by paragraph markers in red. It would seem that they must have originated as a note added by the author in an autograph manuscript, which was then simply incorporated into the text by a later copyist (whether of the present manuscript or of an intermediary). The reference to "the one who will correct the text" (*correctori*) indicates that Giovanni Colonna expected someone to smooth out the version he had produced.

141. The Latin is "ad alterius ministerium"; the referent is not clear.

which was flowing a *fountain of living water*,[142] where, as she was commanded, she placed her mouth, drinking as much as she wanted, because the cup produced no loathing, and there she sipped *all that is delicious of taste*.[143]

CHAPTER VII. ON HER PIOUS WORKS AND ABSTINENCE, WHICH SHE PURSUED AFTER ASSUMING RELIGIOUS DRESS

Her brother [Giacomo], who was away and living in Bologna, heard of the things being done at God's command concerning the virgin; how she had left her brother [Giovanni] and her home and had given herself over completely to divine guidance. Moved by the spirit, he returned to his own estate, so that he who had preached in support of this holy idea might lend his hand to the accomplishment of the holy work now under way and assist in *confirming what God had done* within the virgin.[144] He arrived and discussed many arrangements regarding his sister's situation and devised several means of building a monastery for her. But some difficulty arose for each of them, because such was the will of God as to her placement.

He obtained from his brothers what was due to his sister as a dowry, which he intended to spend on the construction of a monastery. But an obstacle arose,[145] and so the two of them began to spend this money, and the other money they had, on the poor of Christ. They set aside—or to say it better, they gave to Christ—only the amount spent in support of the poor virgin of Christ and her household. And her brother attended to these expenses and others out of his own income only in the way he would for a poor person of Christ. For the poor virgin of Christ had stripped herself entirely, as though *leaving all things*.[146] And thus in de-

---

142. Numbers 20:6; Jeremias 2:13; John 4:14.

143. Wisdom 16:20.

144. Cf. Psalm 67:29.

145. Exactly what "obstacle" prevented this course of action is never explained.

146. Luke 5:11, 5:28.

ciding how to spend her dowry, she left it to her brother to spend where he pleased for the support of the poor and the servants of Christ. The virgin showed that this was so, and proved it specifically, by asking her brother [Giacomo] about the matter. For she said to him, "What motivates you, brother, in managing my requirements for me as you are doing? Are you doing it because I am your sister? If so, I will have no part of it! For you have paid your share, just as my other brothers have, so no burden for my support falls to you beyond what falls to them." Therefore her brother, acknowledging her richly appointed desire for the poverty of Christ, answered that if he were spending more for her than he was accustomed to spend, he would rather believe that this was because God prompted him to spend on others and not on himself, and he thought it more pleasing to God to spend on these things.

From then on, firm in the knowledge of her brother's desire concerning the doling out of distributions for the poor of Christ, she was prepared to help every known want: now clothing the naked; now nourishing the starved; now providing lodging for pilgrims and strangers; now placing at her own expense those women who longed for the service of Christ; now increasing donations for the promotion of saints for whom she had great devotion; first aiding those who had been set apart for the worship of God, thereafter setting her hand to every perceived want. O wondrous supplier of alms whose yearnings in such matters were never diminished by what was given! Either she thought that she had done only a little, because her passion outran her aid, or she gave such attention to the needs of others that the spark of her compassion remained even when everything was used up. And just as she fulfilled the needs of the poor, so she spared the honor of many who were ashamed to receive help. For if some man or some woman of noble or middling status came into need, and she knew about it and some help was at hand, she would come to their aid, but not in the same way as for the rest. First she would find out what their needs were, and then she would supply her charity either in secret or in the guise of a loan while stipulating that it would not be repaid unless and until asked. For others who were not of such quality but were ashamed to beg at her door, she provided for them at home. While handing out aid to other pilgrims and strangers arriving at her door, she also brought some of them inside to be revived and restored by her personal attention and that of her household.[147]

Behold the purpose around which this brother and sister whirled! On one hand they were withdrawing to Christ through contemplation, on the other reaching out to their neighbors in compassion. Alas, poor me, who was there with them, that I did not then return my spirit to its God, being busy and removed from them! I well know what I should think of myself. The mere memory of them comes to me from time to time, and leads me to weep and pray that God may grant that I should come to such sensibilities before I die. For their glowing love could not help but set their neighbors' hearts aglow.

Indeed, where there was greater suffering, the virgin's compassion increased, especially among the sick. During the summer she would prepare with her own hands honeyed remedies and syrups with which she treated the sick. She would prepare their daily meals herself, and because her sympathy ran so deep she was hardly able to believe that she could fulfill her longing through service carried out by someone else, but only through her personal involvement. Therefore, with the whole household bearing on their heads wicker baskets in which she hid supplies for the sick, she would gather her upright company and personally go forth visiting each one at their door. One by one she would see them and inquire about them, for she was well enough instructed in such matters that she could tell those who had a fever from those who did not. She would revive this one with daily provisions, while strengthening that one with a meal of chicken. She would prepare syrups for one who was suffering from a fever, for another she would concoct honeyed remedies that strengthened the weak, just as she saw fit for each case. And when she returned home she would not forget those whom she had gone to see; but overflowing with greater compassion she would give her assistance with daily visits until she had heard that the sick had gotten well.

---

147. As Bianca Lopez has pointed out, Margherita's "poverty" here is directed toward using her family resources for charitable support of the poor (as opposed to Clare of Assisi's embrace of absolute poverty for its own sake). See Bianca Lopez, "Between Court and Cloister: The Life and Lives of Margherita Colonna," *Church History* 82 (2013): 554–75.

From time to time, with her brothers' help, she even got a doctor to visit the sick. I will relate two quite marvelous examples of her deeds in this regard.

Once her more worthy brother [Giacomo] was lying in one part of the houses, *taken by a great fever.*[148] She was caring for him herself, while not neglecting her daily worship. And her other brother [Giovanni], *whom* she *loved,*[149] was likewise lying fever-ridden in the lower houses.[150] Yet because of the severity of their illnesses, each one's sickness was hidden from the other. The virgin of Christ heard that the Franciscans [*Fratres minores*] who were then staying at a place in Zagarolo[151] were all so sick that the guardian and the lector[152] who had arrived had to beg for daily sustenance for the Friars and even for themselves, since not one of them was well on his feet. Then, moved by marvelous compassion, forgetting the illness of her brothers because of Christ (since it was for Him that she worked when working in obedience to them), she came to the bedside of her more worthy brother [Giacomo] to whom she had pledged obedience. She told him that she had heard the Friars were in need, and she asked permission to go to Zagarolo so that she might be obedient to them by caring as a caregiver. And she added, "I serve you freely because I should, especially when you are sick. But I am driven to

---

148. Luke 4:38. The passage refers to one of Jesus's cures and thus places Margherita in a Christ-like light.

149. Cf. John 13:23. As Oliger noted, the reference is to the disciple "whom Jesus loved," generally understood to be John. Thus the author may be obliquely naming the "other brother" as John/Giovanni (that is to say, himself).

150. The "lower houses" (*in inferioribus domibus*) may indicate that Giovanni's sickbed was in the family residence in Palestrina, at the foot of Mount Prenestino.

151. Zagarolo is due west of Palestrina and was firmly under Colonna influence. The present text is the earliest reference to a community of Friars there. Documents otherwise attest to the community only from 1277, although hagiographical tradition records that the house was visited by Francis himself. See Gelasio Zucconi, *La Provincia Romana dei Frati Minori dei SS Apostoli Pietro e Paolo* (Rome: Sede Provinciale Convento Aracoeli, 1972), 162. Mariano d'Altri considered that early foundation plausible; see "Gli insediamenti Francescani del Duecento nella custodia di Campagna," *Collectanea Franciscana* 47 (1977): 297–316.

152. The "guardian" is the Brother in charge of a specific Franciscan community; the "lector" is the educated Brother in charge of teaching at the community.

show myself where there is greater need for the servants of Christ. So Christ commands, and so we should wish." Her brother marveled at such sensibility in her and such perfect will to take part in such inspired good work, and he gave his permission and he ordered that the things necessary for such care be transported. Then, seeing to it that honeyed remedies and syrups were brought over, the virgin came to the place and inquired, from those who were healthy, of the condition of each and every one of them and prepared with her own hand what was required. Coming each morning to hear Mass at the Friars' place, she would ask the condition of the sick; hastening back she would send over the required items that she had prepared, while at the same time taking care to provide what was required for those in good health. When the astonished lector said to her, "What is this, that you have abandoned your gravely ill brothers to come here?" she replied that she would willingly attend to them, "But in all truth they have people to care for them without me, which is not the case for you. Therefore I must show myself where I see the greater need among the poor of Christ."[153] The lector, hearing this and praising it as a saying of great perfection, repeated it to many people because he recognized thereby that this virgin was truly following in the footsteps of Christ.[154]

Nor will I keep silent about another memorable deed. When she heard that a certain leprous woman had recently been expelled from the town of Poli and had found no other home where she might be received,[155] and that there was no help for this woman who had been so impiously shunned, [Margherita] detested the detestable conduct of the men of that village, since she remembered Christ, to whom *there* was *no beauty nor comeliness*,[156] and who for our sake had been thought a

---

153. Margherita's way of life and the Franciscan way of life are both repeatedly referred to as *pauper*.

154. Cf. Thomas of Celano, *Legenda S. Clarae* 16.13, in Boccoli, *Legenda*, 150; Armstrong, *Lady*, 303.

155. Poli is just north of Palestrina but belonged to the Conti family, another Roman baronial family. Cf. chapter 9, where the text's anti-Conti animus is clear.

156. Isaiah 53:2.

leper.[157] And at once she saw to it that the woman was brought, and she received her into her home. Having compassion for the woman, she tended her sores with her own hands, changed her dressing, nursed her herself, and brought her food and drink. And she wanted her own meals and drink to be given at a table where the leper had eaten and in a cup from which she had drunk. She kissed her sores out of love for Him who wished to be and to appear bruised and *wounded* for us sinners.[158] After this woman had received much comfort through medical attention to her sores, good food, and gentle sleep, [Margherita] sent her off to a certain place in Campania where those so infected are taken in,[159] having made all arrangements for her maintenance. She who had come to them virtually naked was now well clothed and bandaged, with the dressings and funds she needed.

---

157. Cf. Isaiah 53:4.

158. Cf. Isaiah 53:5. Evoking Margherita's care for lepers may have been intended to echo a transformative moment in the conversion of Francis of Assisi, recently stressed by Augustine Thompson, O.P., *Francis of Assisi: A New Biography* (Ithaca, NY: Cornell University Press, 2012), 16–17.

159. Oliger suggested that this place might be the leprosarium founded by Pope Alexander III at Veroli in 1170, according to the *Annales Ceccanenses*. It is not certain that Veroli is indicated, but it might be particularly likely because the town was also home to another hospice and confraternity dedicated to caring for sufferers of deforming diseases, after the supposed relics of Mary Salome (Jesus's aunt and mother of two of the apostles) were discovered in a cave outside the town in 1209 and moved into a shrine in the cathedral; a cult soon developed (with the support of Innocent III) celebrating healing miracles experienced there. See Brenda Bolton, "The Absentee Lord? Alexander III and the Patrimony," in *Pope Alexander III (1159–81): The Art of Survival*, ed. Anne Duggan and Peter D. Clark (Farnham: Ashgate, 2012), 155–89; Brenda Bolton, "Signs, Wonders, Miracles: Supporting the Faith in Medieval Rome," *Studies in Church History* 41 (2005): 157–78. Veroli is located southeast of Poli and the Colonna territories around Palestrina. Although the boundary of the modern province of Campagna begins farther south, in the thirteenth century Veroli fell within the papal province of Campagna and Marittima, according to Daniel Waley, *The Papal State in the Thirteenth Century* (London: Macmillan, 1961), 91.

CHAPTER VIII. ON THE UNDERSTANDING THAT SHE HAD CONCERNING THE SCRIPTURES,[160] AND THE REVELATION MADE TO HER ABOUT THEM

Who, indeed, would be able to describe all the preludes of holiness that occurred in these days to this brother [Giacomo] and sister as they earnestly pursued their celibate life?[161] It would be a very long story just to relate those things we know about, let alone those that are unknown to us. How they incited one another to the love of Christ in their discussions! Now brother, now sister impelling each other in joy! And how deep was the understanding of the virgin in holy matters, so that often she resoundingly propounded obscure points of the scriptures with such clarity that, to us who were listening, it seemed as though we were hearing Christ himself answering the questions. For she was drinking from His own breast, and what He *hid from the wise and prudent* He *revealed to this little* woman.[162] I will relate what now comes to mind.

Once when these two were engaged in holy discourse, their hearts impelled each other in joy as was their habit. They asked each other, reviewing the opinions and pronouncements of the saints, whether the blessed Thomas *put* his *finger into the places of the nails, and* his *hand into His side* as Christ directed him.[163] They worked over the collected opinions together but ended by having reached no firm conclusion, since they

---

160. Oliger pointed out the similarity to the title of chapter 11 of Bonaventure's *Legenda maior*, "On His Understanding of the Scriptures, and His Spirit of Prophecy."

161. The way Giovanni now presents his two siblings as a holy pair is notable. On such brother-sister relationships, see Fiona J. Griffiths, "Siblings and the Sexes within the Medieval Religious Life," *Church History* 77 (2008): 26–53.

162. Matthew 11:25; Luke 10: 21.

163. John 20:25. This episode is retold in *Vita II*, ch. 21, where the date is given as Easter 1280. Stefania in *Vita II* indicates that Margherita had this conversation with Giovanni, but it seems far more likely that her interlocutor was Giacomo, not only because the cardinal was the more likely discussion partner for this question, but because Giovanni (the author here) would be unlikely to be confused on this point.

were not able to. The following night a certain hand was shown to the virgin; a hand of marvelous beauty and splendor that surpassed the beauty and splendor of any flesh, and that was swollen from a nail wound in the very middle. The virgin then felt the apostle's exclamation, speaking as he beheld that very sight, which teaches the faithful: "My Lord and my God!"[164] She herself was not able to relate the matter, because when emotions are felt in this way "one does not show one's source."[165] After this taste of those emotions, a voice spoke to the virgin: "Thus Thomas did behold!" Once she had been taught by this revelation, if those who spoke with her suggested otherwise, she laughed at them.[166]

CHAPTER IX. ON HER DEPARTURE FROM HER KINDRED AND HER FATHERLAND, AND HOW SHE WANTED TO SERVE AS AN OBLATE IN THE CHURCH OF ST. MARY IN VULTURELLA

Her burning desire left her restless, so that she always yearned for greater things regarding God. Thus, as is the case with those who long for something, the tiresome anticipation made difficult the wait, which was due to the delay in building the monastery where she might confine herself with those women who wished to join in service to God. Indeed, the virgin's very greatest passion was gaining souls for Christ, because she

---

164. John 20:28 (these are the words of Doubting Thomas).

165. This line of verse is found in the *Tobias* of the twelfth-century Cistercian author Matthew of Vendôme. See *Mathei Vindocinensis Opera*, ed. Franco Munari, vol. 2 (Rome: Edizioni di Storia e Letteratura, 1982), 245 (line 2218). Although Oliger did not spot this borrowing, he was correct to speculate that the manuscript reading of *actorem* should be emended to *auctorem*. The passage in its original context reads: "Te laus nulla canit quia significatio vocum / Deficit auctorem significare suum."

166. This passage suggests that Margherita's mystical vision gave her a superior understanding of this event, beyond that of the learned biblical commentators whose opinions she and Giacomo had compared. This contrast between mystical women and learned clerics represents a common trope in contemporary medieval writing. For an overview of this theme and examples, see Anneke Mulder-Bakker, ed., *Seeing and Knowing: Women and Learning in Medieval Europe* (Turnhout: Brepols, 2004).

knew many women her age and other nobles of her own land, and she wished that Christ would provide for them as He had for her, before they might be ensnared by the allurements of this world. And so that they might not (God forbid!) fall into wrongdoing due to poverty, which would have been worse, she strove all the harder and wanted her brothers to strive on by building a monastery rather than by [settling for] a building already built. For she said that any building at all would do for her, but that they were really working toward what needed to be built for the sake of those who would come afterward, and what needed to be done for those women of her own house who wished to be wed to Christ, whose wish so brightly shone forth thereafter.[167]

For once the building of a monastery was understood to be nearly impossible (which I cannot say without shame and sorrow!), the virgin, burning for God, wished to go to the Monastery of Saint Clare at Assisi.[168] And she obtained from the minister general[169] a letter stating that she would be received upon her arrival. But illness prevented her, and so she remained where she was, for this was the Lord's decision for her. And now we see that, to a great degree, her desire has been fulfilled, that many *virgins*, especially her own relatives, *should be brought to* God *after her*.[170] For in those houses where she was then abiding we now

---

167. The sentiment attributed to Margherita here is ambiguous; Giovanni portrays her as desperately wanting a monastery, but more for her followers in the future than for herself.

168. The Latin is "cenobium sancte Clare." That is, Santa Chiara in Assisi, where the sisters had moved in 1260 from their original location at San Damiano outside the walls of the city.

169. Oliger plausibly puts this moment right around 1274. In that case the unnamed minister general referred to here could have been Bonaventure, who died in July 1274. But it seems more likely that it was his successor Jerome of Ascoli, later cardinal bishop of Palestrina and then Pope Nicholas IV (r. 1288–92). Jerome emerged as a strong ally of the Colonna, but this passage (if indeed it refers to him) would be the earliest evidence for his association with the family. See Giulia Barone, "Niccolò IV e I Colonna," in *Niccolò IV: Un pontificato tra oriente ed occidente*, ed. Enrico Menestò (Spoleto: Centro Italiano di Studi sull'alto Medioevo, 1991), 73–89, who points out that if Bonaventure had been the man in question the author here would likely have given this late, illustrious theologian's name for reasons of prestige.

170. Psalm 44:15.

know many virgins, handmaidens to the Lord. Let us hope, with God's blessing, that the monastery she longed for may still be completed![171]

As she believed that her brothers were not acting seriously in their preparations to found a monastery, she learned of the holy reputation of a certain place, the Church of St. Mary in Vulturella. It was called by this name because the Mother of God, the Virgin Mary, had appeared at that very place, so that it was held in great reverence by the local people.[172] She therefore most earnestly begged her brother [Giacomo] to be allowed to go there. This permission was denied repeatedly, but she received it at last and took herself there, intending to remain. With her went all her religious household, among whom were the virgins she had begun to form into a flock for the service of God.

Because the temporal lord of this place misunderstood what was happening, he acted disgracefully toward her.[173] He believed that she had come to steal his church and turn it into a monastery. But this was not

---

171. This passage clearly indicates a date of composition before 1285, when Margherita's followers moved to the house of San Silvestro in Capite in Rome.

172. The earliest evidence for Santa Maria in Vulturella (now known as Mentorella—presumably a contraction of Maria and Vulturella) dates to the fourth century. Tradition ascribes its foundation to the Emperor Constantine's desire to mark the spot where a second-century Roman tribune named Eustacius had converted after witnessing a vision of the Virgin. Benedictines affiliated with Subiaco held the church from the sixth through the late fourteenth centuries. The reference to the local lord's opposition to Margherita's presence there, however, reflects the way local comital families—here the Counts of Poli (see the next note for more detail)—regularly took an interest in such religious sites. The Conti may have funded the refurbishing of the church during the twelfth and thirteenth centuries and supported the shrine. See further Angelo Lipinsky, "Il tesoro del Santuario di S. Maria in Vulturella," *Atti e memorie della Società tiburtina di storia e d'arte* 51 (1979): 97–145.

173. According to Sandro Carocci, *Baroni di Roma: Dominazioni signorili e lignaggi aristocratici nel duecento e nel primo trecento* (Rome: École française de Rome, 1993), 379, Giovanni Conti, Lord of Poli, died by 1261, leaving his sons Nicolas and Pietro. It seems that the former was the older brother and thus inherited lordship of Poli; but the latter was in fact married to Margherita Colonna's older sister Giacoma. This tie may explain why Margherita thought such a move into Conti territory would be possible, and also perhaps why this account by Giovanni Colonna is so bitter at what he may have perceived as Conti betrayal and familial disrespect.

true, for she had not come in a spirit of strife. Rather, she was advancing peacefully in the service of the peaceful King and had dedicated her efforts to that work, if she could do it with the peace and goodwill of those whom it concerned. But this lord saw to it that the prior and priests of the church left, and the ropes were removed from the bells so that they could not be rung, and all the church's furnishings were put under lock and key. And he fortified the rocky outpost of the place with armed men, so that she would be deprived of the solace of the Mass and would be denied the local supplies made available for pilgrims and would leave all the sooner, worn out by all of these aggravations.

But, as God would have it, the more she was assaulted by troubles from without, the more she exalted within, and in her heart, which *God created clean*, the love of the Holy Spirit *renewed a right spirit*.[174] And a work of such true *joy of her salvation*[175] was prepared for the virgin that she confided to her brother[176] and other religious people that she had never before experienced such a renewal of her spirit. Her more worthy brother [Giacomo] witnessed this. When he heard about the trouble she had encountered on her arrival, he immediately ordered her to return. The virgin was unwilling and did not comply, because she scorned these exterior trials and was delighted more by joyous interior exaltations. Her brother therefore ordered that, since she had not returned, the usual daily supplies should not be taken to her. Yet she still did not leave, but rather laughed even more! In truth, the local men and women, knowing that a virgin of widespread and holy reputation was staying among them, brought loaves of bread to her so that she might pray for them and for their dearly departed. She most eagerly accepted these loaves, calling them *the bread of angels*,[177] brought to her in her poverty. And then she proclaimed the Hours to be sung by her Sisters in prayer for those who had brought the bread, and she herself sang along with them.[178]

---

174. Cf. Psalm 50:12.

175. Cf. Psalm 50:14.

176. Presumably Giacomo Colonna.

177. Cf. Psalm 77:25.

178. This sentence is evidently corrupt in the manuscript; we have followed Oliger's speculative addition of the word *horas* to make sense of it.

Therefore *grace did more abound*[179] in the virgin dwelling there—so much so that it did not escape the notice of her brother [Giacomo], who was then staying at Mount [Prenestino] and who had not been disturbed by his vision.[180] He remained silent, understanding that her delay advanced her spiritually, and he did not trouble her to return for many days. But as the days passed, he entrusted the other brother [Giovanni] to go up and see about bringing their sister back. [Giovanni] was quite ready to fulfill this charge but criticized the difficulty the virgin was causing about returning. He was then told, "Go, for you will not find her stubborn." How marvelous! For the virgin had decided that if it were not possible to have the above-mentioned church for the construction of a monastery with the consent of those involved,[181] then she would remain there as an oblate to minister in all humility.[182] Who would not marvel at the depth of such humility, that one of such high status should so eagerly plunge to such servility? But she believed this was nothing at all compared to the stain of sin for which she would feel ashamed in the outside world, so great were the emotions that seethed within her for the Mother of God. So she held to her pledged intent. And she would not have changed her mind if she had not been warned in a vision that the Mother of God willed otherwise.

For she had seemed (as it had appeared to her) to stand with Mary the most blessed Mother of God and other virgins on a certain dome of a house, a *semmnum* as it is called in the local vernacular.[183] Not far away was a road and wide street down which I, the one writing this, was

---

179. Cf. Romans 5:20.

180. It is not clear what vision is being referred to here; perhaps it is implied that Giacomo had experienced a vision that revealed Margherita's state and intentions.

181. Giovanni here seems to contradict his earlier statement that Margherita did not intend to claim the church for her own use as a monastery.

182. The Latin is "sicut oblata manere." In medieval usage the word *oblate* could refer to a child given by her parents to a monastic institution; here it is apparently being used in the alternative sense of a person who dedicates herself to a monastic or religious community without taking formal vows.

183. An obscure word, apparently of Roman dialect.

coming as a traveler; and I stopped as though I were waiting for some-one.[184] Then the Virgin Mother of God, said to her, "Go, for this person is waiting for you." It was difficult for the virgin to hear this and to lose the company of the one by whom she was so gladdened and comforted, and the company of the virgins standing around, but still she had to obey. Then, in answer to a look she made rather than to any word, the Mother of God said, "Go now, free from any worry, because you will never be far from me, nor any less gladdened by me." Departing, [Margherita] then saw that a new cable had been prepared, down which her descent was accomplished to the road where the traveler was waiting.[185] And, indeed, quite miraculously it appeared to her that as she made her way down she was not moving away from the Virgin Mother of God. Rather, on the way down [the Virgin] stayed right beside her, and as close as she had been before when she had remained with her on the dome mentioned above.

Hearing that her brother was arriving, a little before the foreseen time,[186] the virgin of God entered the church. Prostrating herself in prayer before an image of Mary the Mother of God,[187] she rose up fully instructed as to what was *the good and acceptable will of God*.[188] Recalling *the vision that* she *had seen*,[189] and now made more confident through prayer as to the divine will, she said to the Sisters, *"Rise, let us go!* For

---

184. As Oliger noted, Giovanni Colonna is the one who has just been sent to fetch Margherita. She now has a vision of a man approaching, whom the author identifies as himself. This passage therefore provides one of the strong indications that Giovanni Colonna is the author of *Vita I*.

185. In Margherita's vision, the cable that appears to aid her descent empha-sizes just how arduous the trip up and down the steep and lofty Mount Prenestino really was.

186. The wording again strongly suggests that Margherita's brother Giovanni must be the person in her vision and therefore the author of the text.

187. This may be a reference to a Romanesque statue of the Virgin and Child, studded with gems and pearls, that was installed on the high altar. Lipinsky, "Tesoro del Santuario," includes photographs of the statue (see plates 10–11), but modern restoration has stripped all traces of medieval polychromy.

188. Cf. Romans 12:2.

189. Cf. Acts 10:17.

behold,[190] this person has come for us, and it is the will of God that we depart from here." When he arrived, after their meal, she *left and departed.*[191] Everyone[192] marveled at this event, grieving because she had gone away. They had heard that she was strong in her resolve not to return, and so they marveled. But they grieved because they had thought she would remain with them there in the service of God and of His mother, for which they had longed.

These events had been predicted to her by the venerable father Friar Giles of the Order of *Minores*, whose reputation for holiness was growing after long and pleasing service to God in these hills.[193] For this holy man had heard of the virgin's arrival and her praiseworthy plan. Therefore he came to visit her, and upon his arrival he saw the opposition raised against the virgin, which we have described and which he loathed.

---

190. Matthew 26:46; Mark 14:42; John 14:31. Interestingly, the biblical quotation ("Rise, let us go; behold, he is at hand that will betray me") puts Giovanni Colonna (the author) in the position of Judas.

191. 2 Kings 3:24.

192. Oliger emended the feminine *admirat[a]e* to the masculine *admirati*. The former would indicate that it was particularly the Sisters who marveled, but the emendation seems justified, since it does not seem that Margherita's band of female followers stayed behind when she departed.

193. Oliger tentatively identified this Franciscan as Giles Capocci, whom early Franciscan historians remembered for his piety and for unspecified miracles. The sixteenth-century Franciscan chronicler Mariano of Florence described him as "de Assisi" and "vir magne sanctitatis, qui in caritate floruit, ac miraculis corruscavit." The Franciscan annalist Luke Wadding followed this description of Giles as "from Assisi," but this was probably incorrect. The Capocci were in fact another of Rome's noble families, whose members served in the city's urban government as well as in the ecclesiastical hierarchy. While we cannot be sure that this Brother Giles was a Colonna client, the career of another Capocci suggests a possible connection. Niccolò Capocci (d. 1368) began his ecclesiastical service in the household of his uncle, Cardinal Pietro Colonna (who in turn was Margherita's nephew). Among his diplomatic missions, in 1325 Niccolò negotiated a reconciliation between Cardinal Giovanni Colonna (grandnephew of Margherita) and Pope John XXII. See Bernard Guillemain, "Capocci, Niccolò," in *DBI*, 18:600–603. Moreover, Carla Keyvanian, *Hospitals and Urbanism in Rome, 1200–1500* (Leiden: Brill, 2015), 276, asserts that Cardinal Pietro's sister Aloisa married a Capocci; we have, however, been unable to verify this assertion, which is contradicted by Carocci, *Baroni di Roma*, 366.

And with one word, by his authority he restrained the hearts of those who were enraged, saying that such things should not be done but rather that solid support should be given to the virgin's praiseworthy plan. "Now then," he said. "Behold, virgin devoted to God! You have departed *from your kindred, going forth from* the land *of your father.*[194] And now a monastery prepared by you has been offered to God, in which you wished *to lead* many *virgins* with you to Him.[195] This has all been accomplished because of you. The goodwill that endures in you is the only sacrifice *acceptable* to God,[196] and by your sacrifice you have shown such a result is possible with effort. Therefore, when your brothers shall send for you, depart; for your reward will be no less in the eyes of God."

Now without doubt this must be believed, just as the holy man said, for she wished to leave her home and people for the sake of Christ. And the most humble virgin wanted not only to put up a monastery, if she had been able to do so without opposition, but also to act as a handmaid to the Mother of God. The wondrous Mother of God deigned to speak to her and to come as the messenger of her salvation, making herself the guardian of [Margherita's] mind and body, for which the virgin did not know any greater recompense and thanks than to offer her whole self.

CHAPTER X. HOW FOR THE SAKE OF OBEDIENCE SHE SUBJECTED HERSELF TO A RELIGIOUS LADY IN HER HOME

Another of the virgin's deeds of great perfection and holiness, not so very different from the last, is worth remembering. Her ears were always open to hearing the Lord's teachings, her heart was eager to carry them out, and she did not ignore good counsel. Therefore, holding fast to Jesus as if to a guiding rod, she was mindful of His *words* and deeds, *pondering*

---

194. Cf. Genesis 12:1.

195. Cf. Psalm 44:15. The author is stretching the point by insisting that Margherita deserves credit for founding a monastery, since this was her intention, even though the plan failed.

196. Cf. Leviticus 22:20.

them[197] so that she could become His imitator, like a dearest daughter. Then, since she recalled Him saying that He *came not to be ministered to but to minister,*[198] and that He had *become obedient unto death,*[199] and since she had learned from elsewhere in the Gospel that He *was subject to* His mother and to His foster father Joseph,[200] following His example she herself longed to be subjected and to obey another while *denying herself,*[201] even though she had always reaped the fruit of obedience because she had subjected herself to her brother [Giacomo] and had not *transgressed* his *commandment.*[202] So she began asking her brother [Giacomo] to provide her with a religious woman to whom *she herself and her entire household could be subject.*[203] Finding such a woman was not easy, because the monastery had not been built and it was hard to wrest someone away from a monastery that had already been built, and to provide for her there. But because impatient "love will not accept the excuse of impossibility nor be stilled by any difficulty,"[204] she hit upon a wonderful way to achieve self-subjection.

She had heard of and known about a certain religious woman in the city [of Rome], who from childhood onward had pledged her virginity to her Spouse, serving in deepest humility even *to good old age,*[205] and who had spent her goods on the poor. This woman therefore acquired a name among the poor and was known as Lady Altruda of the Poor, for she was herself a poor woman of Christ.[206] Seizing this opening, [Margherita]

---

197. Cf. Luke 2:19.

198. Matthew 20:28.

199. Philippians 2:8.

200. Luke 2:51.

201. Cf. Matthew 16:24; Luke 9:23.

202. Cf. Luke 15:29.

203. Cf. John 4:53.

204. Cf. *Sancti Petri Chrysologi collectio sermonum*, pt. 3, ed. Alexander Olivar, Corpus Christianorum Series Latina 24B (Turnhout: Brepols, 1982), 912 (sermon 147).

205. Cf. Tobias 14:15.

206. "Lady Altruda of the Poor" must have been from a noble or at least respectable background, since she is accorded the title *Domina*. She appears to have been well known in pious Roman circles, but to our knowledge this text is the only extant historical reference to her existence. There was a long tradition in Rome of

urged her brother [Giacomo] to allow her to go and see the image of the face of Christ that is venerated with such veneration in the city [of Rome] in the Church of the Prince of the Apostles. For indeed [Margherita] was overflowing with emotion at the sight of this image that offered a view of the One for whom she always longingly seethed. Permission was given, and in the company of another brother[207] she went at night and saw it, venerating it with indescribable veneration. She did not want to leave but had to be dragged away.[208]

After this viewing, she asked her brother to turn off to the house of that most holy virgin [Altruda]. Her brother assented, since he could not decently do otherwise. As he was leaving, he noted the habits of this

---

pious women living independently in their homes or small groups, outside any formal monastic structure. See Brenda Bolton, "Daughters of Rome: All One in Christ Jesus," *Studies in Church History* 27 (1990): 101–15. This tradition persisted into the later Middle Ages, as Katherine Gill has shown in "Open Monasteries for Women in Late Medieval and Early Modern Italy: Two Roman Examples," in *The Crannied Wall: Women, Religion, and the Arts in Early Modern Italy*, ed. Craig L. Monson (Ann Arbor: University of Michigan Press, 1992), 15–47.

207. Presumably Giovanni Colonna.

208. This is a reference to the *Sudarium*, a popular relic believed to be a cloth used to wipe sweat from Christ's face, which came to be known as "Veronica's Veil" or just the "Veronica." It had long been located in (Old) St. Peter's Basilica, but it gained vast new popularity after 1208, when Pope Innocent III instituted an annual procession in which it was carried from St. Peter's through Rome to the Ospedale Santo Spirito. This procession took place on the second Sunday after Epiphany, but in this case the text implies that Margherita received special permission to visit it ("at night"), so the date does not seem clear. For the complicated history of the *Sudarium* and other Holy Faces, see Herbert Kessler and Gerhardt Wolf, eds., *The Holy Face and the Paradox of Representation* (Bologna: Nuova Alfa Editoriale, 1998); Neil MacGregor, *Seeing Salvation: Images of Christ in Art* (New Haven, CT: Yale University Press, 2000), esp. 90–94; and Alexa Sand, *Vision, Devotion, and Self-Representation in Late Medieval Art* (Cambridge: Cambridge University Press, 2014), ch. 1. Interestingly, the nuns at San Silvestro in Capite had their own relic purporting to show Christ's face. The origin of this early image is obscure, but in 1518 Mariano of Florence wrote in his pilgrim's guide to Rome (*Itinerarium urbis Romae*) that the sisters were forbidden to display it lest it compete with the St. Peter's relic. See the discussion in Eileen Kane, *The Church of San Silvestro in Capite in Rome* (Genoa: Edizioni d'Arte Marconi, 2005), 22–26.

Lady [Altruda] and the mode of life with which she served in her house. The good Lady was accustomed to go at dawn to the Mass of the Brothers.[209] And after Mass was celebrated, she would visit the shrines of the saints[210] until Nones and sometimes even later as the length of her trip required. Since she did not want to go alone, [Lady Altruda] would take with her a certain religious woman. This was a virgin who lived with her and served her needs, and yet it was [Lady Altruda] who was always obedient to her.

When these two went out each day on their pious mission, the virgin [Margherita] would remain behind and shut herself in at once. She had not brought even one person from her own household with her lest she be a burden to the Lady; instead she herself had come to perform household service for her. Having shut herself in and gone through her Hours and divine service, she would do the cooking so that when the two returned they would find a meal prepared to restore them in their weariness. She would sweep with a broom, wash the dishes, and see to preparing all the other things just as any maid of the lower house would have done. Thus it was that for no few days this virgin, so dear to God, gave service in that home with such humility. Word spread of the virgin's behavior there, and many came to see her, but she would show herself to only a few. She did not blush at her service to Christ, though many marveled to see her so cheaply clad. She, however, avoided gossip, and after a few polite words would return to her solitude.

---

209. Lady Altruda may have regularly attended Mass at the Franciscans' main church, Santa Maria in Aracoeli, on the Capitoline Hill. The Colonna family chapel to the right of the high altar there still depicts Giovanni Colonna kneeling beside Francis and praying to the Virgin and Child. The Friars also had smaller communities in Trastevere and other parts of the city. See Giulia Barone, "I Francescani a Roma," *Storia della città: Rivista internazionale di storia urbana e territoriale* 9 (1978): 33–35.

210. The Latin is "limina visitabat sanctorum," which taken literally would mean she visited the "doorsteps of the saints" or "holy men." But the phrase "ad limina sanctorum apostolorum" was routinely used to mean simply "to Rome" (that is, the place of the holy apostles), so presumably here the phrase means loosely "the holy sites/shrines of Rome." Cf. for example Thomas of Celano, *Vita prima*, 34.

For some little time she hid from her brother [Giacomo] her plan not to come back until a monastery in which she would be enclosed had been made ready. But when he pressed her about her return, she revealed her humble and pious plans, because it was more beneficial to her to be subservient in this way to that Lady and to live a religious life guided by her fine example than to remain in her own home. For without a doubt she was making progress on each of these paths of service to Christ, proceeding down both at the same time.[211] Indeed, the virgin marveled so much at the vigor and driving goodwill toward God in such an elderly person that she found her own dedication to holy service more heated still. The old woman delighted in the virgin, who drew steady, impassioned breath only when engaged in lowly service to Christ.

After many days dedicated to placing herself in subjection, which was why she had gone there, she wanted to obey her brother's command. And so she returned, if not willingly, then as one subject to obedience. Behold her true self-*denial* in which, *taking up* her *cross*, she proceeded imitating the deeds of Christ![212]

CHAPTER XI. ON HER SUFFERING AND THE PATIENCE WITH WHICH SHE BORE IT

The more the virgin conformed to Christ through obedience to his commandments, the more her desire was kindled. For He himself had said, *If you love me, keep my commandments.*[213] Therefore, after the display of many holy acts, this most powerful desire flashed forth in her mind—to be crucified together *with Christ* whom she loved.[214] *A bundle of myrrh* was her *beloved* to her, who *abided between* her *breasts.*[215] When she sought a physical imitation of His suffering, then truly marvelous things

---

211. That is, active and contemplative paths.
212. Cf. Matthew 16:24.
213. John 14:15.
214. Cf. Galatians 2:19.
215. Canticles 1:12.

happened to her, which I relate with trembling hand and a pen that fails as I write.[216]

When she was armed with meditation on the suffering Christ, she saw a king lying as though ill upon a bed, and she began to burn with desire to render obedient service to him as the needs of sick people require. She did not dare, however, unless she was called. Then a sign was made to her that she should come. She came forward in obedience and asked whether it would please him if she massaged his feet, since sick people are often cheered by this. He nodded his consent that this was pleasing. She then genuflected and began to work, rubbing his foot with her hand; and with her hand or hands that were working and rubbing, she encountered nail wounds. Realizing that this was the wounded Christ, her soul remained transfixed as though the points of the nails had gone straight through her middle. And more incredibly—or rather not incredibly at all, for what is truly incredible is that we are not all transfixed in this way!—it was as if the sorrow remained in her soul while her body was pierced through, so that she could not move for three days, and her body was no more mobile than if she had been transfixed by a spear.

Therefore, when she was enflamed like an *elephant* at the *blood*[217] of that wounded One whom she kept always before her mind's eye, suddenly there came upon her a certain ulcer that broke her flesh and skin and took root in her bones.[218] It produced such a flow of blood and pus that it ran down to her ankle, as though the humors of her whole body, especially of her side, created the flow.[219] She sustained this *without blame*,[220] enduring great suffering until the end of her life.

---

216. Cf. Psalm 44:2.

217. Cf. 1 Machabees 6:34.

218. *Vita II* returns repeatedly to the suffering caused by the ulcer in Margherita's leg at the end of her life.

219. Medieval medical texts described the human body as composed of four "humors"—black bile, yellow bile, phlegm, and blood. Balance between the humors was believed to be necessary for good health.

220. Luke 1:6, etc.

For a long time, she hid this from her brother [Giacomo] and even from her household, not letting up at all in the rigor of her usual abstinence and vigils. But it was particularly trying to her in her austere sleeping habits, insofar as she lay down only when turned on the other side. At last, when she was at the end of her strength, she revealed this to her brother, who was taking care of her, and he sensibly directed her austerity toward *reasonable service*.[221] Truly then, at that point, with great sorrow and streams of tears, she changed her accustomed practices, but she did not fail in her emotional, prayerful vigils. And the more her body failed, the more she progressed to higher things with a rising spirit. Her brother sought the assistance of many doctors and medicines for her, but they brought no relief. And once when a certain physician, who was celebrated but a Jew, had come to cure her, she shunned him and did not allow herself to touch medicine from one who denied her Christ. And indeed she said, "If you want me to take your medicine, you take mine and become a Christian!" Hearing this, the stubborn man departed.[222]

Her suffering, the form it would take, and even the length of time for which she would need to bear it, had all been revealed to her. For three roads were shown to her,[223] of which she chose to go down the middle one. And as she started down this, it was shown to her that if she made her way through the middle road she would have to go through blood, but she did not give up on that account, though her *foot was dipped in blood*[224] right up to her ankle. And it turned out this was quite correct, because she trod the middle path, the royal path,[225] the path that

---

221. Romans 12:1.

222. The anti-Judaism of this passage is notable. The attitude displayed here was not, however, universal. For instance, Pope Nicholas IV (Jerome of Ascoli), who was a close ally of the Colonna, employed the Jewish doctor Isaac ben Mordecai, according to Robert Brentano, *Rome before Avignon: A Social History of Thirteenth-Century Rome* (New York: Basic Books, 1974), 47.

223. This passage seems directly related to the "three roads" vision related by Stefania in *Vita II*, ch. 5, but there Margherita takes the third path.

224. Cf. Psalm 67:24.

225. *Via regia* (Numbers 21:22) and *via media* were oft-used phrases for holding to a middle path between potential vices on either sides of an issue, here used in combination (*viam mediam et regiam*).

Christ had taken, for the whole course of her life, not turning off to either side. She crossed through blood, for such was her suffering. And her ankle was steeped in blood, for the ankle is the finishing point of the body and her suffering lasted all the way to the finish, to her end. While enduring this suffering the virgin would sometimes say that a Christian neither could nor should be beaten down just because something happened to him. And with the blessed Job often and more often she would say, "Let the one who does this finish and *not spare* me sorrow!"[226]

Once when she was tortured by severe pains due to her troubling ulcer, as happened quite often, in the heat of the suffering she said to the Sisters, summoned in these scourgings, "My Sisters, what do you request when you pray for me?" Then she added, "Do not ask God to remove my sickness or to lessen my pains, but pray that He may cut and burn me,[227] so that there He will not upset me! Let Him swell trouble upon trouble, so that He not deny me his presence!"

CHAPTER XII. ON THE APPARITION MADE TO HER IN THE GUISE OF A PILGRIM

Now by her self-denials and fasting, now by her vigils and weeping, now by the suffering that for three years had eaten away at her body,[228] the virgin was so worn away in the flesh that it was as though her flesh were already dead and only the seething desires of her soul remained! She carried out these things unfailingly and was renewed in them each day. And as she advanced in the things with which she seethed, others followed. Therefore, with *all things accomplished*[229] and done in conformity to her

---

226. Job 6:10.

227. The phrase "secet et urat" echoes Bernard of Clairvaux's *De gradibus humilitatis et superbiae* 6, ed. J. Leclercq and H. M. Rochais, *S. Bernardi opera*, vol. 3 (Rome: Editiones Cistercienses, 1963), 45.

228. Since Margherita died at the end of 1280, and the text states that the vision that is about to be related occurred in the last year of her life, this passage would indicate that she was beset by her troubling ulcer at the end of 1277 or early in 1278.

229. Cf. John 19:28.

Beloved, she now desired nothing but *to dissolve and be with* her *Christ*.[230] This had long been preached to her by her brother [Giacomo]. At the call of Mary, Mother of God, she, a virgin, had followed the Virgin, as a poor woman following the poor, wishing wholly to leave her people and country.[231] And having once left, she followed a young pilgrim. Denying herself,[232] she imitated Him whom she *obeyed unto death*,[233] whose command she served and whose advice she did not disregard. Finally, out of loving longing for the crucified One, she bore the scourge in her own body.[234] This [suffering] stamped her with the privilege of Christ's love, and it is a sure sign to us of her election by her Betrothed.

During her final year, as the end of her life grew near, in kind thanks for her obedient service and so that we might be inspired by this virgin's example, Christ himself, who had summoned her through His mother, came to visit her and deigned to demonstrate that He had consecrated the virgin as his accepted betrothed. That year she was holding the Feast of the Nativity of the Blessed John the Baptist[235] in an even more holy and earnest fashion than usual, and had expended funds to feed the poor both on Mount [Prenestino], where she was living, and also in the town below,[236] having her household take meals door to door. And she brought within the gates[237] of her own house a rescued host of poor women and children for her personal attention and that of her followers. After Mass was celebrated and heard with deep devotion, weeping copiously with great emotion, she returned and gave orders to her household that they

---

230. Philippians 1:23.
231. Cf. Genesis 12:1.
232. Cf. Matthew 16:24; Luke 9:23.
233. Philippians 2:8.
234. That is, the suffering caused by her ulcer.
235. Since this vision is set in the last year of Margherita's life, the date should be 24 June 1280. It is worth noting that San Silvestro "in Capite," where Margherita's followers eventually established themselves, was believed to possess the head (the *caput*) of John the Baptist.
236. That is, Palestrina.
237. Although the phrase "in claustris" might evoke the idea of a formal nuns' cloister, these were not in fact cloistered nuns at this point.

should cause all who had come *to sit down* at table,[238] which they did. After stepping aside briefly to finish her prayers, she at once returned to her service. And nearly everything had been distributed, because even as some children were departing, others were still arriving and being served.

A certain virgin among the Sisters, who had arrived as a follower of the virgin after Christ, was one of those engaged in this service.[239] She was reluctantly carrying out the task assigned to her by her mother, Lady [Margherita].[240] She did not have that passion for serving which she should have had but was only doing what she was told out of obedience. As she stood in the doorway of the house, a pilgrim dressed in pilgrim's garb appeared within the enclosure, and she saw his face, all lit up and aflame, [from] beneath the branches of a certain almond tree that stood in the garden of the enclosure. The branches of that tree are more than twice as tall as a man, and yet she saw his approaching face shining from above, as though it were above [the branches] laid out below.[241] Marveling at this sight, she shouted to her mother at the top of her lungs, "Lady! Behold a pilgrim whose face burns with fire!" Her mother warned her about this outcry and ordered her to prepare the water, although speaking in a low voice as though she understood what was happening. Then, as though weakened, [Margherita] sat back on a chest that was placed there. And as if she were fainting, she placed her hand on the shoulder of the other Sister standing there. The Sister who had turned

---

238. Cf. Matthew 14:19, etc.

239. This "other Sister" is never named, but at the end of the chapter the author states that she is now leading the community after Margherita's death.

240. The *mater/materfamilias/domina* in this long sequence is Margherita. The source of this story is eventually revealed to be "the Sisters," and in particular the Sister who saw the pilgrim along with Margherita (thus the reference to "reluctance" and lack of zeal is humility rather than criticism). As noted below, it is not impossible that this Sister was Stefania, author of *Vita II*. It is thus interesting that here Margherita is *mater* and *materfamilias* (as well as *virgo*), apparently reflecting the label by which her followers referred to her.

241. The imagery is confusing here, with the face seeming to be both below the branches ("infra ramos") and above them ("super prostratos," where *ramos* seems to be the only masculine plural noun to serve as referent). We have thus conjectured a reading that suggests that the Sister was looking "from below" the branches and saw the face up above.

to call her mother had hardly turned her head back around after her mother's whispered order to fetch the water, when she saw that the pilgrim whom she had spied at a distance was now standing right before her. Nor could she find or tell that he had taken any time at all in covering the length of the garden approaching the house.

The pilgrim, now standing at the door, begged alms in honor of the blessed John the Baptist. The order was given that he should enter; and the virgin mother of the family, looking for a jug to wash the hands of the guest, found that the Sister who had seen him and had shouted at the sight had ministered to him with another jug that had by chance been prepared for her. Everyone in the house heard him whispering a blessing, but what it was no educated woman knew.[242] They saw, however, the sign of blessing being raised, and the blessing being given to the whole house.[243] And after the blessing he sat down. The bench on which he was seated (which the ladies venerating their images had caused to be built)[244] has space for four or five people to sit. Miraculous—and yet, not miraculous!—as he sat down he filled the whole seat, so that there was no space for anyone else. The virgin who had first beheld this and recalled it, likened his sitting there to a certain image in the apse of the Church of the Blessed San Pietro of Mount [Prenestino] that depicts the Lord enthroned in his majesty.[245]

---

242. The term *litterata* in the medieval context means "woman literate in Latin." It would seem that the pilgrim recited his blessing in Latin, but not even the educated women present could understand what he said.

243. Thus one of the points of the entire episode is to demonstrate Christ's direct blessing for the community.

244. The idea seems to be a bench on which multiple people could sit while contemplating sacred images or statues.

245. This church no longer exists, having been destroyed as part of Pope Boniface VIII's campaign against the Colonna in 1297. In a document seeking restitution for the destruction, Cardinal Pietro Colonna (Margherita's nephew) complained that even if there were sufficient funds, the antiquity of the town could never be recovered. He described ancient temples and buildings from the time of Julius Caesar, along with medieval fortifications, palaces, homes, and, of course, churches that were destroyed at Boniface's direction. Interestingly, Pietro's complaint does not list the houses in which Margherita and her companions had lived, suggesting that the site was no longer central to her cult (or canonization efforts) after the transfer

The heart of that same Sister, who had first beheld the radiance of his flaming face and had been reluctantly attending to the poor of Christ, now began to burn with passion after seeing him sit down to table. Thus she realized that she was seething within, so that she freely devoted herself to serving him food at table and did not go to distribute charity elsewhere; and all who were standing about were honoring him as though he were the Lord, even if they did not yet recognize him. The virgin mother of the family placed down the only bit of meat that was left from what remained of the supplies that had been purchased. The Sister who had seen him placed before him a jug of wine, shaking as she served.

Behold! Another man came, seeking nothing.[246] The pilgrim, who had sat down, made room for him at his side, although to the observers it had appeared there was no space. And she who had provided water to the pilgrim did the same for [the other man], and he asked her if the liquid she provided was wine. She answered that it was not.

The virgin mother of the family was standing there watching, thinking to herself and wondering if this could be the same one that she had seen another time.[247] [In this earlier vision] she had seen an old man, a father as it were, who was grieving over a spiritually dead son whom he was severely threatening. The virgin's own more worthy brother, Lord [Giacomo], was respectfully restraining his arm, calling for forgiveness and repeating, "Have pity!" When the virgin asked [Giacomo] what was happening, he put his finger to his lips, signaling her to be silent; she recognized that this was God, who was offering pains and threats for someone's offenses, for whom her lord brother was praying that He might refrain and not punish.

---

of her body to San Silvestro in Capite. For an overview of Boniface's campaign, see Pierre-Yves Le Pogam, "La lutte entre Boniface VIII et les Colonna par les armes symbolique," *Rivista di storia della chiesa in Italia* 61 (2007): 47–66; for the document, see Ludwig Mohler, *Die Kardinäle Jakob und Peter Colonna: Ein Beitrag zur Geschichte des Zeitalters Bonifaz' VIII* (Paderborn: F. Schöningh, 1913), 215–18.

246. The Sister recounting the story hints below that the community believed this second man to be John the Baptist.

247. She seems to be referring to the "pilgrim" (Christ) and not the second man (John the Baptist).

So she now asked herself if this man was that same one. Her soul groaned and sighed with this question, and by these sighs she was made certain that indeed it was He. And at once, praying, she asked Christ, who was there, for that which she was accustomed to ask of Him when His suffering on our behalf is recalled at the altar.[248] As her prayer poured forth and she emitted more sighs and groans, she knew that she had been heard, and she had the conviction that those who pray are accustomed to having[249] when they know that they have been heard. For if they have prayed in true devotion, they are less able to be fooled than those who see something right before their eyes. Indeed, we know that illusions have been dispelled by prayer, but we have known no one to be fooled by prayer, unless the person was lying about praying.

Then [Margherita] began to weaken, and her spirit briefly began to fail, and she doubtless would have fainted. But suddenly she was wrenched away, as though hands were pushing her, all the way to the interior of the house, where she lay down all weak and unable to speak for as long as the pilgrim was to be seen in the house. When the other Sister, who has so often been mentioned in this vision, noticed the mother's absence and was eager to go to her, the lord pilgrim signaled her with three taps on the jug, and she understood that the wine was gone. She genuflected and took the jug and filled it and brought it back, and she would not have dared serve in this attendance had she not genuflected.

The Sisters know and bear witness that such things were set out. But as to whether or not the pilgrim ate or drank (though they assume he did), they really cannot swear for certain. Yet they do not remember seeing or cleaning away anything left behind where He was sitting. They believe that the other one who had come along (for whom a vacant space to sit was made and given, which seemed to emerge from the full space occupied by the sitter) resembled a certain image in the above-mentioned church [of San Pietro of Mount Prenestino]; this was an image of the blessed John the Baptist, whose feast was being celebrated, and for love

---

248. In *Vita II*, ch. 26, Stefania clarifies this passage by explaining that Margherita was accustomed to ask for the salvation of her soul and of her brothers' souls.

249. Oliger's edition contains the misprint *babere* for *habere*.

of whom the expenditures were made, just as that image appears to the eyes of viewers.[250]

Just *as He was sitting at table*,[251] [the other Sister] came to her mother and said, "My lady! Is there something holy about this man?" Then, first recovering her power of speech, [Margherita] replied, smiling as though fully aware, "Is He still here? Go see." She went but did not find Him. For He had departed, in the same way that no one had seen Him come and go except these women in the events recorded here.

Her brother and guardian [Giacomo] was not present there when these things happened to [Margherita] and the Sisters. Out of devotion he had gone to the doorstep of his holy church in the city [of Rome],[252] intending to remain there in that city until celebrating the coming Feast of Peter and Paul[253] in worthy devotion on this pilgrimage. After the rites of these days were completed, he came back and was told what had happened. Giving thanks in devout humility, he was greatly moved by such worthiness of Christ's goodness that He had shown to those aspiring to Him. He sent the virgin and the Sisters to their quarters and stirred up their emotions with the idea of atonement, alleging that they had welcomed Him with less than proper reverence. He ordered that they were to afflict themselves and seethe with desire to see Him again, until the Lord should deign to indicate his goodness to the humble women awaiting another view of the pilgrim they had seen. They fell to praying, therefore, for these, their deepest desires. And, indeed, because of their earnestness, not long afterward they saw again other things, to the greater confirmation of the first vision.

---

250. There are few remains of the thirteenth-century Church of San Pietro on Mount Prenestino, but John the Baptist appears linked with the Colonna in several other extant frescoes in the Lateran as well as mosaics from the Aracoeli (discussed above in the Introduction). For the Lateran scheme, see Donal Cooper and Janet Robson, *The Making of Assisi: The Pope, the Franciscans, and the Painting of the Basilica* (New Haven, CT: Yale University Press, 2013).

251. Cf. Matthew 9:10.

252. As of 1278, Giacomo Colonna was cardinal deacon of Santa Maria in Via Lata.

253. 29 June 1280.

When that Sister who had first seen Him was sitting all alone weaving, and the virgin mother of the family was in the chapel praying, that Sister began to think to herself about the future presence of the pilgrim. She wanted Him to come and enter through the window that provided light for her there; but if that happened, should she call her mother, as [Margherita] had ordered her to do? [The Sister] was of two minds here, but she decided that it would be better not to do so, lest He leave her. Immediately after these thoughts and the resolution she had made to rejoice alone with Him if He should appear, He came as imagined, and granted comfort to her desire for Him, for as long as the human mind is able to take, and then left. On this occasion He did not offer a bodily presence to her eyes but rather made his presence known to the eyes of her mind,[254] giving just as much delight that way.

Another worthy event—no less worthy a marvel!—occurred just after the departure of Him who, when He so wishes, shows Himself to the eyes of the mind or the eyes of the body; now one, now the other; *the spirit breathes where He will* and no one *knows whence He comes or where He goes.*[255] The virgin mother of the family, aware of what had occurred, came to the Sister, asking her at some length if she had thought anything about the pilgrim. [The Sister] did not hide her thoughts from [Margherita, but] because she had decided not to call her if He came, she wished to pass over the rest in silence. But truly this could not be concealed from [Margherita], for she spoke like one who was well informed in the matter. And she commanded, under obedience, that [the other Sister] tell her all that had transpired. So [the Sister] told her mother, and both of them told me. There can be no doubt that the virgin was in pleasant favor with the pilgrim, since He shared his secrets with her about what was done with that Sister.

He appeared *in those days*[256] to the more worthy brother [Giacomo], who had been absent when these things occurred and so was seething,

---

254. Cf. *Sancti Odonis abbatis cluniacensis II Collationum*, bk. 1, *PL* 133, col. 538. The echo of the phrase "sed mentalibus oculis" may be coincidental but seems worth noting in light of *Vita II's* extensive use of (pseudo) Odo of Cluny.

255. John 3:8.

256. Genesis 6:4; Mark 1:9, etc.

wanting to see for himself. One day when [Giacomo] had fasted and then dined, and with the household resting inside, he went outside to the front of the house. And behold! A young pilgrim was there and sat down beside him. [Giacomo] led Him inside and *set him down to table*[257] with another poor person who had been brought in and was sitting there. Since almost everything else had already been given away elsewhere, he placed a bunch of grapes before [the pilgrim]. Going off to fetch Him something to drink, [when Giacomo returned] he did not find the young man, who had left; and thus He disappeared. This troubled [Giacomo], but he discovered nothing else. And he himself was left, if it is proper to say, guilty of the same thing for which he had blamed the virgin and the Sister! Namely, that they had not shown Him due respect. But neither he nor they [showed this due respect] because they could do no more unless it were granted them. The disciples themselves did not show proper honor to the Lord walking the road as a *stranger*,[258] yet He then, just as now, fulfilled the purpose of His appearance.[259]

There is further confirmation of the appearance of the pilgrim to the more worthy brother [Giacomo]. On the night before the day when this had occurred to him, the Sister who had first seen the pilgrim saw Him again in her sleep. But this time His face was not so fiery and He was united with the more worthy brother [Giacomo], the guardian and foster parent of her mother and of the women. They were joined as though they were one body, head to head and face to face and body to body, so that whatever one of them might do would be done with the other to whom he was joined. As He sat upon a higher seat, with her seated lower down, He leaned toward her, and the pilgrim was resting over her shoulders with the one joined to Him.

By means of what has been shown, we are able to understand that He who considered that whatever was done *to one of* his *little ones* was

---

257. Cf. Luke 12:37.

258. Cf. Luke 24:13–25.

259. The point of the two concluding sentences seems to be that although neither Giacomo, Margherita, the unnamed Sister, nor the disciples honored Jesus as they should have when he appeared unexpectedly, Jesus's intention was still fulfilled by displaying the importance of seeing Christ in every poor traveler.

done to Him[260] was mightily pleased by the worshipful observance of the brother and sister in the largesse they expended on the poor of Christ; and He showed this by appearing to them in the dress of a pilgrim.

Nor was the following fact by any chance lacking in secret significance: that although the virgin wished to offer water to the newcomer, it was the other Sister who actually provided it. By this we could understand that the performance of the virgin [Margherita]'s holy work for the servants of Christ was going to end swiftly because of her death, for which her desire was always ready. Thus it was fitting that the virgin offered what was left of the largesse, according to what was recorded next. In fact, it happened that the one coming along and following, who is now in charge of her family,[261] actually provided the service, because she followed [Margherita] in the honor of service. Because they used up the wine, which no one witnessed being drunk, and whose bitter taste stands for the harshness of her penance, Christ gave us to understand that because the virgin had *brought forth fruits worthy of penance*[262] in her own suffering, He was now eager to remove her from the tasks of Martha.[263] And He moved her, as though pushed forward by hands, away from the obedience of service, to rest apart from the others, because she should enter into his *joys* in calming quiet.[264] Therefore near the end of her life, He deigned to confirm with his presence that the virgin had

---

260. Cf. Matthew 25:40.

261. The Latin is "que nunc sue familie preest." The "other Sister" in this story is now revealed to be leading the community after Margherita's death. Oliger speculated that this woman might therefore have been Herminia, who was made first abbess of San Silvestro in Capite in 1285, but since *Vita I* was completed before 1285 there seems no strong reason to make this identification. Another possibility is surely Stefania, author of *Vita II*, who describes herself there as "sororum cenobio presidentem." The latter interpretation seems particularly compelling, since if Stefania was already providing an extended narrative to Giovanni for incorporation in his *vita*, it might have been logical for Giacomo to then solicit additional writings from her a few years later.

262. Luke 3:8.

263. "Martha" stands for the active life; see note 269.

264. Cf. Matthew 25:21 and 23.

been heard in her constant prayer, and that He had not forgotten calling her to Him[265] while she lived.

That [other] Sister saw more clearly what was going to come about; when the pilgrim (who was joined with the virgin's brother, her guardian and lord) was leaning over her shoulders, He was leaning over the very woman who displayed her own servitude in serving the Sisters in Christ at the command of her father and foster father,[266] following after the ministry of the virgin. And what followed showed why she had at first seen His face as though on fire: for she, who was cool in offering service, as has been explained, later was afire with the flames of love. Therefore, Christ brought it about that she and the other daughters, through the example of their mother, would be able to please their Betrothed as she did.

Other things have been seen of this pilgrim by other Sisters and shown to the religious man,[267] but let what has been written suffice, lest there be greater delay in the weaving of this narrative.[268]

CHAPTER XIII. HOW THE BLESSEDNESS THAT SHE WOULD ATTAIN WAS SHOWN TO HER IN A VISION

Just as Christ confirmed his virgin in the works of Martha through His taking up the guise of a pilgrim, so [He confirmed her] in the leisure of Mary because of the earnestness of the desires by which she was brought to Him, and He showed His mother to her in a most beautiful vision. For just as [Martha's] efforts through compassion for one's neighbor were

---

265. Cf. Psalm 21:25.

266. "Que de mandato sui patris et alumpni suis ministrans Sororibus." It is not clear whether this is a reference to this Sister's biological father and a "foster father" (Giacomo Colonna?), or to the pilgrim and his companion.

267. Presumably a reference to Giacomo Colonna.

268. As Oliger notes, the Latin in the manuscript here requires emendation; our translation is somewhat conjectural (changing *ut* to *ne* to result in a counter-factual "lest" clause).

perfected in [Margherita], so [Mary's] contemplation through withdrawing into God completed the evidence for [Margherita's] holiness.[269]

When she had come to the Church of San Pietro of Mount [Prenestino], standing where she used to hear the celebration of Mass, in a place apart where she set herself in prayer with her household, it appeared to her that her more worthy brother, Lord [Giacomo], was listening to the singing of a psalm of faith before the altar, dressed in the robes of a deacon and exercising great preaching.[270] And then she saw a bed, spread in beauteous delight, on which a little boy of about three years of age was lying. Standing in front of the bed was a lady who appeared to be the boy's mother. As she gazed, [Margherita] thought, and indeed knew, that this was the only born Son of God [and] His mother Mary who bore Him. It appeared to her that the boy who was lying there was filling the whole bed. And so, feeling for the mother because no empty place had been left for her on the bed, she touched the boy with faith and great daring, thinking to move Him with her hand so that there would be space for His mother. But she was not able to do it! Indeed, a great resistance opposed her push, as though she had wanted to push a mountain into a valley. She grew pale, trembling in awe of his divinity. But after a while she regained her courage through prayer, saying, "You are not allowing yourself to be moved because it does not please you. But remember that she carried you in her womb for our sake!" Immediately after her appeal and prayer, the boy moved away and left an empty space for His mother.[271]

The virgin did not dare look into the boy's eyes, nor was she as yet being taken within that gaze, but she looked at the boy's whole body. Thereafter the boy turned His gaze upon the virgin. His gaze bored through her heart and limbs so that nothing whatsoever within her, corporeal or spiritual, escaped His look. At this gaze her body turned all light and clear, as she had sometimes heard preached of the blessed.

---

269. In medieval interpretations of Luke 10:38–42, "Martha" stands for the active life and "Mary" for the life of contemplation.

270. Giacomo Colonna was cardinal deacon after 1278.

271. Margherita's bold rebuke of Christ is noteworthy; by contrast, she has just had a vision of Giacomo more timidly imploring Christ's mercy.

After this she was permitted the sight of the boy's eyes. Faint and trembling, she later described this, saying that the bright clarity of those eyes exceeded all the peace of heaven, and in their observation she beheld *heaven and earth*, the sea *and all things that are under* their *cope*.[272] Then, recalling His divinity, she repeated most worshipfully the prayer she was accustomed to recite when Christ's suffering was recalled at the altar, and that she had poured forth to the arriving pilgrim. We know fully and entirely what she asked of Him, that Christ might bring all remaining things to completion through her merits and endless prayers.[273]

CHAPTER XIV. ON HER LAST ILLNESS AND WHAT OCCURRED DURING IT AND AT HER PASSING

The virgin had been made *ready* so that she might *go in to the marriage* with her *Bridegroom*,[274] because the gaze of the Christ Child had readied her. [Christ] *gazed on Peter*[275] and called the apostle. And naming him Peter after the rock itself,[276] He crafted the name of the person acknowledging Him. He gazed on [Peter] when he denied Him, so that he wept *bitterly*.[277] He did not *depart from* his disciple but [commanded] that he *should wait for* his *promise* with the others.[278] [In the same way, Christ] gazed upon this virgin, and He called her through His mother, and He inspired his follower with a plan for her virginity. He gazed upon her in the form of a pilgrim, received by her hospitality, so that He might show the truth of her deeds and these might remain as models for our imitation. And He gazed upon her once more in the last vision, because He wished to show that she was to be blessed in heaven.

---

272. Cf. Esther 13:10.
273. Cf. Note 248 above, and *Vita II*, ch. 26.
274. Cf. Matthew 25:10.
275. Luke 22:61.
276. The well-known but untranslatable pun (Peter is *Petrus* in Latin, rock is *petra*) is from Matthew 16:18.
277. Cf. Luke 22:62.
278. Acts 1:4.

Now only the prison of the flesh separated the virgin from her Betrothed, whose ever-present spirit breathed within her. For near the end of her life she said that for the previous three years nothing here below had occupied her emotions even for a moment;[279] rather, she was constantly yearning for higher things. And she had been warned that she should do so. For once when she was praying that God would guide her actions "in accordance with His will"[280] so that she might see what she should do, a certain eagle was shown to her, turned so that it was flying with its back parts to the earth and its head pointed to heaven. When this was shown to her, it was said to her that this was how she should proceed, that she should not *look back.*[281] And without doubt she did fly in this manner. She therefore prayed for nothing else but to be *led* from this prison *to praise* her Betrothed.[282]

Thus it was once said to her, *Behold, the* desired *king will come.*[283] And then, through other means, she was made certain about the place from where she was to depart, but she was not then made certain as to when this would occur. But before her passing, in her illness, she was given the answer to this, and she foretold the exact day of her death. She had the holy scriptures searched as to when the church sang this line [*Behold the king will come*], believing that this would be the day of her passing. And learning that the church most devoutly recalls those very words at Advent,[284] and hearing all this with great joy in her heart, she exalted what is recalled from the scriptures at that time; for those are the words of a soul in eager expectation, exactly as she was herself.

---

279. In *Vita II*, ch. 26, Stefania asks Margherita to elaborate on the meaning of this passage.

280. The phrase echoes a collect used variously in the Christmas and Epiphany liturgy. *CO*, 3830; Van Dijk, *Sources*, 2:38; Lippe, *Missale Romanum Mediolani*, 27.

281. Cf. Luke 9:62.

282. Cf. Psalm 141:8. Note the way this claim relates back to Giacomo Colonna's interpretation of his first vision in the text, at the end of chapter 2.

283. Zacharias 9:9.

284. Invitatory for the First Sunday in Advent. Cantus ID, 1074; Van Dijk, *Sources*, 2:29.

Therefore, the day came when she began to grow weak; that is, on the vigil of the blessed Thomas the Apostle.[285] No further weakness followed this one,[286] which put an end to all her labor and increased her longing to go off to her Betrothed. The moment she felt the stiffening fevers, she raised her eyes to heaven, saying, "It is time that you entrust my body to the earth."[287] And looking at her hands, whose flesh she saw was wasted away and merely skin and bones, she *gave thanks*,[288] saying, "Thank You, Lord, because You have allowed my flesh to be worn away like this." And at once she called out in hope, with the blessed Job, *And in my flesh I will see God, my* Savior.[289] And, as if addressing her flesh in consolation of its suffering, she said, "For your reward there will be greater than your trouble here." So she lay down weakly upon her bed, overwhelmed by the double weakness of the fever and her ulcer. She was in great physical agony for the five days before the birthday of Christ,[290] but she suffered them patiently in great equanimity. The tempter, the enemy of the human race, came; but he found nothing in the virgin whatsoever with which he could accuse her.[291] Unable to do anything else, he left a fetid stench in her left nostril that lasted three days and that she could not get rid of even with much perfume. And then the virgin explained where that foul stench had come from, and mocking the one who had left it, she *gave thanks* to God and His mother because [the tempter] had been able to accomplish so little against her. And after those three days the stench was entirely gone.

The Lord's birthday came; and so she greatly venerated the glorious night of His birth, pouring herself into total devotion. And it is believed that the Virgin Mary, Mother of God, for the exaltation of the virgin at the time of her passing, showed her own childbirth to her, and showed

---

285. The Feast of the Apostle Thomas is 21 December, so the vigil would be 20 December 1280.

286. That is, this was her last, terminal, illness.

287. The phrase comes from an Antiphon for the Feast of Saint Andrew (November 30) *Cantus ID, 0023*, Van Dijk, *Sources*, 2:121.

288. Cf. Luke 22:17.

289. Job 19:26.

290. 20–24 December 1270.

291. Cf. John 14:30.

her the flaming star that had led the Magi to their adoration. Her more worthy brother [Giacomo] knows more about this, because he questioned her and she told him some things, though not everything, about this vision. But after this vision, all of us who were standing there saw a marked change in her, from which we surmise these things. For her eyes were all full of joyous sparkle; her *face* was more bright and *comely* than usual.[292] Then I, the one writing this, beheld that jubilation which the holy authors describe, the happiness that the jubilant cannot hide. For this jubilation stayed continually with her from that day until the day she left this world and was taken up to an even greater jubilation. Her face, as I have said, became even brighter. Her eyes were suffused with eager joyousness. She could not contain her laughter, and yet she was not completely laughing. While she was in this jubilation we noticed that she again and again repeated a phrase said before, that is, *over where the child was*.[293] This phrase erupted from her in her jubilance! And she was again in jubilation when she recalled in the quiet of her heart the flaming star, about which this phrase was spoken, that guided the Magi, leading them to the boy. She was overheard speaking to the Mother of God, saying, "My Lady, gather me into the company of this court." And when a woman standing by asked another woman what she was saying, the woman answered very quietly, "She is speaking with the Mother of God." [Margherita] added, "And she does not *leave me alone*."[294]

Another thing happened to her during that illness. She asked her other brother [Giovanni] to give her a mixture of water and vinegar to drink, since he was carrying a cup of it. The brother answered, "I am afraid to let you have this, since the doctors may not approve." So she said, "Then give me a cup of ordinary water." When those standing there poured some in a glass, she raised her eyes to heaven, saying, "*God is able*[295] to give this liquid the flavor that his serving maid desires." And she made the sign of the cross, blessing it. After making the blessing, she

---

292. Cf. Canticles 2:14.
293. Matthew 2:9.
294. Luke 10:40.
295. Matthew 3:9, etc.

put the drink to her lips and drank. When she had finished *she gave thanks*,[296] because He had given that liquid the flavor to her taste that her *soul desired*.[297] She directed the Sister who had given her the drink to preserve carefully what was left. A certain religious woman who was standing by and considering what had happened said to the virgin, "Lady, let me taste it." But she was unwilling. Indeed, right away she caused to be brought to her what was left in the cup, which she had ordered should be saved; and when it came, she drank it right down in great haste.

Since she drank it all herself, we have no other firm evidence that the flavor had been changed, beyond her words as she tasted it, through which we infer [the change]. But we do know that something similar was done by her during a Sister's illness. One of the Sisters fell ill a short while before her own illness, and [the Sister] wanted to taste bitter pomegranates. When none were offered to her, since there were none to be found there, she endured two days of suffering in her longing. The virgin, taking pity on the invalid, directed that this Sister be brought sweet pomegranates, which were to be found there but whose taste did not please her. [Margherita] nevertheless had them brought, and with her own hands she pulled out the seeds. When they were cleaned and sifted she blessed them and gave them to the invalid, who ate some and found in their taste the flavor that she had desired. Her hunger for them was so well satisfied that during her illness she asked for no more pomegranates to eat. Since we know that this was done for another, we surely believe that [Margherita] was able to accomplish as much for herself.

Having strayed a little from the path in order to tell of this miracle, let us now return to the orderly course of events concerning her passing. As day by day [Margherita] was approaching her end, she asked those standing near how many days had passed since Christmas, and when the fifth day thereafter would arrive. *This she said knowing*[298] that it was the third day of her passing. Then, when those who were there asked whether she was inquiring about the fifth day before Christmas (because that

---

296. Luke 22:17.
297. Cf. Psalm 41:2.
298. Cf. John 6:6.

was when she had fallen ill), she answered that she wanted to know the fifth day after Christmas. And when the day was named, that is, the Monday that was the fifth day after Christmas,[299] she said, "That day is my day." A secular person said to her then that he would ask God not to take her from us so quickly; and she replied to him that she would not listen to a request for even one more hour of life. To another certain religious woman who was citing the blessed Martin, who had said that he would not refuse to work if he were still necessary for the Lord's people,[300] she replied, "Will I stay behind for this? Because I shall go! My people? My people are a flock of hens!"[301]

As a poor woman of Christ, she had nothing to put in a will, since everything had already been distributed in alms. In humble subjection she entrusted her household, which had gathered about her in loving pursuit of Christ, to her more worthy brother [Giacomo]. *Knowing* that upon a certain day, that is, the fifth day after the Lord's Nativity, she would pass *from this world to the Father*,[302] three days before this she had asked to be administered the viaticum of the Body of Christ, which is customarily delayed until dawn. She directed that she be renewed and dressed in clean tunics, for such was always her custom when she was to receive the Body of Christ; just as she would cleanse her soul, so also her body. Her brother [Giacomo] was one of those attending to her, so that his attention, which he diligently offered to the virgin in life, would not be lacking at the end. As soon as she heard the ringing of the bell that the bearer carries before the Body of Christ, she leapt from her bed; and

---

299. Oliger used this passage to date Margherita's death exactly. In the decade before 1285 (by which time she was demonstrably no longer alive), 30 December fell on a Monday only in 1275 and 1280. But the former date is too early, since Margherita's death came after Giacomo Colonna was raised to the cardinalate in 1278. Hence 30 December 1280 is certainly correct.

300. The Latin "qui dixerat se *non* recusare *laborem, si populo* Domini *necessarius* foret," echoes an Antiphon for the feast of Martin of Tours (November 11). Cantus ID, 2382; Van Dijk, *Sources*, 2:171.

301. We agree with Oliger's suggestion that while Margherita's remark is not entirely clear, it should probably be read as a mix of humor and humility.

302. Cf. John 13:1.

genuflecting as though she were no longer weak, with joined hands she eagerly received her Christ with all her devotion. And having been taken back to the place from which she had descended, she went to bed.

And she said to her brother,[303] "Though God has anointed my soul it is good that I should still receive extreme unction, since He commands that in no case should His command be overlooked." Her brother agreed but put it off until late. Again the virgin's household asked her brother to see that they would be blessed by their mother. Her brother humbly requested this for himself as well as for the household. Marveling at his humility, the virgin said, "On the contrary, you must bless me!" Hearing this, her brother did not refuse her any more than he had in all other matters that led her to Christ. But unobtrusively making the sign of the cross over her as though he were the father who had given birth to her in Christ, he blessed her. Clasping his head to her breast where she lay, the virgin did not sign another blessing, but she said, "Brother, great are the rewards laid up for you from the good things you have brought to me and my family in our pursuit of Christ." Her other brother [Giovanni], *whom* the virgin *loved*,[304] asked if she would say what she wanted of him. And she advised him, saying that he should not part from his more worthy brother [Giacomo] but that he should always follow in his footsteps. He replied to her, "I will do this, but I fear that he may leave me." To which she said, "He will not be able to do that unless it will seem good and pleasing to God."[305]

Thereafter she blessed her whole family one by one. She especially sought to bless the young son of her brother [Giovanni], the foster son

---

303. In *Vita II*, ch. 27, Stefania says "older brother," which would be Giovanni; but clearly here it must be Giacomo—not only because the brother in question offers a blessing and is thanked for his spiritual gifts, but also because the "other" brother below must be Giovanni. Presumably *Vita I* is to be trusted on this passage, since Giovanni himself is the author.

304. John 13:23; the same phrase is used to describe Giovanni Colonna in chapter VII.

305. Giovanni Colonna's report about his own conversation with his sister, on the subject of their brother Giacomo, is fascinating. The meaning of his fear that Giacomo would "leave him" is open to interpretation.

of her more worthy brother [Giacomo].[306] And blessing him on his arrival, she desired that he be privileged over his brothers. And when a girl
was offered to her, the daughter of her brother [Giovanni], whom she
understood to follow in the footsteps of Christ, she blessed her.[307] And
she also blessed the remaining sister, who was ill, naming her by name,
upon whom the blessing so fell that after her passing she had no use for
this world and followed after [Margherita], pursuing her Betrothed.[308]
So, *in the end*, as did Christ, [Margherita] displayed her joy to those
whom she *had loved in the world*,[309] and she turned her mental longing
completely toward the One to whom she was longing to go.

And when it was late her brother [Giacomo] came with the Friars
to anoint her with extreme unction. She who had offered her whole body
and soul to Christ, offered all her limbs, one by one, for anointment in
the greatest devotion, and she answered to the Friars that she should at
that moment make of herself the *evening sacrifice*[310] to her Christ. When
this was done and the Friars with their attendants were leaving, she
began to say to her brother [Giacomo], "Does it befit a Christian man or
woman to die in bed?" Saying this, she wanted to leap from her bed and
stretch out on the ground. But her brother did not allow this, lest (although she was already failing) it might turn out to cause more harm;
and he said that her goodwill would suffice. Then she fell silent, and after
a while she said to her brother that he should give her a little space. Her
brother left for a little while, going into another room. As best she could,

---

306. This was Pietro Colonna, the future cardinal (*Vita II*, ch. 29, removes
any doubt).

307. This is almost certainly Giovanni's daughter Giovanna, future nun and
abbess of San Silvestro in Capite.

308. This is Mateleone, daughter of Giovanni, as specified in *Vita II*, ch. 29.
The wording here ("ad sponsi sequelam post ipsam transivit," coming right after the
noun *transitum* is used to indicate Margherita's death) might seem to suggest that
Mateleone had already died when this life was written; *Vita II*, however, states clearly
that she was still alive and had "devoted her celibacy to God," presumably at San Silvestro in Capite.

309. Cf. John 13:1.

310. 4 Kings 16:15, etc.

she slid down off the bed, while those in attendance held her by her knees.[311] She was doing this, however, so that death coming to take her should find her lying flat on the ground. Upon his return, her brother prepared for her another bed that was much lower and sloped downward, where she might rest, and he wholly forbade the virgin's intent. She repeatedly tried to slip or cast herself off from [the bed] but was not allowed.

She herself had said to her brother, "After my passing, with what expression will you first break out in song for me in praise of God?" Her brother said to her, "What would please you?" And he asked if she would like the hymn *Salve regina*.[312] She answered that this was good, but truly she proposed that the first thing to be said for her should be *They shall entreat your countenance*, and so on.[313] And certainly the verse *I have sought your face; your face, o Lord, I will seek*[314] never left her lips, repeated often as she was passing.

Therefore, at break of day, as "dawn was ending,"[315] she said to the Sisters that they should send quickly for her brother [Giacomo] so that he might come with the Friars to commend her soul for her as is the custom. And because he put off coming for a short while, she ordered him to hurry. But realizing that her hour was at hand, she fixed her eyes on heaven and returned her spirit to her Christ. Her *eyes*, remaining *lifted up* in this way,[316] could not be closed by those in attendance, until her brother arrived and closed them.

---

311. Compare the description in *Vita II*, ch. 29.

312. "Hail Holy Queen," one of the most popular Marian antiphons.

313. This chant text, derived from Psalm 44:13, 15–16, is used for the Common of several virgins, for individual female saints, and for a number of Marian rites. See Cantus Index, 6029a, g01385, g01390, g01760; and Van Dijk, *Sources*, 2:275, 279, 294, 316, 320.

314. Psalm 26:8–9. Echoed in the liturgy of the Ascension and elsewhere. See Cantus Index g00733, g01084, g02097; Van Dijk, *Sources*, 2:256, 262, 225.

315. The Latin phrase *"cum aurora finem daret"* echoes an Antiphon for the Feast of St. Cecilia (Nov. 22). See Cantus ID, 2437; Van Dijk, *Sources*, 2:172 (Benedictus).

316. Cf. John 11:41.

CHAPTER XV. ON THE SIGNS AND PRODIGIES THAT OCCURRED THERE

Many Friars staying in the vicinity were called, and they came together from all directions.[317] And of these, a great many holy men came who had not been called but were present. And thus was Christ causing his virgin to be honored by the most worthy respects of his ministers, who solemnized her solemn watch just as much as we did. Her brother [Giacomo], the guardian of the virgin, saw to it that her body was washed in the customary way by the holy religious women, who handled her limbs [and found them] quite flexible and as though still living. She was dressed in haircloth, the same way she dressed in life. Her face was not pale but appeared radiant, as though she were not dead but sleeping. Meanwhile the rituals of the Mass were celebrated in the central hall as usual, with the introit that she had specified: *Your face, o Lord*, and so on. When the rites were finished, we carried her venerable body out. No sad or sorrowful emotion was displayed by the visitors and bystanders, for joyful piety and pious joy had so filled the hearts of us in attendance that we felt no sorrow for her. However much we were joined to her in affection, still we rejoiced together for her going now *to life*.[318] Showing their piety, because they were being separated from her sweet words, many poor women and children raised their voices, saying, "Where are you sending us, dear mother? Who will feed us? Who will come to see us in our daily need?" If tears were shed, they were shed because of piety, not sorrow.

After she had arrived at the Church of San Pietro of Mount [Prenestino], where her body was buried, the solemnities of the Mass were again celebrated, with the *Eternal rest*, so that all humility was preserved

---

317. Oliger suggests that these brothers came from the friaries in Zagarolo (see note 151) and/or Civitella, a town near Tivoli. Tradition ascribes the founding of the latter community to Francis, who established a hermitage there ca. 1223, around the period of his visit to Subiaco, although it is hard to date his stay there with much precision. See Candido Mariotto, *Il ritiro di S. Francesco presso Civitella* (Rome: Tipografia Sallustiana, 1899), esp. 33–42.

318. Matthew 7:14, etc.

and ecclesiastical order was observed.[319] A certain holy religious man sang, Friar Niccolò of Catino,[320] who was then staying in the household of the Hermit Friars of Civitella. And I could describe what happened to him, but it is better to ask him, since he is still alive. When he came to the sacrifice of the Mass, he saw the virgin's soul standing there, seeing it in the form of a maiden with a beautiful face, who presented her image; she stood by until *the sacrifice was* over[321] and afterward flew off into the highest heavens.

I will not keep silent about what occurred at that hour to me, the sinful man who is writing this. I felt an absolutely enormous change within me, as though all my faults and sins had been gathered together and rolled up into a ball, and the prayer of the one who was still lying on her bier was turned to their destruction and dispersal and removal—and all, I felt, because at that very hour the virgin had interceded for me.

Following the celebration of the rituals of these Masses, in which many Friars took part, her brother and guardian [Giacomo] went out, and lifting her from her bier with his own hands, enclosed her in her tomb, which is located right in front of the image of the Virgin Mary, Mother of God. Afterward, so that the tomb would be more greatly honored, he supplied it with iron railings and saw to it that it was always venerated with burning lights. There, too, is situated the body of a holy, religious man, her paternal uncle.[322] Seeing thus to her interment, her brother, who until this moment had been in full command of his emotions, could control himself no longer; and he wept and hastened back as

---

319. That is, after performing the Mass with the introit *Vultum tuum Domine* as Margherita had requested, a Mass for the dead was now celebrated, with the introit *Requiem aeternam*.

320. Mariotto, *Ritiro di S. Francesco*, cites a necrology for the Roman Province recalling the death of Fra Nicolò "da Canino" at Civitella on 5 September. He was praised as a very pious brother (*vir utique sanctitate famosus*) who celebrated the funeral Mass and witnessed Margherita in heaven. This brother's correct place of origin, however, was Catino, northeast of Rome and southwest of Rieti.

321. Cf. 2 Maccabees 1:30.

322. This is probably an elder Giovanni Colonna, a brother of Margherita's father Oddone. A Dominican, he served as archbishop of Messina before dying in 1263.

his tears interrupted the chorus. Let no man censure such tears! For he ought to have cried, and it was proper—if not because he was her flesh-and-blood brother, then because he had now lost this daughter in Christ, in whose sweet company he knew such delight.

With [Giacomo] so upset because of the extreme vigils and fasting that he undertook while she passed away, it fell to the other brother [Giovanni] to console him. And he did console him, telling him what he himself had experienced and I have related,[323] and that he ought rather to rejoice for her, who was now with Christ. [Giacomo] listened to these things and considered others about the virgin, saying, "You will yet see and hear better things."

We returned home and dined well with the Friars. And I will tell you how Christ laid out the feast for his ministers who came to render honor to the virgin. For we had all been so intent on her passing that we gave little or no thought to entertaining guests. But the Lord caused a great abundance to be brought from the chase in these sparse surroundings, from which we had never received so much, so that we were better supplied without having given any forethought than we were when we had earnestly planned ahead.

For a great many days before the virgin departed, as I have said, her brother [Giacomo] wore himself out with many vigils, much weeping, and extreme concern over the dying virgin. And his distress only grew after her passing; for while his body was held here, his spirit was there with her who had departed. Nothing else would please him but to pray and remain alone, longing for the *wings of a dove* that he might fly off and go to her at rest.[324]

So one evening I sat down at table with him [and] with the Friars, at his request. Although he himself had not eaten, nor had many of the Friars,[325] he was attending to the table of those who were eating and

---

323. This is another clear indication that the "other brother," Giovanni, is the author, who has just related in the first person the "huge changes" he felt within himself at his sister's death.

324. Psalm 54:7.

325. We follow Oliger's suggested emendation of this passage, where something seems to be missing from the Latin.

seeing that they had everything necessary. Then he stepped aside to talk with his priest. And in front of the houses and below the cloister he began, with this same priest, to sing with great devotion the vigils of Our Lady, because he had known his sister was most devotedly dedicated to her praises while she lived. As he sang, there appeared to him virgins who had "received their shining seats"[326] and were enjoying their long-desired Betrothed. And they appeared in that glory that the blessed receive from their Betrothed. Among these he saw and recognized his virgin Margherita, counting her the sixth. The other five were those whom the church celebrates with the very highest honors: the most blessed Agnes, the most brilliant Cecilia, the blessed Agatha, the holy Lucy. He could not tell whether the fifth one was the blessed Catherine or the holy Margherita,[327] but the others (whose identities were clear) offered themselves to the observation and notice of the viewer. This vision went on right before his eyes, delighting him with its appearance until he had finished the whole vigil. When the vigil was done, the vision was wrenched from him, and he went back inside and found the Friars, who now had eaten,[328] discussing among themselves the *discourses that*

---

326. The phrase echoes an Antiphon for the Feast of St. Agnes (January 21). Cantus ID, 1886; Van Dijk, *Sources*, 2:125.

327. Oliger suggests that this vision might have been related to a mosaic commissioned by Cardinal Giacomo Colonna for the outer wall of the apse of Santa Maria Maggiore in Rome between 1292 and 1297, since that mosaic included saints Agnes, Cecilia, Lucy and Catherine. A seventeenth-century renovation scheme destroyed this mosaic, but it was described in P. De Angelis, *Basilicae S. Mariae Maioris de Urbe a Liberio papa I usque ad Paulum V Pont. max. descriptio ac delineatio* (Rome, 1621), 90. See Julian Gardner, "Pope Nicholas IV and the Decoration of Santa Maria Maggiore," *Zeitschrift für Kunstgeschichte* 36 (1973): 1–50, esp. 21–23, reproducing several early modern sketches, including one that shows a separate portion of the mosaic that depicts both Colonna cardinals. See further Serena Romano, "I Colonna a Roma: 1288–1297," in *La nobiltà romana nel medioevo: Atti del Convegno organizzato dall'École française de Rome e dall'Università degli studi di Roma "Tor Vergata" (Roma, 20–22 novembre 2003)*, ed. Sandro Carocci (Rome: École française de Rome, 2006), 291–312; and Herbert Kessler and Joanna Zacharias, *Rome 1300: On the Path of the Pilgrim* (New Haven, CT: Yale University Press, 2000), 128 (plate 125).

328. We follow Oliger's suggestion of emending "non comederant" to "iam comederant."

they knew in praise of the virgin.[329] He stood there in silence a little while, and then he went into his room, taking with him one of the Friars, a holy man of his household. And leaning at the window where he was accustomed to stand in prayer, with growing emotion over the things he had seen, he began to repeat the vigil with the Friar. And at once he saw what he had seen, and he recognized his sister again with those he had recognized before.

CHAPTER XVI. ON THE SIGNS AND MIRACLES THAT OCCURRED AFTER HER PASSING

I will tell what was shown to me, an unworthy sinner, about her, on the fourth day after she died.[330] Even if these things are not as great, because I was not worthy of those things or others that were shown to her other devoted follower,[331] I do this because "I owe greater emotion where my own sight compels belief, than where only my thoughts urge my faith."[332]

After [our] sister's passing, a certain relative of ours, a religious,[333] came to console us, but Christ revealed another, more beautiful and deserved consolation concerning his virgin. It seemed to me that our more worthy brother[334] Lord [Giacomo] was standing in the Church of the Blessed Pietro [of Mount Prenestino] in which the venerable body of the virgin had been sealed, and with him was his household. I was among them, as was the religious Preaching Friar, who had arrived. And a *voice*

---

329. Luke 24:17, etc.

330. Four days after her death would be 3 January 1281.

331. Presumably Giacomo Colonna.

332. This saying is found in a sermon by Maximus of Turin (flourished early fifth century). See *Maximi Episcopi Taurinensis sermones*, ed. Almut Mutzenbecher, Corpus Christianorum Series Latina 23 (Turnhout: Brepols, 1962), 414 (sermo CV), lines 10–12.

333. This relative is shortly revealed to be a Dominican, but we have been unable to identify him.

334. Again "frater noster dignior" is an indication that the author must be a brother of Giacomo Colonna.

came down to us[335] of one saying, "Sing *at midnight there was a cry made, behold the bridegroom comes,* and so on."[336] Then we were all singing at the top of our voices the response that is sung in the Feast of the Virgins. As we began to sing, the more worthy brother [Giacomo] said to this religious, "Go, ready yourself for Mass!" And he went at this direction and prepared himself. I wondered at this, saying to myself, "Why is [my] lord brother ordering that Mass be sung at this hour, namely in the middle of the night? Can it be that it is the Nativity of the Lord? For only at the Feast of the Nativity is it customary to perform Mass at such an hour, and not otherwise." And the time at that moment seemed to me to be the middle of the night just as we were singing in the response. And when we reached that place, *Behold the bridegroom comes,* a certain king whom I had seen (I had never seen another king besides him),[337] was entering the door of the church and going straight down the aisle to . . .

[*The conclusion of this episode and the beginning of the next are missing from the manuscript. As the text recommences, an entirely new episode has been introduced, and the subject is now a married older man who is experiencing a vision in the night*].[338]

---

335. Cf. 2 Peter 1:17.

336. Matthew 25:6.

337. Giovanni seems here to indicate that his vision was of a king whom he had actually seen in life and that this was the only king he had ever encountered in person. Although we cannot be certain, the most likely candidate would have to be Charles of Anjou, youngest brother of Louis IX of France and king of Sicily in his own right from 1266 until his death in 1285, since Charles was certainly in Rome repeatedly in these decades and indeed was elected as senator of Rome first in 1265 and then for a ten-year period starting in 1268. Another possibility could be King Philip III of France, who passed through Rome on return from crusade in North Africa in early 1271. See Xavier Hélary, *La dernière croisade: Saint Louis à Tunis (1270)* (Paris: Perrin, 2016), 203.

338. As Oliger noted, in the manuscript a blank space is left that is only the size of a single word. And yet it seems clear that a substantial amount of text has been omitted; perhaps the scribe skipped an entire page in his exemplar. In any case, at least the conclusion of this episode involving the author's vision of an approaching king and Giacomo's demand that Mass be celebrated at midnight has been lost. As the text recommences, it is clear that an entirely new episode has already been

... he was roused by someone: "Why don't you go to the Friars so they may come to lie down?" And at once he got up, and making no delay he went straight to the palace where the Friars had stayed and where the Friars of the ladies were living.[339] Finding this shut, he went in haste to the church [of San Pietro of Mount Prenestino], where he thought they were engaged in the Office; but it was not so, for the hour had passed and the hour for Matins had not yet come. And as he arrived, he looked through the windows and he saw the church all lit up inside. Going to the back door, he pushed it and found it shut and otherwise could not see in. He came to the other door, wishing to see inside through the half-shut fastening; but since the interior doors were closed, they left no opening. But then, when he had bowed down, God opened the inner doors to allow him to see what he was longing for; it was He who made him arise at that hour to see. And he beheld that church so lit up that all the lamps of the world could not add to its splendor, as if the whole place had been made of fiery splendor. Gazing upon it, he fell to the ground. And in front of the image of Mary the Mother of God, right in front of which the virgin's tomb is placed, he saw three young virgins, sixteen years old at most, among whom he saw the virgin Margherita, to whom he was devoted. He also saw an old man who looked to him like a certain holy old former archpriest of the said church. He was holding a censer in his hand and was dressed in white. And as the virgin Margherita turned toward him, the man looking on knew her, and he noted the verse that he heard her singing, although he was not literate,[340] which, as a layman, he called *Lamb of God*.[341] Entering *in ecstasy of mind*,[342] he nei-

---

introduced. It is at least possible that a passage was deliberately removed, if the reference to a specific king seemed politically inadvisable in a changing context; we thank Emily Graham for suggesting this interpretation.

339. These are presumably Franciscans serving the women's community.

340. That is, as a layman, not literate in Latin.

341. The Latin reads "Agnus Dei." Oliger speculated that originally there should have been some humor here, with an incorrect pronunciation of some kind written down, but that a scribe had corrected it to good Latin at some point.

342. Cf. Psalm 67:28.

ther saw nor heard any more, but fell over. His mind was thus restored by these things so that it was filled with all goodness.

When the vigil was done he went home but could not sleep. Rising at dawn, he went to the Friars who were there and confessed and related what he had seen, with great humility, reproaching himself as a sinner. A Friar[343] ordered him to tell it all to me.[344] Because of other things that were said to them that night that concerned me, it seemed to the Friars that these things should be related to the people that very day, under sworn testimony of the one relating them, which was done. For the bells were rung and the people gathered, and the sworn witness retold all the events in order.[345] He spoke of all the other miracles and benefits that God had conferred on his wife and himself through the merits of the blessed virgin and the invocations made to her.[346]

CHAPTER XVII. ON A WOMAN CURED OF A DIZZY HEAD[347]

One evening, as he and his wife sat by the fire, a dizziness suddenly seized his wife. She fell down, and he could hardly raise her up. When he got her up, she was paralyzed on one side. And she lay like that for three days, and all the neighborhood came to see her out of pity. Then, in tearful complaint, she said to the old man, "What will you do? Look, you and I could hardly live when we were well, because of our poverty.

---

343. Oliger interpreted this singular "*frater*" as referring to Giacomo Colonna. This is possible, but in context it seems more likely to us that the author intended to refer to one of the Franciscan Friars who were evidently conducting this questioning.

344. This passage shows that Giovanni was publicly known to be gathering testimony about Margherita.

345. This is a fascinating example of the Colonna family and the local Franciscans giving instant publicity to a miracle occurring just after Margherita's death.

346. These additional miracles are recounted in the final two chapters.

347. The title does not describe the actual contents of the chapter, reflecting instead only the first sentence. This disjunction is one of several indications that chapter headings as found in this manuscript were added by a second hand, not by the original author or the first scribe of this manuscript.

How then will you be able to keep us going, now that I have this paralysis and will be able to give you no support for our living?" Then her husband, *trusting in the Lord*,[348] soothingly comforted his wife. He did not hide from her the devotion that he had for the virgin, and he urged her to have it too. He said to her, "I want you to place your faith in God, and [to believe] that He will free you through the prayers of the blessed virgin [Margherita]. And if we go in all devotion to her tomb and you touch it, with *the Lord granting*,[349] you will be freed by the prayers of the virgin." They did this, since the wife agreed. And the husband and wife lay down in prayer together, and she had the railings opened, and she laid her paralyzed side on the tomb as best she could but thrust in her right arm.[350] Bringing it back out, she at once had it healthy again as she had it before, and that same day she could do everything necessary with it. *Blessed be God*[351] in His gifts, *and holy in all His works*,[352] *who is blessed forever* and ever.[353]

CHAPTER XVIII. HOW A MAN WAS CURED OF AN ULCER OF THE LEG

He described another instance done to himself. He had long suffered from a certain ulcer in his leg that gnawed his flesh right to the bone. When the virgin was still alive, she heard of it and had pity on him and had him come to her. She said to him, "I hear that you suffer greatly from an ulcer. Take care, lest in your impatience you become upset with God! Because if you bear it patiently it will be better for you and for your soul; and God, when He pleases, will cure you." This gave him hope, but at that time she did not provide further help. Yet after she had gone to

---

348. Cf. 2 Maccabees 7:40.

349. Cf. Acts 14:3.

350. If Margherita's tomb was constructed in such a manner as to leave an opening where an ailing limb might be inserted, this would imply an expectation of healing miracles with a view to a future canonization (thanks to Anne Clark for this observation).

351. Genesis 14:20, etc.

352. Psalm 144:13, 17.

353. Romans 1:24; 2 Corinthians 11:31.

heaven, she recalled the devotion that her good son had tirelessly maintained for her. Then as he lay down one night, a voice spoke to him. He heard the voice but did not know the speaker, except that he knew it was a good spirit, [saying,] "Go to St. Mary in Vulturella to that place where the blessed Margherita used to stand in prayer![354] By taking an herb that has a leaf of this shape," and [the voice] described [its] roundness, "and placing it on the ulcer, you will at once be freed by her prayers." He knew this place very well, for it was next to the church where there was a small meadow surrounded by hedges. Without a moment's delay he went to the place that morning, and he saw the herb, and he recognized it according to the shape or form that had been described to him. He applied it and was straightway cured. And to this day marks of great scars remain on his leg.[355]

---

354. See chapter 9. It is interesting that Vulturella—a place with which Margherita was only temporarily associated—is the site of this miracle, rather than her tomb at Mount Prenestino.

355. The text ends two-thirds of the way down folio 26r. There is no colophon or explicit marking a conclusion, but there does not appear to be any reason to think the text is not complete. Folio 27v is lined but otherwise blank.

TWO

Three Papal Bulls on the Foundation of
San Silvestro in Capite in 1285

Nearly five years after Margherita Colonna's death, her group of followers petitioned the newly elected pope Honorius IV to approve their for-
mation of a more formal community and their desire to join the Order
of *Sorores minores*. In three bulls from autumn 1285 Honorius granted
these wishes, no doubt at the urging of Cardinal Giacomo Colonna and
with the support of Cardinal Jerome of Ascoli (former minister general
of the Franciscans and future Nicholas IV). In the bull *Ascendit fumus
aromatum*, Honorius gave the Sisters the newly vacated Monastery of
San Silvestro in Capite, in the heart of the Colonna neighborhood of
Rome, and confirmed the election of Herminia as the community's first
abbess. Two subsequent bulls provided the nuns with an approved copy
of the Rule of the *Sorores minores* and instructed the local Franciscans to
comply with it and even to supply Friars over and above its requirements
to serve the needs of the community. These bulls help to establish the
changed context in which *Vita II* was completed a few years later. They
also demonstrate the nature of San Silvestro's ties to male Franciscans
(*Fratres minores*) and the importance of the Sisters' identity as *Sorores
minores*.

HONORIUS IV, *ASCENDIT FUMUS AROMATUM*, 24 SEPTEMBER 1285

Honorius IV refers to Margherita Colonna's example in founding the community of Sisters living on Mount Prenestino. He grants their request to join the Order of *Sorores minores*, confirms the election of the abbess Herminia, gives them the Monastery of San Silvestro in Capite in Rome, and requires four Franciscan Friars to reside there. Translated from the edition in *BF*, volume 3, 544–46.

HONORIUS, [bishop, servant of the servants of God],[1] to his beloved daughters in Christ Herminia,[2] abbess of the Monastery of San Silvestro in Capite in the city [of Rome], and the Sisters both now and to come professing the regular life there in perpetuity, greetings and apostolic blessings.

The smoke of spices *ascended*,[3] wafted into sight of our notice through widespread report by trustworthy men concerning your reputation and praiseworthy comportment, and the outstanding virtues of your laudable

---

1. Giacomo Savelli came from another powerful old Roman family (the Savelli were in fact intermarried with the Colonna). He was appointed cardinal by Urban IV in 1261 and reigned as Honorius IV from 2 April 1285 to 3 April 1287.

2. Herminia served as abbess from 1285 until at least July 1288. See the documents edited in Vincenzo Federici, "Regesto del monastero di S. Silvestro de Capite," *Archivio della Società romana di storia patria* 22 (1899): 418–23 (documents dated July 1286; February, June, August, and September 1287; and July 1288). There is then no mention of any abbess's name in the published documents until Herminia is again referred to as abbess in February 1293 (431). By December 1294 she was no longer in office (432), though she was still alive if, as seems almost certain, she is the "domina Herminia" who appears in a document of that date. It is thus possible that she retained the office of abbess from 1285 all the way up through 1293 or 1294. At Longchamp (in some sense the "mother house" of the *Sorores minores*) abbesses often— though not always—served three-year terms in this era (See Sean L. Field, "The Abbesses of Longchamp up to the Black Death," *AFH* 96 [2003]: 237–44). It is thus also possible that Herminia served one term from 1285 to perhaps the fall of 1288, was out of office for several years, and then reassumed the position of abbess from perhaps 1290/91 to 1293/94.

3. Revelations 8:4, etc.

progress deserving of encouraging praise. It perfumes the minds of those who hear these tidings in the house of the Lord; it refreshes by huge delight and suffuses by vast fragrance. As we understand, the late Margherita Colonna, despising riches and the grand rank to which she was born, and scorning the other enticements of this world, prudently chose to humbly serve the poor Christ in poverty. In compelling service to Him, she raised you like a swarm of bees to this same end by her own laudable example. And thus, with God inspiring your wishes and directing your feet, being more wisely aware that *the world passes away and the concupiscence thereof*,[4] by turning your back on its false allurements you have more wisely discerned in judgment that He crucified Himself for you and you for Him. For some of you, from your adolescence—indeed, some from your infancy!—have formed a family under a religious habit, giving thanks to the Lord, although not yet bound by any specific religious observance.

And so at length, with your merit following the anticipation of grace, having been roused aloft into such a solid conviction of mind (as is hoped) that you propose unceasing contemplation on behalf of the least among us, should our foe rage about us swirling adversity or should the world entice our minds with ambition, and, truly wanting to more securely carry on the struggle against such enemy attacks within an enclosed fortress under the observance of the Order of the *Sorores minores inclusae*, you have come before us in humble supplication, seeking that the Apostolic See mercifully assign to you the rule granted to that order by Alexander [IV] of blessed memory and then revised and amended by Urban [IV] of holy memory,[5] who were pope before us, as well as assign to you some place appropriate and proper for the observation of this rule.

---

4. 1 John 2:17.

5. On 10 February 1259 Alexander IV approved a rule for the Abbey of the Humility of Our Lady (better known as Longchamp) just west of Paris, which had been composed by Isabelle of France with a team of Franciscan advisers including Minister General Bonaventure. A revised version, granting Isabelle's coveted title *Sorores minores*, was approved by Urban IV on 27 July 1263. For details and English translations, see Sean L. Field, *The Rules of Isabelle of France: An English Translation with Introductory Study*, additional documents translated by Larry F. Field (St. Bonaventure, NY: Franciscan Institute Publications, 2013).

Since we were of the same mind, willingly consenting to these requests fashioned for the salvation of your souls, we then spoke directly to our venerable brother, the bishop of Palestrina, who was then present, since you were living within his diocese on Mount Prenestino and are said to be living there still in proper enclosure.[6] And we directed him to assign to you the rule you seek; and that, receiving your profession of this rule, he should affirm by apostolic authority your choice of an abbess as provided in that rule. In due course he examined your vows more diligently with due reflection, and finding that you remained firm in what you proposed, he assigned to you the rule as mentioned. At your immediate request, he accepted your profession of this rule. Then, by the authority we had vested in him, he confirmed your election as abbess, Herminia, beloved daughter in Christ, as you were so chosen by appropriate ballot, an agreeable choice that he deemed canonical and solemnized upon a suitable person. A credible report of all this progress was made to us by this same bishop upon his return to our presence. We considered the steps well taken, agreed upon, and welcome, affirming them by apostolic authority.[7]

And desiring to consider the pressing need for an appropriate location mentioned in your petition, we have decided to grant to you the Monastery of San Silvestro in Capite in the city [of Rome], which is

---

6. Jerome of Ascoli became minister general of the Franciscans in 1274, was named cardinal priest in 1278 (stepping down as minister general), and then became cardinal bishop of Palestrina in 1281. He would be elected pope as Nicolas IV in 1288, dying in 1292. Note that he was probably the minister general referred to in *Vita I* as giving his approval for Margherita to enter Santa Chiara of Assisi, though she never followed through on this request. As former minister general, bishop of Palestrina, and a firm Colonna ally, by 1285 he was well placed to aid Margherita's followers in their attempt to join the Order of *Sorores minores*.

7. This passage demonstrates that the Colonna family, working with Cardinal Jerome of Ascoli, had already organized Margherita's followers into an enclosed community, chosen an abbess, and adopted a rule *before* Honorius's bull was issued in confirmation of these steps. The bull itself was clearly secured by Giacomo Colonna, since Brentano notes that on the dorse (where it was customary to inscribe the name of the person for whom the bull was written) appears "Cardinal' de Columpna." Robert Brentano, *Rome before Avingon: A Social History of Thirteenth-Century Rome* (New York: Basic Books, 1974), 241.

within the immediate grant of the Roman Church. Previously [it pertained to] the Order of Saint Benedict, [but it is] now empty because its abbot has been removed to the Monastery of San Lorenzo of the same order beyond the walls of the city, while the monks of the monastery have been settled elsewhere as we have thought beneficial to their salvation, for the Monastery of San Silvestro could not easily be reformed by individuals of the same order. Because we have concluded that the place is appropriate to your occupancy as well as the observation of your order, we have decided, upon the advice of our Brothers,[8] in a specific benefit, to grant to you this monastery together with its homes, gardens, vineyards, land, farms, chattels, vassals, and all other goods, privileges, immunities, and all else pertaining thereto, and all rights whatsoever, decreeing that the monastery moreover shall be called the Monastery of San Silvestro in Capite of the Order of the *Sorores minores inclusae*, and that your same order shall be observed there in perpetuity; and that you, as well as those who will come after you in the same monastery, shall freely be able to use all privileges, indulgences, immunities, and benefits granted to your same order by the Apostolic See; and that this same Monastery of San Silvestro shall remain directly subject to the Roman Church, as it has been.

We desire as well that four Friars of the Order of *Minores*, proven through long service, shall remain continuously at the monastery to perform the solemnities of the divine office for you as well as the church sacraments. We also desire that each and every thing that pertains to you from the practice of your rule, concerning the election of the abbess and anything else whatsoever, and other things that pertain to the aforesaid Order of *Minores* or the individuals thereof from the practice in monasteries of your oft-mentioned order, shall remain intact and unaltered for you and this same Order of *Minores* and its individual members. Nor, in these respects, should any loss or diminishment whatsoever occur from the fact that, as was mentioned, this same Monastery of San Silvestro remains directly subject to us and the Roman Church.

---

8. That is, the College of Cardinals.

Moreover, by this communication we grant you leave to travel to that Monastery of San Silvestro without seeking or awaiting further permission. We add this express provision: that if it should happen that this, your oft-mentioned Monastery of San Silvestro, be abandoned by members of your order, or if it be deemed deserted, we desire that the monastery with all the goods thereto pertaining and rights above mentioned will remain in the free gift of ourselves and of the successor popes and the same Roman Church.

Therefore, we decree that no human being may counter this writ of our affirmation, grant, constitution, and command, or violate it in daring recklessness. If, however, anyone should presume to attempt this, let him know that he will incur the indignation of almighty God and the blessed apostles Peter and Paul.

I, Honorius [IV], bishop of the Catholic Church, have subscribed.

I, Ordono [Alvarez], [cardinal] bishop of Tusculum, have subscribed.[9]

I, Brother Bentivenga [Bentivengi], [cardinal] bishop of Albano, have subscribed.[10]

I, Brother Latino [Malabranca], [cardinal] bishop of Ostia and Velletri, have subscribed.[11]

I, Brother Jerome [of Ascoli], [cardinal] bishop of Palestrina, have subscribed.[12]

I, Bernard [of Languissel], [cardinal] bishop of Porto and Santa Rufina, have subscribed.[13]

---

9. Former archbishop of Braga, created cardinal by Nicholas III in 1278, died 1285.

10. Franciscan and former bishop of Todi, created cardinal by Nicholas III in 1278, died 1289.

11. Dominican, from the Orsini family on his mother's side (and thus a relation of Margherita Colonna and her siblings), created cardinal by his uncle Nicholas III in 1278, died ca. 1294.

12. See note 6 above.

13. Former archbishop of Arles, created cardinal by Martin IV in 1281, died ca. 1290.

I, Anchero [Pantaléon], cardinal priest of San Prassede, have subscribed.[14]

I, Gervaise [of Clinchamp], cardinal priest of San Martino, have subscribed.[15]

I, Conte [Casate], cardinal priest of Santi Marcellino and Pietro, have
subscribed.[16]

I, Geoffroy [of Bar], cardinal priest of Santa Susanna, have subscribed.[17]

I, Goffredo [of Alatri], cardinal deacon of San Giorgio in Velabro, have
subscribed.[18]

I, Giacomo [Colonna], cardinal deacon of Santa Maria in Via Lata, have
subscribed.[19]

I, Benedetto [Gaetani], cardinal deacon of San Nicola in Carcere, have
subscribed. [20]

Given at Tivoli, by the hand of master Pietro of Milan, vice chan-
cellor of the Holy Roman Church, VIII Kalends of October, in the fourteenth indiction, in the 1285th year of the Lord's incarnation, in the first
year of the papacy of Lord Honorius IV.

HONORIUS IV, *IN MANDATORUM SUORUM*, 9 OCTOBER 1285

After having granted permission to the abbess and nuns of the newly
founded Monastery of San Silvestro to follow the Rule of the *Sorores mi-*

---

14. Created cardinal by his uncle, Urban IV, in 1262, died 1286.

15. Created cardinal by Martin IV in 1281, died 1287.

16. Created cardinal by Martin IV in 1281, died 1287.

17. Created cardinal by Martin IV in 1281, died 1287.

18. Created cardinal by Urban IV in 1261, died before 1287.

19. Brother to Margherita Colonna.

20. The future Boniface VIII, created cardinal by Honorius IV in 1281. By
1297 he was the mortal enemy of the Colonna, severing their ties with San Silvestro
in Capite as part of his crusade against the family. His signature here is thus of some
interest.

nores, in this follow-up bull Honorius forwards the text of the rule itself, to provide the nuns with a papally approved master copy.

Translated from the edition in *BF*, volume 3, 548.

HONORIUS [bishop, servant of the servants of God], to his beloved daughters in Christ, Abbess Herminia, and the convent of the Monastery of San Silvestro of the city [of Rome] directly subject to the Roman Church of the Order of *Sorores [minores] inclusae*,[21] greetings and apostolic blessings.

For a long time now the Lord has been leading you down the pathways of His commands in praiseworthy fashion, although you were not bound in strict obedience to any specific form of religion, and you have led a religious life, as we are told by trustworthy people. Progressing from virtue to virtue, by the virtue of the Most High, you have now come to the Rule of the *Sorores minores inclusae*, promulgated with a forthright disposition of devotion by Alexander [IV] of blessed memory, revised and approved by Urban [IV] of holy memory, our papal predecessors, and you have asked in supplication that this rule be assigned to you. And when it was assigned to you by our particular command through our brother the bishop of Palestrina, for you were at that time staying in proper cloistered fashion in his diocese, you freely and immediately made profession of the rule, in accordance with our command, and this profession was received personally by the bishop.

Therefore, so that with God's guidance you may be able to observe this rule and its provisions more fully and more accurately, since you will have been more fully instructed by examining it, we have provided to you, under surety of our seal, for future memory, the rule itself, as revised and approved, which is patently clear from the letter of Urban [IV], our above-mentioned predecessor, which was found in his register and which we have had copied, word for word, and attached hereto. The content of the above-mentioned letter and of the rule is this:

---

21. The word *minores* was apparently omitted, at least as the bull was edited in *BF*.

Urban, bishop and servant of the servants of God, to the beloved daughters in Christ, the abbess and the convent of the Sorores minores inclusae[22] *of the Monastery of the Humility of the Blessed Mary,*[23] *Diocese of Paris, greetings and apostolic blessing. [We procure] the increase of religion, and so on.*[24]

Given at Tivoli, VII Ides of October, in the first year of our papacy.[25]

HONORIUS IV, *NUPER DILECTAE IN CHRISTO,* 2 NOVEMBER 1285

The Rule of the *Sorores minores* required that resident confessors and the visitor be from the Franciscan order, and Honorius accordingly instructs the Franciscans of the Roman province to fulfill these terms, and also to be ready to supply six additional Friars to the Monastery of San Silvestro in Capite if they are asked, and even more for particular occasions. Translated from the edition in *BF,* volume 3, 549–50.

HONORIUS [bishop, servant of the servants of God], to his beloved sons . .[26] the minister general and minister of the Roman Province of the

---

22. Interestingly, the word *inclusae* was not found here in Urban's original bull.

23. The abbey founded by Isabelle of France in 1260, which became better known as Longchamp.

24. The entire rule is included in the original bull. For English translation, see Field, *Rules of Isabelle.*

25. Cardinal Giacomo Colonna also composed "constitutions" for San Silvestro, apparently intended to augment the rule itself. Oliger, who edited these constitutions, thought they probably were first written between the reign of Nicholas IV (when Giacomo formally became protector of San Silvestro) and 1297 (when Giacomo was excommunicated and stripped of the cardinalate by Boniface VIII) but also allowed the possibility of between 1306 (restored to the cardinalate by Clement V) and 1318 (the date of his death). See Livario Oliger, "Documenta originis Clarissarum Civitatis Castelli, Eugubii (a. 1223–1263) necnon statuta monasterium Perusiae Civitatisque Castelli (saec. XV) et S. Silvestri Romae (saec. XIII)," *AFH* 15 (1922): 83–86, 99–102.

26. Papal bulls routinely include two dots (gemipunctus) instead of the name of a specific officeholder to avoid any legal questions about whether an order applies

Order of *Fratres minores*,[27] those now and those to come, greetings and apostolic blessings.

Recently our beloved daughters in Christ, Abbess Herminia and the convent of the Monastery of San Silvestro in Capite of the city [of Rome] of the Order of *Sorores minores inclusae,* who, although living religiously on Mount Prenestino under proper enclosure, had never been bound to any specific form of religious life, and wishing within an enclosed fortress etc.

[*The bull here repeats the contents of* Ascendit fumus aromatum, *up to the penultimate paragraph that begins, "Moreover, by this communication we grant you"*]

Although you should properly attend, without having to be asked, to the decrees of the above-mentioned rule that involve you, still, so that you may seek to carry them out more willingly, and so that you may realize that you are encouraged in this way more eagerly by the Apostolic See, directing your judgment through apostolic writing, in strict merit of obedience, we command that while you are satisfactorily, thoroughly, and effectively carrying out the things assigned to you in this Monastery of San Silvestro as provided by the decrees of the said rule, if either your four [Friars] or the abbess and the convent of this Monastery of San Silvestro, in light of its actual resources, should request six such Friars of your order to continuously carry out the prescribed services there, you will oblige the said abbess and convent without raising any difficulties.

We wish, moreover, and by the contents of this letter we grant, to you or in your absence to your custode and guardian of Rome, or one of them, or in their absence their vicars, or others acting for them, that it shall be permitted upon request from the above-mentioned abbess and convent, to dispatch even more Friars to the above-named Monastery of San Silvestro to assist during feast days at the same Monastery of San

---

only to a specific person, particularly if the name of the current officeholder is in doubt.

27. The minister general at this moment was probably Arlotto of Prato, who briefly held the office in 1285–86.

Silvestro and for other holy duties and occasions that from time to time will happen to be performed in the said Monastery of San Silvestro, [such as] the consecration of Sisters, rites for the dying, and other instances where there will be even more need of holy service.

No provision of your order's rule or any prohibition there to the contrary shall impede or defer in any way the effect of this grant; nor shall any indulgence that is said to have been granted to you or to your order by the aforesaid see that you not be held to involve yourselves in this work that is entrusted to you by letter of this same see; nor shall any other indulgences or privileges of that same see concerning which special mention ought to be made in your letters, which are not expressly referred to in the present letter or completely inserted in this mandate.[28]

Given at Rome at Santa Sabina, IV Nones of November, in the first year of our papacy.

---

28. See also the letter from Matthew of Acquasparta (in consultation with Cardinal Giacomo Colonna) dated 31 August 1288 that deals further with the question of Friars entering and staying at San Silvestro. Oliger, "Documenta," 85.

THREE

A New Statement on Margherita Colonna's Perfection of the Virtues, by Stefania

The "second life" of Margherita Colonna was authored by "Stefania," apparently a leader of the newly established Franciscan community of San Silvestro in Capite and possibly a Colonna relative. It was written (or at least completed) between 1288 and 1292.

Our translation is based on the text in *DV*, 189–222, compared with Rome, Biblioteca Casanatense ms. 104, folios 27–38. The work does not have a title in the manuscript, and we have drawn from the first sentence (particularly the phrase "nove editionis eloquio") in an attempt to encapsulate Stefania's conception of the work as a "new publication" or "new statement" on Margherita's virtues, intended to complement *Vita I*.

1. [Dedicatory Letter to Cardinal Giacomo Colonna]
Since I am attempting to set forth, with the declaration of a new statement, some part of the perfection of the virtues with which Margherita, of bright and blessed memory, blazes in astounding brilliance like a great beacon for the present and the future, although I am of *unclean lips*[1] and

---

1. Isaiah 6:5.

parched tongue, may He who with two sharp blows from the *rod* of Moses forced the dry rock to give forth flowing drink for the refreshment and thirst of the people of Israel[2] pour down his nourishing rain upon my inadequacy and upon this modest little oration! You, however, most holy father, burn with such praise for the noble virtues with which this same sister first stood forth, guided by your teaching, that I wish that I—who, though unworthy, am now presiding over our prodigious[3] and impoverished band of sisters and the whole gathering entrusted to me— could be taught by daily observation of your holy comportment.[4]

Yet was it not the case, most glorious father, that you could find no one except your devoted little Stefania to ask about such virtue, and es-

---

2. Cf. Numbers 20:11.

3. Oliger emended the manuscript reading of *ingenti* to *indigenti*, but we have returned to the manuscript reading, in accordance with the source for the passage (see next note). The source contained only the adjective *ingenti*, and Stefania apparently wished to add a self-consciously paradoxical opposite ("ingenti inopique"; literally "large/great and poor") presumably to contrast spiritual strength with physical weakness.

4. This first paragraph of the dedicatory letter is in large measure adapted from John Cassian's *Collationes XXIIII*, ed. Gottfried Kreuz and Michael Petschenig, 2nd ed. (Vienna: Verlag der Österreichischen Akademie der Wissenschaften, 2004), 311–12. English translation in John Cassian, *The Conferences*, trans. Boniface Ramsey (New York: Newman Press, 1997), 399. Oliger (unaware of this borrowing) suggested that in the passage "me... sororum cenobio presidentem," the word *presidentem* indicated that Stefania might have held the formal position of president, as established in the Rule of the *Sorores minores*. But since the passage is simply adapted from John Cassian ("ut unus quidem vestrum ingenti fratrum coenobio praesidens") this inference is probably unwarranted. From this point onward, the dedicatory letter is almost entirely an adaptation of the second prefatory letter of pseudo-Odo of Cluny's *De reversione beati Martini a Burgundia*. See André Salmon, ed., "De reversione beati Martini a Burgundia tractatus," in *Supplément aux chroniques de Touraine* (Tours: Guilland-Verger, 1856), 14–34, at 16–17. This treatise was actually written in the mid-twelfth century; it is preceded by a first letter supposedly from Count Fulk of Anjou (d. 958) to Odo of Cluny (d. 942) soliciting the treatise, and a second (from which Stefania draws heavily) supposedly containing Odo's response. These borrowings demonstrate Stefania's erudition, as well as her technical ability to adapt an old source to new purposes.

pecially about that shining woman of virtue, Margherita?[5] I suppose that you did not have access to the outstanding talents of your older brother,[6] whose lofty eloquence is equal to such a lofty subject. Though he is busy with many serious endeavors, he embodies the emulation of virtue. In truth I confess that the task is one for him who *is able from these stones to raise up children* of Israel![7] It is obvious, I think, why I mention these things at the outset. For behold! *The whole world is seated in wickedness,*[8] and yet does not claim as its own the most noble Giovanni,[9] by whom in no small part it has been claimed. He truly deals with the business of this world as a man of power, but it seems to me he does this out of necessity,[10] for at heart he is more occupied by divine matters. I am happy to dwell on such things and describe his goodness, but I am sparing in my praises, lest I seem to adulate rather than to praise. Yet perhaps I might be allowed to make this one remark—that rarely, if ever, is one found whom such an emulation of virtue steals away from this world to give over to honor and integrity. Still, the force of pure love unavoidably compels me to deal with some of those things that were passed over by your most well-spoken brother,[11] and I must not avoid the steep challenge of writing. Although at first I may seem to build on his foundation, I will avoid it in what follows.

As I understand it, and I would say this with all due respect, personal love shuts the mind's eye, and thus the simplicity of a poor woman is

---

5. This reference is the sole evidence for the author's name.

6. Senator Giovanni Colonna.

7. Matthew 3:9; Luke 3:8.

8. 1 John 5:19.

9. Putting together the evidence from the letter to this point, there is no doubt that Stefania is referring to Senator Giovanni Colonna, and hence that the recipient of the letter must be his younger brother Cardinal Giacomo Colonna.

10. Our translation is somewhat conjectural. Oliger's reading, *contraticitus*, appears correct in the manuscript but makes little Latin sense. The passage that is being adapted from the *De reversione* reads, "sed hoc, ut perpendo, specie tenus in divinis vero medullitus occupatur." Stefania (or her scribe) has "sed hec, ut perpendo, contraticitus in divinis vero medullitus occupatur."

11. This essentially amounts to a statement that *Vita I* was composed by Senator Giovanni Colonna.

more pleasing to you than the ornamented sophistication of others. But because, to speak truthfully, I will not hesitate to obey you, even if it is beyond my powers and even if some ignorance is involved (let that objection be assumed!), love does not shrink back. I will therefore comply, writing not as a gifted speaker to the learned but as a poor follower to her lord, and I will endeavor to be found truthful rather than eloquent. What I have to say neither allows nor requires the tinsel trappings of high-flown rhetoric, concerned with appearances rather than the essence of the matter. If, in truth, these flights of spirit that I have rendered in common prose are not able to satisfy the holy thirst of your zeal, then you may read over again your brother's composition,[12] and it will soothe the passion of your longing in wondrous ways. Since it is the habit of some people to take a very sharp file[13] to the writing of others, and yet, if they have published anything themselves, to hardly even run a bleary eye over it, I beg you to be content with reading this in private, so that what I have composed in private you may read in private. Otherwise, I might fall into the hands of critics and be mauled and torn apart by those who delight not in the truth but in the bizarre.

Here ends the letter.

2. Our Redeemer, Lord Jesus Christ, Son of the Eternal Father, most glorious in His majesty, beholding from the height of heaven that human glory had been defiled by a great course of misery since the sin of Eve, provided, through an ineffable plan, to show His virtue to those *sitting in the shadow of death*,[14] and to recall to the homeland of freedom those now in exile.[15] Accordingly, because the redemption of His creation per-

---

12. That is, *Vita I*, by Senator Giovani Colonna.

13. The phrase *ad unguem* is a common image derived ultimately from Horace, *Satires* 1, 5, 32.

14. Luke 1:79.

15. This paragraph is copied nearly *ad litteram* from Pope Gregory IX's bull *Gloriosus in majestate* canonizing Elizabeth of Hungary, dated 1 June 1235. A critical edition of the text can be found in Leo Santifaller, "Zur Originalüberlieferung der Heiligsprechungsurkunde der Landgräfin Elisabeth von Thüringen vom Jahre 1235," in *Acht Jahrhunderte Deutscher Orden in Einzeldarstellungen. Festschrift zu Ehren Sr. Exzellenz P. Dr. Marian Tumler O.T. anlässlich seines 80. Geburtstages*, ed.

tained to no one more than to Himself, and insofar as it was right and proper for the Creator, through His power, to return to its original state what He is known to have created in more beautiful form (having been ruined by whatever happenstance), He took himself off the royal throne of nature into a small container that, however small it might have been, still received a guest of wider scope than all else: that is, into the hall of the Virgin replete with the fullness of sanctity. From there He brought forth a work that all could see and through which, having expelled the prince of darkness, He triumphed in the redemption of His creation, leaving secure instructions for believers by which an easy passage back to their homeland was restored.

Giving thought therefore to the course of virtues of such piety, the sparkling Margherita, born to the renowned lineage of the Colonna, distinguished by even more renowned miracles, bestowed fame not only on her family but also on her country.[16] She chose to follow the above-mentioned teachings, with unremitting effort, in order to render herself worthy of the notice of eternal fame, as though *from the rising of the sun to the setting thereof*.[17] Abandoning herself to the cultivation of virtues, she never ceased to find delight in the embraces of pure love, with a mind devoted to sanctity in profession of the true faith and by loving the Son of the Queen of Heaven, with whom she would be able to achieve the sweetness of a heavenly marriage. And she *loved* her *neighbor*[18] so

---

Klemens Wieser (Bad Godesberg: Verlag Wissenschaftliches Archiv, 1967), 73–85. We have had the benefit of the translation in Nesta de Robeck, *Saint Elizabeth of Hungary: A Story of Twenty-Four Years* (Milwaukee, WI: Bruce, 1954), 200–203, but have preferred to stay closer to the Latin wording. On the canonization (but not translating this document), see Kenneth Baxter Wolf, *The Life and Afterlife of St. Elizabeth of Hungary: Testimony from Her Canonization Hearings* (Oxford: Oxford University Press, 2011).

16. This paragraph continues to be copied from Gregory IX's canonization bull for Elizabeth of Hungary, with only small necessary changes to pertain to Margherita's case (in particular, passages that referred to Elizabeth of Hungary having been married are here omitted). The borrowing actually extends to the first two words of the next paragraph, "Quid ultra?"

17. Psalm 49:1.

18. Cf. Matthew 5:43; 19:19, etc.

much that she established a household composed of the poor, because she understood that the reward of eternal life comes from God through worthy service to the beloved poor. She held so dear their condition, which pride normally despises, that indulging her pleasure there she made herself penniless, abundantly and in many ways concerned for the poor. Withdrawn from the world of women that she held in contempt, she continuously beat down her delicately tender body by frugal self-denial, advancing so much in the scope of her merit that the more it was of her own free will, the greater she was rewarded in grace.

What more? While she was still in the flower of her girlish youth she was called upon by her older brother to marry a certain young pro-consul of the Romans.[19] And while the men were drawing up the mar-riage agreements,[20] mutually pledging the amicable bonds that come from intermarriage, and looking to the guarantees of welcome future off-spring, their human minds freely arranged these human affairs. But any such arrangement is in vain if divine goodness does not bring it about. For while that proconsul lusted for the marriage bed and for the conjugal embraces of that nubile girl whose high birth, striking beauty, and vir-ginity so recommended her, a heavenly arrangement was preparing celi-bacy for the glowing Margherita to preserve the flower of her youth in the glory of beauty and virtue. Happy is she whom heaven by the exer-cise of such blessed goodness preserves untouched, who rises above the

---

19. The title *proconsul Romanorum* appears in various contemporary sources and could apparently refer to a Roman sent to govern as *podestà* in another town (the meaning cited by Oliger); but Du Cange equates it to the title of senator and in fact cites a document from 1303 referring to "Nobilis et magnificus vir dominus Petrus de Columpna Romanorum Proconsul, miles ac familiaris illustrissimi principis domini Francorum regis, etc." See the entry for *proconsul* in C. Du Cange, *Glossarium mediae et infimae latinitis*, enl. ed. (Niort: Le Favre, 1883–87), vol. 6, col. 518c, http://ducange.enc.sorbonne.fr/PROCONSUL. In any case the reference should indicate that the intended groom was from one of the highest-ranking families of the Roman aristocracy.

20. From this point the rest of the paragraph is largely adapted from a letter by the twelfth-century bishop Arnulf of Lisieux "to G., a nun." See Frank Barlow, ed., *The Letters of Arnulf of Lisieux* (London: Royal Historical Society, 1939), 7–9; English translation in Carolyn Poling Schriber, *The Letter Collections of Arnulf of Lisieux* (Lewiston, NY: Edwin Mellen, 1997), 27–30.

wanton enticement of lust and pleasure so that, bolstered by the gift of eternal virginity, she may *follow the Lamb wherever He goes* and sing out that *new song* with the other virgins![21] Therefore the marriage vows were not forced upon her but altered so that now she should be wed not to a man but in spiritual union to God, whose longed-for embrace clasps and enfolds her so that *his left hand is under* her *head and his right hand embraces* her.[22]

Guided by the saving teachings of her more worthy brother [Giacomo] (who in worthy fashion earned a summons to the tribe of the Levites[23] as minister and apostle of the universal sacrosanct Church of Rome),[24] she at last left the valley of misery and ascended to Mount Prenestino, or really ascended to Him, who is Christ, so that from the tower of the high mountain she might more clearly behold the *land* running *with milk and honey* that God will give to the sons of Israel.[25] *And there*, sustained by frequent heavenly nourishment, she *pitched* her *tents*,[26] keeping with her a loyal and righteous band of noble women who feared God with a pure heart and who received with deepest devotion their first anchoritic customs[27] from the venerable and reverend man just mentioned

---

21. Revelation 14:4; 14:3.

22. Songs 2:6.

23. The reference could be taken to indicate that he entered the priesthood (the tribe of Levi, including Aaron and Moses, formed the first priestly class of the Israelites). But Giacomo was never ordained a priest, so the passage must refer to his status as deacon.

24. Giacomo Colonna was made cardinal deacon by Nicholas III on 13 March 1278, some years after the events described here.

25. Cf. Exodus 3: 17; 13:15.

26. Cf. Exodus 19:2.

27. This phrase "prima anachoreseos instituta ... susceperunt" is taken directly from Cassian's *Collationes XXIIII*, 311; trans. Ramsey, *Conferences*, 399. In the Middle Ages the term *anchorite* could designate an individual who vowed permanent enclosure in a single cell. But because here the word is simply taken from John Cassian, where it is used in the older and looser sense of "one who has retired from the world," it probably should not be taken too literally as specific evidence for the exact status of Stefania's group.

above.[28] This uprooter of vice and sower of virtue, although raised to the summit of honor, preserved the undiminished principle of most solid goodness throughout his life, so that he was never flattered by any rank that had accrued to him and never abandoned in any way the humble character of his past.[29]

3. And it came to pass by the arrangement of divine providence (which, *before the foundation of the world*,[30] had claimed the glowing Margherita as its own so that her *candle* should be *set on a candlestick*[31] in order to blaze like a solar light for wayfarers) that, not wanting to be without the compassion of her pearly treasure,[32] I speedily sought out this modest, pure, and holy woman in order to perform with her the rites of the birth of the Lord.[33] And as the time for the midday meal approached she asked only for *spare bread and short water*,[34] saying that strict fasts are the strongest weapons against the temptations of the demon. When I heard this, I suggested that such a fast with such sparseness of food should be practiced by all the individuals of our holy band, because it was the final Friday of Advent and the vigil of the blessed Thomas the Apostle.[35] But

---

28. Cardinal Giacomo Colonna did author "constitutions" for San Silvestro in Capite, but probably not until after 1288. It seems likely he could have given the loosely defined community some kind of form of life to follow in its early days, but again we should use caution before investing too much meaning in a phrase drawn directly from a fifth-century source (Cassian).

29. The last two clauses, here used to flatter Giacomo Colonna, are adapted from Cassian, *Collationes XXIIII*, 314–15 (*Conlatio abbatis Chaeremonis prima. Capitula II [De episcopo Archebio]*), trans. Ramsey, *Conferences*, 409.

30. Ephesians 1:4; 1 Peter 1:20.

31. Mark 4:21.

32. Stefania employs the same pun on *margaritalis*, meaning "pearl-like," as Giovanni Colonna did repeatedly in *Vita I*.

33. Stefania's own voice and experiences enter the narrative here.

34. Isaiah 30:20.

35. The vigil of St. Thomas would be December 20. As Oliger noted, this day fell on a Friday in 1275 and 1280, so this episode must refer to one of those two years. Oliger thought 1275 was the more likely because *Vita I*, ch. 14, describes Margherita as weakening and falling into her final illness on that date (she would die on 30 December 1280), whereas in Stefania's account Margherita does not yet seem to

she was compassionate with the love of a mother's compassion, for the Sisters were worn out from excessive vigils and the harshness of self-deprivation, and she stayed me with this reply: "I know," she said, "dearest Sister, that you are suggesting for us what is best and truest. But because love alone holds first place among the sacred virtues, without its complete realization neither martyrdom, nor contempt of this world, nor mortification of the flesh, nor largesse of alms can please God. Therefore, let a meal be prepared for me and for the others from the regular Lenten dishes." And this was done. And in this way she was refreshed with spiritual joy on days of abstaining from food for the body, so that in works of mercy she burned brightly with the flame of love.[36]

And a short while later she spoke to me with this proposition: "Because I foresee that the demise of my body is quickly approaching, and I will no longer be able to carry out a fast of such self-denial for the mortification of the flesh, with urgent prayer I entrust to your innermost love, out of our state of piety, that straightway upon my death you promise to pay my debt to Christ, my creditor, on the eve of the next Sabbath."

Oh, happy woman! Oh sweet Margherita, who earned the angels' share for nourishing the poor! Oh famous virgin, fertile in virtues by lineage, who sought to attain the power of such courage from the virtues of grace in order to conquer the formidable enemies of the soul with the *shield of faith*, the *breastplate of justice*, the *sword of the spirit*, the *helmet of salvation*, and the spear of perseverance![37]

---

be gravely ill. Nevertheless, given that virtually Stefania's entire narrative concerns the last month of Margherita's life, and that here Margherita is already referring to her coming demise, we are inclined to believe that Stefania intended to refer here to December 1280. Since she was writing some eight to twelve years later, her memories might not have matched exactly with Giovanni's concerning the specific date of the onset of Margherita's last illness; or she may overtly have intended to correct Giovanni's version of events.

36. Cf. *Vita I*, ch. 6, where Giovanni Colonna gives a harsher description of Margherita's eating habits. Stefania may be offering a correction or defending the practices of the community at San Silvestro as in line with Margherita's desires.

37. This paragraph returns to Gregory IX's canonization bull for Elizabeth of Hungary. The biblical quotations (found in that bull) are from Ephesians 6:14–17.

4. When one and all were fortified with solid food and revived with the spiritual sustenance of her consoling speech, with modest gravity she unlocked to me the secret revelations and the stream of gifts coming forth to her from the secrets of our Lord Savior—not in swollen bombastic pride or unbearable loathsome hypocrisy, but burning with the sevenfold Holy Spirit. Revealing these things to me, who was joined to her by the intimate bond of overflowing love and with longing for the scope of her revelations with seething soul, she warned me that I should long more ardently for eternal joys than for the worthless dust of this world.

5. Indeed, she had seen three roads, differing from one another in their nature and in those who traveled them.[38] The lower road was the widest, so that it might be considered the public highway. Over it ran a mass of people beyond number, all trusting in their skills and abundant riches; and they rushed with ruinous headlong speed, although some went along with shorter, some with longer strides. And right in the middle of it there was a great open market area[39] that took up the width of the road, leaving no paths around it, no matter how far off to the edge, that seemed to offer the pleasure of an inn to the travelers' feet. And the more they strove to proceed with great haste, as though their heels were greased with the oil of adulation, the more heavily and grievously they sank into this area, and all their hope of rising was in vain. And *under* them *was strewn* the *consuming* and burning *moth*, and the *worms*[40] of hell clung to them like an irremovable winding sheet, and they were seen wracked and worn by a suffering more violent than childbirth.

---

38. This vision is clearly related to—but in several ways contradicts (or consciously corrects)—*Vita 1*, ch. 11.

39. The Latin phrase *area palestrata* seems to imply an open square, perhaps a marketplace (Cadderi translated simply as "piazza"). See, for example, the usage in a 1317 document cited in Laura De Angelis Cappabianca, "I beni del monastero di S. Maria Teodote di Pavia nel territorio circostante Veghera ed a Zenevredo (Pavia) dalle origini al 1346: Ricerche di storia agraria medioevale," *Studi di storia medioevale e di diplomatica* 5 (1980): 15–153, at 65n145. We thank Professors Jacques Bailly and Robert H. Rogers for consultation on this point.

40. Cf. Isaiah 14:11; Matthew 6:19–20.

The middle road appeared thorny, dry, and dark, surrounded on all sides by the densest thistle hedges of sorrow and by thorn bushes. Terrified at the horrid, frightful sight, the passersby were sickened at the passage through it. Only a very few—shedding their cloaks of empty momentary pleasure so that they would not be snared by the curved points of *thorns and briars*,[41] not running but proceeding step by step, afflicted by many sorrows and toils and taking with them nothing from the charred remains of this world—were making their way along this happy road[42] to heaven.

She, herself, truly panting after the third road and leaving behind a world frozen by winter cold, would fly like a supremely pure dove to those lands that Christ, the Sun of Justice, looks upon and illuminates, overflowing with the fruits of virtue where none had gone before her and few were following far behind.

6. O wondrous working of divine piety for the human race![43] How boundless the worth of His love, by which He has given over His Son to redeem a slave! Not abandoning the good things of His mercy, and

---

41. Isaiah 7:25.

42. Oliger read "per eam feliciter," but the manuscript actually reads "per eam felicem."

43. This chapter is taken entirely from the first two paragraphs of Gregory IX's canonization bull for Francis of Assisi, *Mira circa nos* (19 July 1228), printed in *BF*, 1:42–44 (in these initial quotations Gregory cites the *Exultet*, the Proclamation at the Easter Vigil). Stefania's text, however, makes small changes. For example, compare the canonization bull, "Mira circa Nos divinae pietatis dignatio, et inestimabilis dilectio charitatis, qua filium pro servo tradidit redimendo," with Stefania's "Mira circa humanum genus divine pietatis operatio et inestimabilis dignatio caritatis, qua filium pro servo tradidit redimendo." It is not entirely clear whether a change such as *dignatio* to *operatio* was intentional, the result of a faulty copy of the bull, or a later scribal error. In light of these uncertainties, we translate as the manuscript of Stefania's text actually reads (for instance, in the next clause where Stefania has *bona* rather than *dona* as found in the bull; later a number of clauses are omitted, and obviously Francis's name and some descriptive and gendered language are changed). We have had the benefit of the translation of Gregory's bull in Regis J. Armstrong, J. A. Wayne Hellmann, and William J. Short, *Francis of Assisi: Early Documents* (New York: New City Press, 1999), 1:565–66, but have not followed it directly.

protecting with continual care the vineyard[44] *which* His *right hand has planted*,[45] He sends those to cultivate it healthfully with hoe and plow-share, rooting out the *thorns and briars*.[46] Even *at the eleventh hour*[47] He sends workers so that when the overgrowth has been cut back and the weak-rooted weeds and the thistles have been pulled up,[48] they may gather the sweet and pleasant fruit.[49] This fruit, when purged by the winepress of suffering, may be taken to the storehouse of eternity, even while the *charity of many grows cold*[50] and impiety proceeds as though lit by fire, and the Philistines, overcome with the drink of earthly pleasure, rush in[51] to demolish the garden wall.

But behold! *At the eleventh hour,* God, who was destroying the earth with the water of the flood, *not leaving the rod of sinners upon the lot of the just*,[52] raised up a woman *according to His own heart*,[53] the resplendent Margherita. Indeed, she was a beacon made to shine forth at the appointed time, replete with the oil of holiness, sent *into His vineyard*[54] to pluck up the thorns and nettles and, with the attacking Philistines laid low, to reconcile people to God by illuminating our homeland and warning with earnest entreaty.

7. But why linger any longer over these things? Immediately after recounting her visions, as the first fevers began to render her wretched, she said, "I thank you, Lord God our Father, because you have found me

---

44. Oliger read *unicam,* but the manuscript actually follows the bull in reading *vineam.*

45. Cf. Psalm 79:16.

46. Hebrews 6:8. Note the way in which Stefania makes the redeployed wording of Francis's canonization bull work to "clear" the path filled with thorns and briars described in Margherita's vision in chapter 5.

47. Matthew 20:6.

48. Cf. Wisdom 4:3.

49. Stefania has the plural verb *afferant* where the bull reads *afferat.*

50. Matthew 24:12.

51. Cf. 1 Kings 31:2.

52. Psalm 124:3.

53. 1 Kings 13:14.

54. Matthew 20:2.

worthy to receive the care of your attention,[55] chastising your daughter whom your mercies have called back from hellish error." And seeing in her mind's eye that I was going to follow her in the sacrament of burial, with all the passion of her heart she proclaimed to me, saying, *"For I am even now ready to be sacrificed,*[56] and it is time that you entrust my body to the earth.[57] And because I see that in time to come you will ride the waves of sundry whirlpools, my spirit groans in overwhelming sympathy and almost faints in wonder, beholding the bravery of your endurance under such stress.[58] But do not quail before any coming peril, as though you lacked comforting help, for Christ will immediately come to your protection, walking over the waves of your distress,[59] and will command *the sea* of your sorrow and *the winds* driving you to destruction, and will render the raging whirlwinds *calm,*[60] and will bring your little ship to safe haven; and He will open the treasure of your love for our brothers[61] and will provide what is fit for your time and place."

8. Meanwhile a petitioner was beseeching her, very earnestly, that when she took her position in the Kingdom next to her wedded Husband she would profusely intercede on behalf of a certain notable highly born man

---

55. The Latin "Gratias tibi ago, Domine Pater, quod mihi dignatus es sollicitudinem tue visitationis impendere" strongly echoes the *Passio S. Agathae*. Compare the "Cistercian" version edited in Carla Morini, "Una redazione sconosciutta della *Passio S. Agathae,*" *Analecta Bollandiana* 109 (1991): 305–30.

56. 2 Timothy 4:6.

57. Antiphon for the Feast of Saint Andrew (November 30). Cantus ID, 3923; Stephen Joseph Van Dijk, *Sources of the Modern Roman Liturgy: The Ordinals by Haymo of Faversham and Related Documents (1243–1307)*, Studia et documenta Franciscana 1–2 (Leiden: E. J. Brill, 1963), 2:121.

58. Although the language is ambiguous, the implication seems to be that Margherita knows that Stefania will both outlive her and assume her place as leader responsible for their band of Sisters.

59. Cf. Matthew 14:25; Mark 6:48; John 6:19.

60. Cf. Matthew 8:26.

61. We interpret "nostrisque fratribus" as referring to Giovanni and Giacomo, rather than to the *Fratres minores.*

who was in the bloom of strength and known to be serving overseas,[62] so that He should open to him the flow of his mercy, that he might be able *to keep himself unspotted from this world*[63] and advance in virtue day by day, and thus might be worthy to behold with the other saints *the God of gods in Syon,*[64] *face to face.*[65] She granted that she would do this, and announced that this worthy noble who was serving in those regions was going to depart this world and, moreover, "was already gone from my bodily sight." This was shown by true and compelling experience. For while there, before he could return, he discharged his debt to nature. And I think it is beyond all doubt that, as the bravest champion of Christ, he enjoys the holy vision and reigns[66] with the saints in heaven.

9. Therefore Margherita, turning the rights of blood lineage into a longing for heavenly joy, bound herself to the yoke of obedience under whose law she was placed, because she put on the religious habit of the most blessed Clare, in which she unfailingly pursued the mystery of the Lord's passion until her final day.[67] Thus she made herself beloved to her immortal Spouse; thus she bound herself in continual delight to the Queen of Virgins by reducing her noble status to that of a household servant; thus she attuned herself to the holy progress of the earlier Margherita[68]

---

62. The Latin is "in ultramarinis partibus." Presumably this man was a crusader reinforcing the remaining Christian outpost of Acre.

63. James 1:27.

64. Psalm 83:8.

65. 1 Corinthians 13:12.

66. Oliger read *concregnare* where the manuscript has *conregnare*.

67. This paragraph (except the final sentence) returns to a literal borrowing from Gregory IX's canonization bull for Elizabeth of Hungary. This first sentence is cleverly altered so that "sub lege posita" refers not to the authority of a husband (that clause from Gregory's bull is omitted) but directly to the habit. The phrase "religionis habitum induit" is then modified by the addition of "Beatissime Clare." Stephania suggests more directly than Giovanni Colonna that Margherita literally donned a habit akin to Clare's, not just a habit modeled on the one worn by the Sisters of the Order of St. Clare.

68. That is, her example conformed to that of the early martyr St. Margherita. The text of Elizabeth of Hungary's canonization bull had placed the earlier St. Elizabeth here.

while she walked plainly *in the commands and justifications of the Lord without blame.*[69] Through her passion, in the depths of her mind, she received the grace of God. And she demonstrated this grace in her accomplishments and nourished it in her progress, because it is the salvation *of all that trust in Him;*[70] and from on high[71] it urges onward, to the rewards of retribution promised to His own, all those placed in the lowly valleys of innocence. Freed from the coils of death, she was carried by this grace to that sole[72] place illuminated by an unreachable light, by whose amazing and inscrutable brightness her spirit glows in the depth of heavenly splendor and flashes forth with many glorious miracles in the deep of this darkness. These miracles by their virtue bring forth an increase of love and hope to true believers; and the way of truth is set out for the faithless, and much is heaped up to confound heretics while they spin in a numbing whirlwind because of their dread of Margherita's miracles. While still shut in this prison of the flesh, she was truly *poor in spirit, meek* in mind, weeping over her sins, or rather, the sins of others, *thirsting after justice,* given to *mercy, clean of heart,* truly a *peacemaker,* suffering from *persecutors,*[73] if the sword of persecutors had been there, wounded by the torment caused by the unending ulcer of her livid thigh, like a long-suffering ewe who *would not open* her *mouth* in lamentation.[74]

I will now set out in writing briefly and separately some of her miracles. For on the next to last day of December[75] she was released from the bonds of death and went to the source of heavenly joy,[76] where God,

---

69. Luke 1:6.

70. Psalm 17:31.

71. Gregory IX's bull reads *exaltatio* where Stefania (or the scribe) has *ex alto.*

72. Gregory IX's bull reads *ad solium luce* where Stefania (or the scribe) reads *ad solum luce.*

73. Matthew 5:3–10. At this point the use of Elizabeth's canonization bull is suspended, so that presumably the following description of Margherita's physical suffering and her ulcerous thigh can be taken as referring to Stefania's actual memories.

74. Isaiah 53:7.

75. 30 December 1280.

76. This phrase again comes from Gregory IX's canonization bull for Elizabeth.

three in one, who is blessed in the generations of the ages, reigns and rules for all eternity. Amen.[77]

10. A certain noble and religious woman named Risa, from the fortified town of Affile,[78] had been terribly afflicted for twenty years or more with a bloody discharge and other ailments. She took some curls that had come from the head of Lady Margherita and applied them with great reverence and devotion to her body and womb,[79] and immediately the discharge and pains from which she had been suffering ceased, and she was returned to her old health. She is still living, and with many trustworthy witnesses from the same area she *gives testimony to the truth*.[80]

11. Fiordaliso, a sister of that same Risa and from the same town, had long endured weakness from hydropsical swelling. She took some of Lady [Margherita]'s hair and most reverently rubbed it over the limbs of her swollen body; and as it touched each limb the swelling departed, so that she got back her fine health. She herself and many others are witnesses.

---

77. The last four ruled lines of folio 31r are blank following this "Amen," with the miracles beginning on the top of folio 31v. The closing lines "ubi regnat et imperat trinus et unus Deus qui est benedictus in generationibus seculorum amen" are an amalgamation of several common liturgical tropes without directly repeating any single text. The six short chapters that follow relate miracles experienced by people in the surrounding area, apparently in the immediate aftermath of Margherita's death.

78. Near Subiaco, in the Diocese of Anagni.

79. Apparently Margherita had curly hair, though it is not clear exactly when or where these particular locks were cut. The Latin word *utero* here could mean "womb" or just "belly."

80. Cf. John 5:33; 18:37. It is implied that all of these miracles occurred after Margherita's death, but in fact nothing clearly indicates that she could not have been still alive when her hair was used to miraculous effect in these initial miracles. The previous story about the crusader (*Vita II*, ch. 8) suggests that her attention clearly was sought.

12. Mattias of Roiate,[81] who is now a monk in the Monastery of Saint Gregory of the city [of Rome],[82] was afflicted from his earliest youth up through the years of adolescence with the evil of the stone. Upon the invocation of the name of Lady Margherita, he emitted a little stone like a bean through a stalk, and has remained in good health. He himself is a witness, along with the abbess and the convent of the Monastery of Saint Benedict of the same area, who saw this miracle because it was done in their monastery.[83]

---

81. Roiate is a small hill town near Subiaco, also located in the Diocese of Palestrina. A castle was built there in the twelfth century.

82. As Oliger pointed out, the first procurator for the nuns of San Silvestro in Capite (document of July 1286, Vincenzo Federici, "Regesto del monastero di S. Silvestro de Capite," *Archivio della Società romana di storia patria* 22 [1899]: 418) was "Frater Angelus monachus monasterii S. Gregorii [in] Clivo Scauri de Urbe," so clearly there were ties between the two monastic institutions. Oliger speculates that this Angelus may have been the same man as the "frater Angelus" who was a monk of San Silvestro in 1282 and 1283, before the Benedictines were expelled (see Federici, "Regesto," 415–16; he is called "Angelus de Monte Opulo" in the later reference). San Gregorio in Clivo Scauri was one of Rome's oldest and most prestigious monasteries, first established by Pope Gregory I on his own estates in the 570s and reestablished by Pope Gregory II during the eighth century. As this passage makes clear, San Gregorio was still a community of Benedictine monks in the thirteenth century with some connection to the hill towns around the city. See Francesca Carboni, *Via Prenestina* (Rome: Istituto Poligrafico e Zecca dello Stato, 1997), 120–21, and Robert Brentano, *Rome before Avignon: A Social History of Thirteenth-Century Rome* (New York: Basic Books, 1974), 244, as well as the more general description in Christian Hülsen, *Le chiese di Roma nel Medio Evo* (Florence: Leo S. Olschki, 1927).

83. The Benedictine convent in Roiate has received little attention from scholars. According to hagiographical tradition, St. Benedict of Nursia (d. ca. 547)—the "founder" of Western monasticism—once visited the area and rested there on a rock, which miraculously retained the shape of his body. A church was built on this site, and a convent was established that lasted until the fifteenth century when it was incorporated into the Cistercian order. The Sisters appear infrequently in published records, although San Benedetto in Roiate had a reputation as a pilgrimage site for healing miracles and for the miraculous rock, which was believed to "sweat" in times of danger.

13. Giacomo of Campoli,[84] a resident of the same place,[85] was devoted to Lady Margherita and knew her well. He was worn out by the suffering of truly endless fever and fainting spells and delirium, and his doctor abandoned hope of his recovery. Then a certain religious woman reminded the sick man that, if he wished to be cured, he should present himself for help to Lady Margherita. The religious woman returned to her nearby monastery, and the sick man, pulling himself along with his hands and feet (for he had no one to help him), hastened to a certain window. And there, beholding the mist near Mount Prenestino, he gave himself over to prayer. He had not even finished his prayer when Lady Margherita appeared to him, led him back to bed, and soothed the sick man. Unable to stand the splendor and pleasant sweetness, he said, "Please take your leave, my lady!" Soon the lady bathed him in cool water and departed, and *at the same hour*[86] Giacomo was cured of his triple ailment. He is himself a witness, as are many others to whom Giacomo has related this miracle.

14. Lord Alberto of Collemezzo, a knight of Anagni,[87] lay weak a long time in bed, and could not turn himself or his leg without someone to help him; and from lying so long in bed the knight's leg bones began to

---

84. Oliger identified this place as probably Compoli Appenino.

85. That is, Roiate.

86. Matthew 8:13.

87. Collemezzo is south of Palestrina and west of Anagni. This family produced several famous churchmen, but the genealogy of its secular members is less than clear. This "Dominus Albertus de Collemedio, miles Anagninus" is probably the same man as the Alberto of Collemezzo, who is mentioned in various documents from the 1280s and 1290s as the father of Lando (canon of Anagni), Benedetto, and Guido (canon of Arras; apparently not the same man as Guido of Collemezzo, bishop of Cambrai from 1296 to 1306). Although the clerics in the family tended to have ties to Boniface VIII, in 1303 another Guido, Lord of Collemezzo—perhaps Alberto's nephew—sided with the Colonna in the attack at Anagni. This miracle story thus provides evidence for earlier ties between the Collemezzo and the Colonna. See Giovanbattista Ronzoni, *Il castello di Collemezzo e i suoi feudatari* (Rome, 1958), 54, 69–76; and for important genealogical corrections, see Pascal Montaubaun, "'Avec de l'Italie qui descendrait l'Escault': Guido da Collemezzo, évêque de Cambrai (1296–1306)," in *Liber largitorius: Études d'histoire médiévale*

deteriorate and wear away. The sick man's daughter, named Romana, a very religious woman and nun in the Monastery of St. Benedict of Roiate, was then helping her father in response to his suffering. Moved by great sympathy toward her father, giving herself over to prayer, she declared that if her father got back his health through the merits of Lady Margherita she would make a barefooted journey to visit [Margherita's] tomb. At once the said knight called out to her joyously, announcing that he had turned himself and his leg and thigh in bed. And when the next day came, he arose from his bed and was all cured of his sickness. He is himself a witness, as is the said Romana, his daughter.

15. Teodora, a woman of Palestrina, was closing a chest and carelessly caught her little girl's hand between the lid and the chest. The girl's hand was broken, and it withered away and that side of the girl's body even became numb. This Teodora carried her daughter to the tomb of Lady Margherita and tearfully placed her upon it. Then the girl seemed to fall asleep for an hour, and as soon as she awoke she returned to her mother all healed. This Teodora is a witness.

16. On the eighth day after her happy transition,[88] [Margherita] appeared to me in a vision. She was in a very pleasant meadow that was adorned with a variety of spring flowers and had a little stream of clear water running through it. She was wearing a cloak covered with white and red roses. When I asked how she was, she recited to me the verse from the Psalms, from *Who turns the sea into dry land* up to *I extolled Him with my tongue.*[89] Then, commending me and her more worthy brother [Giacomo] and her older brother [Giovanni] to Him, she replied: "Let

---

offertes à Pierre Toubert par ses élèves, ed. Dominique Barthélemy and Jean-Marie Martin (Geneva: Droz, 2003), 477–502.

88. Eight days after Margherita's death would be 7 January 1281. At this point the list of healing miracles attested by others comes to an end. The next three chapters are visions in which Margherita appears, the first one returning to Stefania's own perspective.

89. Psalm 65:6–17.

our brothers beware lest they overstep themselves!"[90] She invited me to view her Husband's palace, and suddenly I found myself with her at the foot of a staircase, whose steps were suffused with exceeding golden brightness. Seen from outside, the house was like the palace of the Sun of Justice, with lofty high columns of emerald and sapphire, bright sparkling gold and flaming garnet, and sunbeams flashing forth, as it were, from a host of precious gems and stones whose bright reflection destroyed my ability to see. In truth I eagerly followed her up the stairs as she proceeded. And after our steps had brought us to the very top, from within the palace *I heard* melodic harmonies as though of *the voice of harpists, harping on their harps,*[91] *and of all kinds of music,*[92] which soothed my ears wonderfully. She, as though rapt in ecstasy, vanished from my sight, having entered the bedchamber of her Husband. And I, awakening, was not worthy to further experience this vision, nor to enter with her into the palace.

17. Friar Bartholomeo of Gallicano of the Order of Friars Minor [*Fratres minores*], a *religious man and fearing God*[93] who was then stationed at the house in Assisi, was sent by the guardian[94] to preach at the house of

---

90. We again take "brothers" here to mean Margherita's biological brothers, not the *Fratres minores*. How exactly Margherita (in Stefania's vision) fears her brothers may overstep themselves is not made clear. It is possible that Stefania is here using Margherita to warn the leaders of the Colonna family that (however much their patronage might be appreciated) they should leave a certain sphere of autonomy to the Sisters of San Silvestro.

91. Revelation 14:2.

92. Daniel 3:7.

93. Acts 10:2. On the basis of antiquarian publications Oliger identified Bartholomeo as a teacher of theology and noted preacher. While we have not found contemporary references to him outside the present text, it seems probable that he had some connection to the Colonna family. Gallicano was a town at the foot of Mount Prenestino that was a part of the family's holdings, and there was in fact a distinct branch of the Colonna family based in Gallicano.

94. That is, the Friar in charge of daily operations of the Franciscan community at Assisi.

Sisters Minor [*Sorores minores*][95] on the vigil of St. Clare.[96] After the sermon was over he returned to the Friars' house and was strolling around the cloister, thinking about what the theme of his sermon should be if he were sent to the same place to preach again the next day. And thinking that he would chose as the topic to introduce his sermon the passage *As the lily among the thorns*,[97] he sat down on a step next to the fountain to ponder this subject. Finally, he drifted off to sleep and saw a company of virgins dressed in white garments decorated with golden stars, proceeding in an orderly fashion, walking two by two. On each one's head rested *a crown of gold wherein was engraved holiness*,[98] that was wreathed with sundry shining pearls.[99] And among this most blessed troop he recognized with his own eyes a certain virgin of the above-mentioned order,[100] Filippa by name,[101] who was quite famous for her lineage but even more famous for the merit of her holiness. When he asked what she wanted, he learned from her that Lady Margherita

---

95. It is worth noting that Stefania apparently thinks of the Sisters of the Order of St. Clare at Assisi (the house Margherita had once intended to join) as *Sorores minores*. Her reference reflects the fact that medieval people may not always have made the institutional distinctions modern scholars emphasize.

96. The day of the visit would have been 11 August, since Clare's bull of can-onization decreed her feast day as 12 August (it was changed to 11 August in 1969). On this vision, see Lezlie Knox, *Creating Clare of Assisi: Female Franciscan Identities in Later Medieval Italy* (Leiden: Brill, 2008), 97–114.

97. Canticles 2:2.

98. Ecclesiasticus 45:14.

99. There is again a play on *margaritis*, meaning "pearl."

100. It is again interesting that "the above-mentioned order" would make Filippa (see following note) a member—in the mind of Bartholomeo or Stefania—of the Order of *Sorores minores*.

101. It is virtually certain that this woman can be identified as Filippa Mareri (ca. 1200–1236), founder of a female community at San Pietro de Molito (Diocese of Rieti) that was incorporated into the Order of San Damiano before her death. Like Margherita Colonna, Filippa Mareri came from a wealthy seigneurial family and preferred a semireligious form of life over an enclosed nunnery. See Knox, *Creating Clare of Assisi*, 101–8, and Robert Brentano, *A New World in a Small Place: Church and Religion in the Diocese of Rieti, 1188–1378* (Berkeley: University of California Press, 1994), 265–74.

Colonna was coming along in the chorus of virgins, pointing her out in the second row of the procession, preceding the most blessed Clare.[102]

Therefore, Friar Bartholomeo looked eagerly and saw Lady Margherita walking joyfully with the other virgins. And wondering at their shining faces, he said to her, "I am frightened, lady, because of the sublime glory of your beauty!" And when he paused in his fright, he heard her say, "Friar Bartholomeo, you cannot see our beauty, for it is not to be grasped by human eyes." To which the Friar said, "O, that what I see could be made known to Lord Giacomo [Colonna]!" "Doubt not," she replied to him, "for he knows full well that I enjoy delights in the glory of my Christ." The Brother replied, "I know, my lady, I know that he is aware; yet I would wish that he might believe that I have seen you in the company of virgins." "I will provide you," she said, "with signs by which he will believe you. When you tell him all that you have seen of this, ask him to recall that our common father was released from purgatory's pains at my passing, and also the vision of the most pleasant pilgrim at the feast of Saint John the Baptist."[103]

He now beheld someone in the procession of virgins who occupied the middle place between Margherita and the blessed Clare, since the blessed Clare was following last in the group as leader and guide to the others. This was a certain most striking virgin, crowned with a gleaming tiara fitted with a flashing red gem that surpassed the stones of the other crowns in size and light, shining like a ray of the sun.[104] But when the

---

102. Clare of Assisi.

103. The reference to their father's release from purgatory has no clear antecedent; the reference to the pilgrim pertains to events detailed in *Vita I*, ch. 12.

104. The identity of this "most striking virgin" remains obscure. The reference to her crown with the red gem may point to a family connection to one of Rome's other noble families and perhaps to a female member of the Savelli or Orsini families, whose family shields were topped by red flowers. All the virgins in this heavenly troop wear crowns, but Stephania's word *cidaris* may point toward the papal tiara, which was known as a *thyara*. Pope Nicholas III (1277–80) and Pope Honorius IV (1285–87) were members of the Orsini and Savelli families respectively. We are not aware of any efforts by either family to promote a female member's sanctity— which may contribute to Friar Batholomeo's surprise. Certainly there must have been

same Friar wished to ask Lady Margherita how that virgin came to merit receiving such an outstanding tiara, just then another Friar woke him up, so that he could not ask what he wanted to, nor could he perceive the vision any longer.

18. After her happy transition to Christ, Margherita left behind among her companions two noble virgins who were without firm commitment to a religious life. Through her merits these two were so illuminated by divine splendor that, *insisting in prayers*[105] and vigils *day and night*,[106] they could think of nothing else but Christ.[107]

And while these mysteries were happening around the handmaidens of God, Lady Margherita appeared in a dream, in the city [of Rome], to a certain lady who holds the first position among all their natural brothers and sisters,[108] saying to her: "Rise and hasten quickly to where the earthly remains of my body rest![109] And take two of your six

---

other contemporary Roman women who were viewed as saintly but for whom evidence of local cults has not survived. See Luigi Pellegrini, "Female Religious Experience and Society in Thirteenth-Century Italy," in *Monks and Nuns, Saints and Outcasts: Religion in Medieval Society. Essays in Honor of Lester K. Little*, ed. Sharon Farmer and Barbara H. Rosenwein (Ithaca, NY: Cornell University Press, 2000), 97–122, and André Vauchez, "Female Sanctity and the Franciscan Movement," in *The Laity in the Middle Ages: Religious Beliefs and Devotional Practices*, ed. Daniel E. Bornstein (Notre Dame, IN: University of Notre Dame Press, 1993), 171–84. On the nomenclature of the papal crown, see Maureen Miller, *Clothing the Clergy: Virtue and Power in Medieval Europe, c. 800–1200* (Ithaca, NY: Cornell University Press, 2014), 192.

105. Cf. Romans 12:12; Colossians 4:2.

106. Deuteronomy 9:18; Ecclesiastes 8:16.

107. The rest of the chapter allows some confusion about how many young women are referred to in total. In the following notes we will call these first two girls "virgins 1 and 2."

108. This would seem most likely to be Margherita's oldest sister Giacoma, who was married to Pietro Conti. If so this passage would suggest that Giacoma was in fact the firstborn of Margherita's siblings.

109. Margherita's oldest sister was apparently in Rome when she received this dream-message, so this passage suggests that Margherita's tomb could be found in "the city" of Rome when these events took place. Generally, the assumption that

daughters,"[110] indicating them to her by name, "for *your heart shall wonder and be enlarged*[111] when you behold Barbara, who has been chosen by God, deeply and passionately loving Christ alone while disdaining all idle affairs!"[112] *And so* her noble sister *rose up*[113] and went with the girls to [Margherita's] tomb, as she had been commanded in the dream.

And thus, concerning these same young women, it came about by divine arrangement that suddenly their mental focus changed from things of this earth to things of heaven, and in that same place they eagerly embraced the reward of religion.[114] Not long after, Barbara followed them into the same rule of seraphic discipline; and Precinta, who so guarded the wholeness of her person that she avoided the lust of

---

her relics were translated from Mount Prenestino when San Silvestro in Capite was founded in 1285 seems warranted, but direct evidence comes only from Mariano of Florence in the sixteenth century (see translation in this volume).

110. Although it is not entirely clear, the rest of the chapter suggests to us that Margherita's older sister's two daughters are Barbara and Precinta, and that they are not the same as virgins 1 and 2.

111. Isaiah 60:5.

112. The ambiguous wording might seem to suggest that "Barbara" had already embraced the religious life, and hence would not be one of the two daughters being brought to Margherita's tomb, but on balance we interpret this passage as saying that Margherita's sister will marvel at seeing what happens once she brings her daughter Barbara to the tomb. As Oliger noted, "Domina Barbara" appears in a document of February 1287 as a nun of San Silvestro, in what appears to be a position of leadership along with Domina Margherita, Domina Sistera, and the abbess Domina Herminia; and in a document of December 1294 "Domina Barbara" is referred to as abbess. See Federici, "Regesto," 419 and 432. It seems extremely likely that this nun is the same Barbara who is referred to in the present chapter, and hence Margherita Colonna's niece.

113. Genesis 21:14, etc.

114. These "ipsas iuvenculas" seem likely to be the original unnamed virgins 1 and 2, who now fully embrace the religious life. The phrase "in eodem loco" presumably implies San Silvestro, if indeed this whole episode can be dated to after 1285; this in turn provides further support for the claim that Margherita's tomb had been moved to San Silvestro by this time.

the eyes,[115] in this way claimed for herself from God the hundredfold [reward], which comes first, for the crown of virginity.[116]

19. In sum, that holy company was led forth with such heavenly gifts[117] by the example and merits of that virgin, their leader,[118] and also of that seraphic man,[119] the guide of these Sisters and of the virgin.[120] Resplendent with works of love and mercy, like another Moses he led the daughters of Israel out of Egypt by his teaching,[121] and he did not abandon them in the desert while he led them, with Joshua,[122] into the *excellent land*.[123]

---

115. Cf. *Concilium Aquisgranense, a. 816: Institutio sanctimonialium Aquisgranensis*, ed. A. Werminghoff (1906; electronic ed., Turnhout: Brepols, 2010), Conc. 2, 1, cap. 5, p. 436, "Quid prodest virgini integritatem corporis custodire, si oculorum concupiscentias noluerit evitare," with Stefania "que sic integritatem sui corporis custodivit, quod oculorum concupiscentias evitavit."

116. In the parable of the sower (Matthew 13:1–8) Jesus refers to harvests of a hundredfold, sixtyfold, and thirtyfold. A common gloss was a hundredfold reward for virginity, sixtyfold for chaste widowhood, and thirtyfold for marriage. See, for example, St. Jerome, in *S. Eusebii Hironymi Opera*, ed. Isidor Hilberg, Corpus Scriptorum Ecclesiasticorum Latinorum 54–56 (Vindobonae: Tempsky; Lipsiae: Freytag, 1910–18), vol. 56, p. 82 (letter 123), "centenarius pro virginitatis corona, primum gradum teneat," where Stefania's passage reads "centenarium numerum, qui primus est pro virginitatis corona." It seems possible that Precinta may have taken a vow of virginity but not become a nun; we have found no record of her in the published documents from San Silvestro. The reference to her "claiming her reward" may well indicate her death.

117. The phrase "divinis carismatibus est" is from an antiphon for the Office of Saint Francis (October 4). Cantus ID, 202188; Van Dijk, *Sources*, 2:165.

118. That is, Margherita Colonna.

119. Cardinal Giacomo Colonna.

120. After the last three visions, Stefania's own voice returns to draw the moral (ch. 19) and then to offer her own prayer (ch. 20).

121. Cf. Exodus 12 and *Vita I*, ch. 4.

122. Cf. Joshua 5:4.

123. Deuteronomy 4:21, etc.

20. But, alas! Tears flow inconsolably from my eyes, because I am shrouded by the mist of my lowly heart's goodness, deprived of the good that I served. I pray therefore that, through the intercession of Lady Margherita, the Lord may illuminate the blindness of my heart; kindle in me the fire of His love[124] and give to me the true faith, hope aspiring to heaven, and *unfeigned charity*,[125] and all the other virtues by which I may love and fear Him; and that I may keep his commandments so that when my last day and the end of my life come to me, the angels of peace may take me up, cleansed of all sin, and pull me out of the power of darkness so that I may deserve to enjoy the company of His saints in blessed rest and be placed at His right hand.[126]

May the most blessed Jesus, Son of the living God, grant this to me "for the praise and glory of His name";[127] He who said, *Ask and you shall receive*,[128] *seek and you shall find, knock and* the door of paradise *shall be opened to you*;[129] He who lives and reigns.

21. In that year when Lady Margherita went to Christ, before her crossing, early on the morning of the Feast of the Lord's Resurrection,[130] she summoned to her chamber her older brother,[131] seeking to learn from him whether that Thomas Didymus, the fit doubter of the Lord's resur-

---

124. The phrase "accendat *in* me *ignem amoris* sui" reflects several prayers from the Pentecost cycle, the votive Mass for the Holy Spirit, and other prayers. Cf. Cantus ID, 5327, 601416a; Van Dijk, *Sources*, 2:258, 260, 340, 343.

125. Cf. 2 Corinthians 6:6.

126. This is an adaptation of a prayer attributed to Odilon of Cluny. See "Un opuscule inédit de saint Odilon de Cluny," *Revue bénédictine* 16 (1899): 477–78.

127. The Latin phrase "ad laudem et gloriam nominis sui" is from the Mass (Oblation). Van Dijk, *Sources*, 2:10; Robert Lippe, ed., *Missale Romanum Mediolani, 1474* (London: Harrison and Sons, 1899), 201.

128. John 16:24.

129. Luke 11:9.

130. Easter was on 21 April in 1280. The narrative suddenly doubles back to the last year of Margherita's life for chs. 21–24.

131. *Senior* indicates Giovanni Colonna. But (as Oliger pointed out) *Vita I*, ch. 8, has *dignior*, which would indicate Giacomo, and the latter would make more sense as a consultant for this theological question (and presumably Giovanni

rection, actually stuck his *hand* and *finger* into the palms and side, the stigmata of the Redeemer.[132] He answered her that the doctors of the church held diverse opinions on this matter. That is, some insist that Thomas did run his hand and finger over the scars, but others assert that when he saw the Lord all hesitation vanished from his heart and he believed that He was indeed the Redeemer, and he feared to handle the stigmata of the glorified body. And so for a time a holy discourse ensued between the two over this mystery. Exerting herself in prayers and vigils and holy meditations, she came to lie back upon the bed so that her weary limbs might take a bit of rest, so that after that rest they might come back stronger for holy endeavors. Truly, she went to sleep as soon as she lay down in bed, and at once she was aroused from sleep by a call: "*Arise, make haste,*"[133] it said to her, "if you long to see the stigmata of your Christ!" As she leapt straight from bed at the sound of this voice, there appeared to her an arm, swollen and strangely livid, whose hand and fingers were streaming with purple blood; and in the middle of the hand was a gaping hole through which a horrid and ghastly rending of bones and muscle was visible. And as she eagerly hastened to embrace the arm and hand, what she saw suddenly vanished; and so she broke out sweating and trembling.

22. In that same year of her passing, she saw in a vision her soul in heaven with a gathering of the saints, and she observed that her body on earth was bursting with worms. As she was lamenting that she had not subjected it to greater abstinences, one of the saints asked whether she would want to be joined to her body again in order to punish it with even greater discipline. But she answered, "My lord, I am happy with the delights which I enjoy. Far be it from me that I should descend to the foul world again for any reason!"

Colonna, as author of *Vita I*, was in a good position to know whether he had been present or not).

    132. John 20:24–29.
    133. Canticles 2:10.

23. On the vigil of the birth of our Lord, around the hour of Vespers,[134] a certain handmaid of the house, Penestrina by name, wanted to prepare detergent in order to wash the clothes.[135] [Margherita], however, ordered her to turn away from the task. But since that handmaiden, as I was half aware, wanted to get around this order, she dumped some of the water, which was not yet warm, over the clothes. When I informed the lady that the handmaid had begun to pour the detergent over the clothes,[136] she began to laugh and said, "And now you too! I know, Sister, I know that the water is not yet as warm as it ought to be to make detergent. Tell Penestrina that she should definitely stop!"

24. When the night of our Lord's nativity was approaching,[137] and our entire group of companions was gathered in prayer, she asked me where Sister Maria of Anagni was and what she was doing. When I told her that the Sister was lingering in the chapel, she answered me saying, "Know, good Sister,[138] that the spirit of this Sister Maria is in a very brave struggle and has never been so stymied by the cunning of the devious one as she is now." As I was recommending this Sister to her, so that she would pour out prayers lest the Sister should fail in her struggle, [Margherita] fell into profound prayer lasting almost two hours. And then she answered, "Be comforted and rejoice! For the strong arm of the most learned warrior has stood beside the aforesaid Sister in the struggle, so that with the crafty foe defeated and the obscuring darkness departed, she can now be calm and peaceful!" This, I have learned from the said Sister Maria, was indeed the case.

---

134. The evening of 24 December 1280.

135. The phrase "liscivium facere" indicates the preparation of a lye-based soap.

136. Chapters 23 and 24 are again from Stefania's perspective, relating stories she recalls herself.

137. The next day, Christmas 1280.

138. In chapter 29, Giacomo Colonna twice calls Margherita "good sister." Thus the phrase here might perhaps suggest the possibility that Stefania was Margherita's biological sister.

25. Adinulfo of San Vito,[139] known as Pelagus, had a sore called a *dranculus* on his groin that was causing him great pain.[140] Seeking to have it removed or cured, he sent a messenger off to fetch a doctor. When the messenger returned, he reported that the doctor had gone up to Mount Prenestino with Lord Giovanni[141] to visit the tomb of Lady Margherita.[142] The sick man waited all day for the return of the doctor, in vain. As evening approached, seeing himself without the doctor's help, shaken by anger and emotion, he said, "Just look at this dismal mockery—how the lords of Colonna are scurrying around trying to force their sister into the chorus of the saints!"[143] His wife took him to task for blasphemy and warned him that, although he was at fault, he should vow himself to the said lady for his illness. He resisted mightily for a while, but at last he was overcome by his wife's warning and vowed to the same lady that if she assisted him in his sickness he would believe in her sanctity. Miraculous result, worthy of wonder! The following morning, the man who had been sick awoke from sleep with no further need of doctors' medicines, and he found himself cured of the sore through the merits of the said Lady Margherita. No signs scarring the flesh remained by which you could tell where he had previously been wasted by the sore. He and his wife and many others are witness to this.

26. On the night of the Feast of John the Evangelist,[144] Lady Margherita, moved by love and sympathy for me, began speaking in this way: "You must have realized that I shall soon travel from this world to my homeland. I know that your spirit is troubled at my departure. If you have in mind making any requests of me, for your love, I ask that you

---

139. San Vito Romano, between Palestrina and Subiaco.

140. Stefania returns here to one additional posthumous miracle reported and witnessed by a layman.

141. Senator Giovanni Colonna.

142. If Margherita's remains were indeed translated to San Silvestro in Capite in 1285, then this episode must have preceded that translation.

143. In this fascinating passage, Stefania highlights public recognition (and suspicion!) of the overt Colonna campaign to see to Margherita's canonization.

144. 27 December 1280. The rest of Stefania's narrative returns to Margherita's deathbed.

make them now." After I had first replied that master Jesus would reward her in heaven for such goodwill, I asked her humbly about the pilgrim upon whom she had waited at table during the Feast of John the Baptist, whether she believed he was really Christ, and what indications allowed her to be sure.[145] And also, how was it that she was at Mount Prenestino for three years and yet had not consciously seen that Mount?[146]

She answered right away, saying, "Since you were extremely upset with me for letting that pilgrim depart,[147] I will point out to you the reasons my spirit was quite certain and knew that that pilgrim was the Lord Redeemer. For when He came and was received as a guest, my mind was not ready for a flood of tears; and yet as soon as He sat down, my eyes seized Him with such devout reverence that a cloudburst of tears soaked the front of my gown from the top right down to the waist, as though a jug full of water had been poured over it. And I could not ask anything of Him with my tongue or my heart, except what I always pray for when I see Him sacrificed for our sins by the hands of the priest above the altar; that is, the salvation of my soul and that of my brothers.[148] And as I longed to throw myself at His feet, I was propelled and felt propelling hands, although I saw no one; and thus I was led into my room and fell down weeping next to the bed, and lay there weeping so long that little fountains of tears sprang from my eyes. And the fact that I did not see Mount Prenestino for three years occurred through divine dispensation, for I was then in the same state of alienation for three whole years that I had been in for the three months when the glorious Virgin appeared to me in her chariot."[149]

---

145. This refers to events recounted in *Vita I*, ch. 12.

146. *Vita I*, ch. 14, makes a brief reference to the fact that for three years before her death "nothing here below occupied her emotions even for a moment." Stefania is here offering further explanation of that enigmatic passage.

147. This indication that Stefania was personally and emotionally involved in the episode around the pilgrim provides further evidence to suggest that she was herself the Sister who provided the account of this incident to Giovanni Colonna, who then wrote it up as chapter 12 of *Vita I*.

148. The last clause here elaborates on a passage that had been left vague at the end of chapter 13 of *Vita I*.

149. This alludes to the vision recounted in *Vita I*, ch. 3.

27. That same night she requested the body of Christ with great devotion. While it was being carried in by the priest, she heard the sound of the bell that is carried before the Savior, and leapt from the bed without any help, even though from the first day of her affliction until that moment she had not even been able to turn herself over in bed. And rising up as if she suffered no affliction, she asked to go out to meet her Redeemer. When her more worthy brother [Giacomo] did not allow this, she threw herself down before the sight of the coming Christ with a torrent of tears, and greeted Him, saying,

> Hail Savior of the world!
> Hail our Redemption!
> Hail sacred flesh of Christ,
> Who has suffered for us![150]
> I adore you, *holy bread of eternal life and chalice of eternal salvation.*[151]

And receiving the body of Christ with the greatest reverence, she requested last rites.[152] In response, her older brother[153] said to her, "Sister, I believe that Christ has already anointed you with His unction, and I do not see that you need another anointing." She responded to him, "The anointing of my soul, which He has done, is clear to Christ. But as I pass

---

150. For the third and fourth lines (Ave sancta caro Christi / que pro nobis passa fuisti), see *AH*, vol. 47, no. 328 (p. 338). For the first two lines (Ave Salvator mundi / Ave redemptio nostra), see later appearances such as those in Edgar Hoskins, *Horae Beatae Mariae Virginis or Sarum and York Primers* (New York: Longmans, Green, 1901), 114; and C. de la Haye and J. Blondel, *Nouveau livre d'église, à l'usage de Rome, pour la commodité universel des laiques*, rev. ed. (Paris: Compagnie des Imprimeurs et Libraires Associés aux Livres d'Église, 1774), 11.

151. From the Canon of the Mass, *CO*, 6267a–b; Van Dijk, *Sources*, 2:11; Lippe, *Missale Romanum Mediolani*, 207–8.

152. That is, extreme unction.

153. "Older brother" should refer to Giovanni, but Stefania's memory here may have been mistaken, since *Vita I*, ch. 14, strongly indicates that this conversation was with Giacomo.

over, I should not be without the sacraments of the church, for He Himself has commanded them and the church has established them." Her unction was put off that day and the next, until evening.[154] Then at last she received the sacrament with such devout reverence that it was evident that the very substance of her soul was anointed in each limb.

Then her more worthy brother [Giacomo] and her elder brother [Giovanni] brought a doctor to her, hoping that she might yet recover. And examining the wound in her right thigh, there was truly then no trace of a gash in her flesh, except for the tiniest [mark shaped] like a hare.[155] Scraping there with his finger, the doctor applied a little wisp of cloth.

28. After the departure of the doctor, she began to shake from the pain and to pronounce in a clear voice Our Lady's greeting,[156] repeating it over and over. Then I took pity on her more worthy brother [Giacomo], who had gone three days without sleep while caring for his sister, and persuaded him that it was time to go and sleep. He agreed and asked if I felt strong enough to care for his sister. As he left, he gave me three honeyed lozenges for his sister's comfort, toast soaked in wine for her to inhale, and warm plasters for her eyes, hands, and feet. But he only pretended to depart, actually remaining behind a hanging tapestry, listening in secret. After what I supposed to be his departure, I offered her a hunk of bread. And having made the sign of the cross, she ate the bread, saying to me, "I do this out of love for you, and so you know this is my last supper, and so that what I do for you will not fade from your memory."[157] And thereafter she took no further earthly food.

---

154. The evening of 28 December 1280.

155. *Cyrogrillus* should indicate a small hare or rodent; the meaning is not particularly clear here.

156. That is (presumably), the prayer *Ave Maria*.

157. There is an obvious echo of Jesus's Last Supper here, without directly quoting a biblical passage. Compare Luke 22:19, "Hoc facite in meam commemorationem" with Stefania's "A tui memoria hoc quod pro te facio non recedat."

After finishing that hunk of bread, she asked me to show her wound to her, so she could see why it was groaning so much,[158] and so it might be visible to her for a little while. But I advised against this, since she was shaking from pain. She asked me to examine her wound for her, lifting aside her garment. The opening of the wound was huge, as though it had been made by a spear thrust. It was rose red in color, and flowing freely with an excess of blood. But she displayed no distress at all from the pain, and she did not want any further medical remedy, except that a certain woman named Sistera pressed cloths over the wound that night at my request.[159]

29. After the wound had been examined, she began to speak of heavenly things. I said to her, "Jesus Christ has rendered you much grace, since He opened your thigh in the way His side was opened, as a sign of His love." And she said, "You speak the truth, but I cry out and do not have the endurance I should, because when Christ was suffering He *did not open his mouth* in grief."[160] And I said to her, "Take comfort, for He will help you out of the abundance of His endurance, and you will overcome this momentary suffering if you cling unswervingly to His love." Then she said, "Yes, because of His love I have torn apart my vitals and the very bonds of my muscles, so that no limb remains joined to another, and now I have thought to tear my garments to pieces. But I ask that you beseech our

---

158. The subject of the verb *murmuraret* is not clear. It could refer back to the doctor muttering about Margherita's condition, or to her brother, but we have interpreted it as the wound itself "groaning" in the sense of causing her distress.

159. As Oliger pointed out, a nun of San Silvestro referred to as "domina Sistera" is mentioned in a document of 1287 and again in documents of 1294 and 1296. A document of May 1298 (in the midst of Boniface VIII's attacks on the Colonna) refers to "religiosa et honesta mulier domina Systera vicaria venerabilis monasterii S. Silvestri de Capite de Urbe." See Federici, "Regesto," 419, 432, 434, 436. Oliger further notes that the same name can be found in an uncdited document in the Archivio di Stato di Roma dated 16 May 1310. Although it is not certain, this woman may be the same as the *mulier* referred to by Stefania here, though it is notable that she does not call her *soror*.

160. Cf. Isaiah 53:7.

more worthy brother Lord [Giacomo] to have me bound and dragged at least a mile in recompense for the scourging of Christ." And held at the knees,[161] she ordered that the family be assembled so that she might bestow the bounty of her blessing.

When all were assembled, she saw that Lord P[ietro], the cardinal, who was then still a young boy, was not present, nor was his sister Mateleone, who has now devoted her celibacy to God.[162] She insisted that they come as well, though Mateleone was sick with a fever.[163] When they appeared she blessed the whole family, saying, "I charge you to let nothing interfere with the accustomed regular rites of the Mother of God. And I ask that, if you wish to offer some ritual for me, you have Lauds and Hours sung throughout the year in her honor, rendering thanks for the blessings heaped on me through her and her Son." When her more worthy brother [Giacomo] tearfully begged her to bless him, she said, "In truth, you must bless me first." When he blessed her and impressed upon her the sign of the cross, she rejoined and said to him, "May God bless you, God who is three in divinity and one in substance. Be assured that in heaven after your happy demise you will receive a double reward from the Lord: the first because of the accomplishment of your good works and services, and the second in recompense for all the blessings that you have brought to us and our household in the footsteps of Christ." Her more worthy brother [Giacomo] said to her in return, "What then may I do for you, good sister?" She replied, "Brother, see that three hundred Masses are sung this year in praise of the Mother of God. And on the vigil of the anniversary of my death, see that the Mass

---

161. The rather odd sounding "Et ligata in genibus" makes sense when compared to the description in *Vita I*, ch. 14, which says that "those in attendance held her by her knees."

162. Pietro Colonna (d. 1326) was the son of Senator Giovanni Colonna and thus Margherita's nephew. He was created a cardinal by Nicholas IV on 16 May 1288. It does not seem possible that he was really much younger than twenty at the time of Margherita's death, contrary to Stefania's description of him as a *puellulus*. This passage dates Stefania's text, or at least its completion, to after May 1288. Nothing further seems to be known about Pietro's sister Mateleone; presumably the reference here indicates she became a professed nun at San Silvestro in Capite.

163. Compare the account in *Vita I*, ch. 14.

with the introit *Vultum tuum* is sung; and on the anniversary itself, *Salve sancta parens.*"[164] To which he replied, "And is there anything else we may do for you, good sister?" She rejoined, "Your rank will be changed to the most exalted. You will perform as will befit your office."[165]

30. Meanwhile, a certain noble lady said to her, "Don't worry, you won't die now, because your face has a rosy red-colored appearance." [Margherita] answered with great confidence, saying that she did not fear death, nor would she for all the world request of the Lord to remain any longer; for she was making a safe crossing, since there was nothing in her that would not be suffused with heavenly love.

31. Then her more worthy brother [Giacomo], *bearing his own cross,*[166] said, "Sister, behold our faith." She ordered that a candle be lit; and looking at her hands and fixing her gaze on her brothers, she said to them, "Beware you do not place your love in any earthly or transitory thing!" And then: "*I thank* Christ, *Father of heaven and earth,*[167] because He deigned to use up my body before my death, according to my desire." And adoring the cross, she said, "*Remember us, O Lord, in the favor of your people; visit us with your salvation.*"[168] And going on she said, "I believe *that my Redeemer lives, and that in the last day I shall rise out of the earth.*"[169] And kissing her hand she said, "*And in my flesh I shall see my God,* my Savior."[170] And touching her eyes with her hand she recited,

---

164. *Vultum tuum* was the introit for the daily commemorative Mass to the Virgin from the Nativity to Purification; *Salve sancta parens* was the introit used from Purification to Advent. Van Dijk, *Sources,* 2:320.

165. In this fascinatingly audacious passage, Stefania seems to have Margherita predicting that Giacomo would be elevated to the papacy. As Oliger wryly noted, "Events turned out rather differently."

166. John 19:17. (Although the passage is probably intended to indicate only that Cardinal Giacomo Colonna held up his cross in front of his sister, the biblical quotation still puts Giacomo in the place of Christ.)

167. John 11:41; Matthew 11:25; Luke 10:21.

168. Psalm 105:4.

169. Job 19:25.

170. Job 19:26.

"*And* these *eyes shall behold.*"[171] Then embracing the cross she declared, "*Into your hands,* O Lord, *I commend* our soul and body and all desire and emotion."[172]

And holding the cross, she longed to see the heavens, so her more worthy brother [Giacomo] ordered that the windows be opened. And when this was done, she still could not see the heavens from there, so she wished to be placed outside under the open sky. But the aforesaid brother would not allow this and ordered instead that she be lifted down from her bed and laid upon the earth. And as she lay stretched upon the earth, lingering her final hour, I said to her, "Remember, my lady, that this bed and everything else that exists are on the earth. I beg that you allow yourself to be put on the bed!" She very obediently did this. And ordering that candles be lit and her brothers summoned, she quickly knelt to meet the Holy Trinity, which she said had come to lead her from the prison of the flesh.[173] Turning her face to the east, fortified by the sign of the cross, she happily went to Christ, though there was no evidence of her death save only for a slight relaxation of her fingertips. Indeed, she did not fall back upon the bed, but remained kneeling, as if she were still alive.[174]

---

171. Job 19:27.

172. Psalm 30:6.

173. Oliger saw this passage as echoing Psalm 142:10 and pointed out that I Celano 8 has Francis of Assisi singing Psalm 142 at his own deathbed.

174. The text breaks off, apparently in the middle of a word: "sed quasi viva genuflexa ma." Oliger conjectured *mansit* for the final word. The text ends in the middle of a line, with eight more ruled lines still remaining on folio 38v (so missing text cannot be the result of quires having been lost or removed). In the bottom margin of the page is a sketch of a male head, added by a later hand. Since the text does conclude with Margherita's death, it is possible that very little has been lost, perhaps only a pious closing and invocation of some kind. But in fact there is no way of knowing how much of the text may be missing; one could imagine the loss of scenes describing Margherita's burial, translation, and the foundation of San Silvestro. Nor is there any very clear explanation for why a scribe ceased his or her work at this point.

FOUR

Three Later Papal Bulls Concerning Boniface VIII, the Colonna, and San Silvestro in Capite

When the dispute between the Colonna family and Pope Boniface VIII broke out into open war in May 1297, Boniface stripped Giacomo and Pietro Colonna of their cardinalate status and powers. San Silvestro in Capite was caught up in this battle in December 1297. Giacomo Colonna had been the informal patron as well as formal protector of the house, and its current abbess was Giovanna Colonna, daughter of Senator Giovanni Colonna (author of *Vita I*) and thus sister of Cardinal Pietro Colonna. On 11 December (just three days before Boniface formally launched a crusade against the Colonna), Giacomo was replaced as protector, and Giovanna was removed as abbess. As Boniface VIII attacked and destroyed Colonna holdings, he also stripped San Silvestro of its distinct status as a member of the Order of *Sorores minores*. After Boniface's death in 1303, his successor Benedict XI reversed his decrees. These three papal bulls demonstrate the extent to which San Silvestro was caught up in Boniface's attacks on the Colonna, and hence how destructive these attacks were for any ongoing attempts to achieve formal recognition of Margherita Colonna's cult. These bulls also indicate the way membership in the Order of *Sorores minores* had become fundamental to San Silvestro's self-identity, and hence a privilege to be attacked by a hostile pope.

BONIFACE VIII, *GENERALIS ECCLESIAE REGIMINI*, 11 DECEMBER 1297

Since Giacomo and Pietro Colonna have been stripped of their status as cardinals and of all ecclesiastical power, Giacomo's role as protector of San Silvestro in Capite is taken from him and given to Cardinal Matthew of Acquasparta, a former minister general of the Franciscans but an ally of Boniface VIII. Giovanna Colonna (daughter of the senator Giacomo Colonna, niece of Giacomo and sister of Pietro) is also removed as abbess.

Translated from the edition in *BF*, volume 4, 456–57.

BONIFACE [bishop, servant of the servants of Christ],[1] to his worthy brother Matthew [of Acquasparta], bishop of Porto and San Ruffino,[2] greetings and apostolic blessing.

Presiding over the governance of the whole church, among other topics dear to our heart we particularly strive to see that churches and monasteries are administered in a healthy fashion, so that, with foul ways eliminated, they may be fortified by flourishing results and may rejoice in the fulfillment of vows. Wherefore, since—because of the compelling sins and unworthy actions of them and their followers—we have recently removed from the office of cardinal Giacomo Colonna and his nephew Pietro, formerly cardinals of the holy Church of Rome, and forever stripped them of every office and benefit of the cardinalate regarding all

---

1. Benedetto Caetani (ca. 1230/1240–1303) was created cardinal in 1281 and was elected pope in 1294 after the controversial resignation of Celestine V.

2. Matthew of Acquasparta (1237–1302) was chosen minister general of the Franciscans in 1287, created cardinal by Nicholas IV (Jerome of Ascoli) in May 1288 (resigning as minister general in 1289), and then named cardinal bishop of Porto. He sided with Boniface VIII in the dispute with the Colonna.

monasteries, churches, and religious and secular hospitals whatsoever in whatever form or way or title by which they were conceded and commissioned or commended, and from every right and jurisdiction in them or any entity pertaining to them or from any one or ones of them within the city [of Rome]; and since the Monastery of San Silvestro in Capite— located within that very city, once the home of the black monks of St. Benedict and now that of the Order of the Poor *Sorores minores* or of whatever profession, order, or rule, and directly subject to us and to the church—was committed to the rule and government of the said Giacomo, at that time cardinal, in a certain fashion, as we understand, by Pope Nicolas IV of good memory, or by one of our other predecessors as Roman pope;[3] and since this same Giacomo has now been stripped, as has been said, of these endeavors and grants made to him in whatever fashion or way or verbal formula while he was yet a cardinal; therefore— looking earnestly with due care to the task of happy management of the said Monastery of San Silvestro, and hoping that through you, a person adorned by God with many fine merits, and who by completion of many difficult [tasks has proved himself worthy], the spiritual and temporal welfare of the said monastery may be advanced in accordance with our wishes[4]—we have decreed by apostolic authority that the protection, governance, and correction of this same Monastery of San Silvestro, and of the abbess, the Sisters, the chaplains, the confessors, the lay Brothers of the household, and all living there, including the personnel of the monastery, of the priories, chapels, churches, hospital, and of the members and other goods and rights pertaining to the monastery in matters temporal and spiritual, shall be committed to you.

We do this deciding that they ought to remain under your governance, protection, and correction, your command, care, and rule, so that

---

3. Thus it would appear that Giacomo was not formally named as protector of the house until the reign of Nicholas IV, although it should be noted that Boniface does not seem sure of this information.

4. Our rendering of the preceding passage is something of a paraphrase, since, as a note in *BF* indicates, there appears to be a scribal error of some kind that impedes a clear reading.

out of concern for souls and supervision over this same monastery, abbess, Sisters, chaplains, confessors, lay Brothers, household, and persons working there, you may strive to fulfill the duty of visitation, correction, and reformation, either in your own person or through another person or other persons, as often as will be necessary, by correcting and reforming there such matters as you find to require correction and reformation. You may thus initiate, terminate, build, plant, separate and eradicate, arrange, decide and dispose, as seems best to you in accordance with God.

Further, we completely remove from the said monastery all Friars, clerics, and laymen, and any persons not professing the order of the said monastery who are staying outside the cloistered section by the authority granted by the said Giacomo [Colonna] before his removal from office or who have been placed or set there later in any capacity. Moreover, we completely remove Giovanna,[5] who is the daughter of the said Giovanni Colonna[6] and is acting as abbess of the said monastery, from the position of abbess of the said monastery, rendering her a person unqualified to exercise any high office or position of service in this monastery. In so doing we command that you not allow anyone from the aforesaid Friars or persons or others to be there or loiter there or even approach the place without your specific and express permission. And, should the need arise, do this by summoning the aid of the secular arm and by suppressing any opposition by church sanction prior to any hearing. No indulgence that may have been granted by the Apostolic See to any person that they not be subject to interdict, suspension, or excommunication, or any other indulgence of the said see of whatever comport as may exist whereby the

---

5. Giovanna, daughter of Senator Giovanni Colonna, is first mentioned in the published records of San Silvestro in December 1294, when she appears as acting on behalf of the abbess, Barbara (very possibly her cousin), and in May 1296, when she is referred to as "reli[g]iosa et honesta mulier domina Iohanna." See Vincenzo Federici, "Regesto del monastero di S. Silvestro de Capite," *Archivio della Società romana di storia patria* 22 (1899): 432, 434. She was evidently elected abbess before December 1297 and was addressed as abbess once more by Benedict XI in 1303 (see below).

6. Giovanni Colonna has not in fact been mentioned yet in the letter.

results of the present letter might be impeded or set aside, of which it would be necessary that our letter make word for word mention, may stand to the contrary.

Now, moreover, to facilitate your task and to allow you more easily to govern the said monastery and see more vigorously to the welfare of those living at the monastery and of the Sisters, we grant to you unrestrained power by virtue of this letter to send to the said monastery clerical or lay Friars of the Order of *Fratres minores*, in such numbers as shall seem appropriate to you, led by God, for the operation and benefit of the said monastery and the said Sisters; and also to place there some persons who are to stay there with the permission and consent of the general minister or the minister of the Roman Province, or of its custode, or of the guardian of the Friars of Rome of the said order;[7] and also to permit Friars of this same order going to that monastery and even entering the interior of the cloister and staying as many times as seems necessary to you.[8]

No chapter of the rule of the said Friars,[9] or of the rule of the Sisters of the said monastery, nor the declaration that our predecessor of holy memory Pope Nicholas III propounded on the rule of the aforementioned Friars,[10] may stand to the contrary, with the caveat that the Friars who by your license will enter the said cloister are to observe those things contained within the rule of the said Sisters.

Given at Rome at Saint Peters, III Ides of December in the third year of our papacy.

---

7. The Franciscan minister general from 1296 to 1304 was Giovanni Mincio of Murrovalle (named cardinal bishop of Porto after Mathew of Acquasparta's death in 1302; cardinal protector of the order in 1307).

8. This is a rather flagrant violation of several provisions guaranteed in the Rule of the *Sorores minores*.

9. Boniface is referring to chapter 11 of the *Regula bullata*, on not entering the houses of nuns.

10. On 14 August 1279, Nicholas III (Giangaetano Orsini, cousin of Margherita Colonna) issued *Exiit qui seminat*, which is presumably the "declaration" referred to here.

BONIFACE VIII, *AD APICEM APOSTOLICAE*, 5 APRIL 1298

Boniface decrees that San Silvestro in Capite may no longer belong to the Order of *Sorores minores* or follow its rule but must join the Order of St. Clare and follow that order's rule. He further notes that since Urban IV specified that the cardinal protector of the male Franciscans would be the protector of the Order of St. Clare, the current cardinal protector, Matteo Orsini, will now fulfill that role for San Silvestro. Translated from the edition in *BF*, volume 4, 468–69.

BONIFACE [VIII, bishop, servant of the servants of God], for the perpetual memory of the matter. Having been summoned to the pinnacle of apostolic honor by arrangement on high, out of a concomitant concern for pastoral duty, we concern ourselves in sagacious thought with the changes of the times, the nature of places, and the state of individuals, so that, having due regard for individual situations, we may, by vigilant concern, develop their healthful and vigorous condition so that they may rejoice by heaven's grace in avowed success and achieve a desired progression. Among the other things that often inspire and sagaciously guide our thoughts, we especially seek to prosperously direct individuals and church properties and particularly religious houses, to ensure for them a flourishing condition so that in greater peace and comfort they may advance their effort for salvation and progress with happy result; and we especially attend to those religious communities that are known to need greater help because of the frailty and weakness of their female sex.

Seeking therefore to provide for the state of the monastery of the nuns of San Silvestro in Capite, located within the Roman City, for some time now of the Order or Rule of the Poor Sisters [*Pauperes sorores*] of the Order of *Fratres minores*,[11] and for the persons within, so that with God's help they may rejoice in progress in their avowed temporal and

---

11. An interesting nomenclature, considering that in the previous bull Boniface and the curia had demonstrated a knowledge of the correct name of *Sorores minores*.

spiritual purpose, we have decided, by apostolic authority and the fullness of apostolic power, that the Order and Rule of St. Clare, given by Pope Urban IV, our predecessor of good memory,[12] shall be observed as well in this same monastery; and that the abbess . .[13] and the Sisters, also the lay brothers and the male and female attendants who may hold vows in the same monastery, shall profess the above-mentioned Rule of St. Clare and be bound to always live according to it; and that the said monastery henceforth shall become and be called a monastery of the Order of St. Clare. If, however, there should be one or more people, male or female, from among the Sisters, lay Brothers, and attendants, bound by vows for some time now in this monastery and who now remain in the said monastery referred to in the present letter—which now is known to lack an abbess[14]—who are unwilling to profess the said Rule of St. Clare, we direct that they be relocated in other monasteries of the order that they will have professed.

Moreover, since this same predecessor [Pope] Urban [IV] directed that whoever at the time should be governor, protector, and corrector of the said Order of *Fratres minores* should also be the governor, protector, and corrector of the monasteries of the same Order of St. Clare, and thus that the same person should be known as the governor, protector, and corrector of both the said Order of the *Fratres minores* and the monasteries of the Order of the said St. [Clare], we do by this letter decide, or rather proclaim, that our beloved son Matteo [Orsini], who

---

12. The Rule for the Order of St. Clare, largely negotiated between Bonaventure as minister general and Giangaetano Orsini (the future Nicholas III and cousin to Margherita Colonna) as cardinal protector, had been approved by Urban IV in October 1263.

13. Papal bulls routinely include two dots (gemipunctus) instead of the name of a specific officeholder, to avoid any legal questions about whether an order applies only to a specific person, particularly if the name of the current officeholder is in doubt; since Boniface has just stripped Giovanna Colonna of the title of abbess, he certainly does not wish to refer to her by name, even though the third letter translated here demonstrates that she very likely continued to exercise authority in defiance of his decree and probably no other abbess had been elected at this juncture.

14. Since Giovanna Colonna has just been deposed by the previous letter, Boniface considers the office vacant.

is now cardinal deacon of Santa Maria in Portico,[15] and other cardinals of the Roman Church who at that time will be governor, protector, and corrector of the other monasteries of the same Order of St. Clare and the said Order of *Fratres minores*, be governor, protector, and corrector of the said Monastery of San Silvestro, of the persons there and of its property, and that they have such power over the persons and property at the Monastery of San Silvestro as the said cardinal now has and that he or others will have in the other monasteries of the Order of the said St. [Clare].

Let no man therefore be permitted [to infringe upon] this page of our command, decree, and pronouncement, etc. . . . .

Given at Rome at Saint Peter's on Nones of April, in the fourth year of our papacy.

BENEDICT XI, *DUDUM FELICIS RECORDATIONIS*, 23 DECEMBER 1303

The new pope Benedict XI recounts the events of 1297–98, reveals that San Silvestro has suffered excommunication and interdict for refusing to obey Boniface VIII's orders, and now declares those orders null and void.

Translated from the edition in *BF*, volume 5, 8–9.

BENEDICT XI [bishop, servant of the servants of God],[16] to his beloved daughters in Christ Abbess Giovanna and the convent of the Monastery of San Silvestro in Capite of the city [of Rome] of the Order of *Sorores minores inclusae*.

Some while ago Pope Boniface VIII, our predecessor of happy memory, decreed upon apostolic authority that your monastery—in which the Order of *Sorores minores inclusae* is and even at that time was

---

15. Matteo Orsini (ca. 1230–1305) was created cardinal in May 1262. He was related to Nicholas III and hence was cousin to Margherita, Giovanni, and Giacomo Colonna. He had been named cardinal protector of male and female Franciscans in 1279. He now replaces Brother Matthew of Acquasparta as protector of the house.

16. Niccolò Baccasini (1240–1304) was master general of the Dominican order from 1294 to 1299. He was created cardinal in 1298 by Boniface VIII and was elected to the papacy on 22 October 1303 but lived only until 7 July 1304.

observed in beneficial piety—should observe from that time onward the Order or Rule of St. Clare, given by our predecessor Pope Urban IV of pious memory; and that the abbess, the Sisters, and the lay men and women who would profess a rule after this decree should profess the above-mentioned rule and be held to it for life; and that the said monastery be and be called a monastery of the said Order of St. Clare. He instructed, moreover, that those persons staying then in that same monastery and professing the said Order of the *Sorores minores inclusae* there, who were unwilling to profess the prescribed rule, should be relocated to other monasteries of the same order that they had professed. Also, our same predecessor decreed that our beloved son Matteo [Orsini], cardinal deacon of San Maria in Portico, who is and was then governor, and the other cardinals of the Roman Church who would be at any later time governors, protectors, and correctors of the monasteries of this same Order of St. Clare and the Order of *Fratres minores*, should henceforth be governors, protectors, and correctors of your personnel and property, and should have such power in the aforesaid monastery with respect to its personnel and property as in the other monasteries of the said Order of St. Clare.

In turn, however, pursuant to this decree, as much through the said cardinal as through our beloved son Pietro Garlengi, canon of the Basilica of the Prince of Apostles of the city [of Rome][17] by authority delegated to him in this matter by this same cardinal, you have been warned and required, within a period of time set by them, either to profess the rule of the aforesaid St. [Clare], or to have those unwilling to profess that rule leave the cloister of the said monastery, so that in accordance with the said decree they may be relocated in other monasteries of your order. And since you have scarcely obeyed the requests and warning, a sentence of excommunication has been passed against you and of interdiction against your monastery by this same cardinal and canon.[18]

---

17. That is, St. Peter's.

18. Thus it appears that San Silvestro continued to resist Boniface's orders and hence was placed under interdict with its inhabitants suffering excommunication.

Wherefore, since you have been wounded by the thorn of heavy sorrow and tribulation from these proceedings and the above-mentioned sentences following from and based on the decree, which you insist was issued without any rational basis; and since to the great detriment of worship of the divine name you have been constrained in the observance of your rule, which was thriving in this monastery; and since upon the issuance of the aforesaid decree some property of the said monastery has been seized and a host of costs have been laid upon you and the monastery; and since you and the monastery have otherwise undergone no small losses in spiritual and temporal matters, you have humbly beseeched us that we should deem it worthy out of apostolic kindness to give you our consideration on your behalf and that of the monastery.

We have, therefore, thought seriously about these affairs and others that must be taken into account here. It is our intention that our consideration offer the assistance of a remedy, whereby you and the monastery can be free of the said burdens and impositions, returned to a calm and peaceful state, and there productively maintained. First, through the agency of our beloved son Gentile [of Montefiore], cardinal priest of San Martino ai Monti,[19] by our command and under our authority to absolve from the bonds of excommunication and interdict imposed according to the rite of the church, your sentence has been annulled. [And] by apostolic authority we revoke the aforementioned decree and all proceedings and sentences and anything else to your detriment or that of the said monastery following upon or by the decree. We hold them empty of effect and consequence, proclaiming that they are of no force whatsoever and that you are in no degree bound to heed them. We wish also that full and complete restitution be made to you of your monastery's temporal properties that were taken away by the enactment of the decree or otherwise from the order of this same predecessor Boniface, and also of the income and returns of the same for the intervening period. Let no man therefore, etc.

Given at the Lateran, X Kalends of December, in the first year of our papacy.

---

19. The Franciscan Gentile of Montefiore (ca. 1240/1250–1312) was created cardinal by Boniface VIII in 1300.

THE ABOVE LETTER was also addressed and sent "To his worthy brother Giovanni [of Murrovalle, cardinal] bishop of Porto"[20] with the following addendum:

BY AUTHORITY of this letter we entrust to your brotherhood and we order the restitution of the said monastery's temporal property, with respect to the said abbess and convent, which had been taken from them by the issuing of the said decree, or otherwise by order of our predecessor Boniface [VIII]. And see to it that such [property] and also the income and profit taken in the interval be restored fully to the said abbess and convent and monastery, out of the monastery's income and profits, which were taken in by the above-mentioned officers or others; and that you compile a strict account of the cost of these things and the amounts laid out in the recovery and preservation of these profits and the pay of these agents or anyone else acting on our authority or another's authority. And see that whatever is left over is consigned to the said abbess and the convent to be directed to the needs of the said monastery, and that a receipt and quittance executed with the said abbess and convent concerning these matters that will have transpired will be received by them in accordance with your order concerning the matters related here. All in opposition, etc. . . .

Given at the Lateran, X Kalends of January, in the first year [of our papacy].

---

20. See note 7 above.

FIVE

Mariano of Florence's Account of Margherita Colonna's Translation

The Franciscan Mariano of Florence (ca. 1477–1523) wrote his *Book of the Worthiness and Excellence of the Order of the Seraphic Mother of the Poor Ladies, Saint Clare of Assisi* in 1519. Mariano based his substantial recounting of Margherita's life (his paragraphs 380–428) almost entirely on *Vita I* and *Vita II*, which were available to him in a manuscript copy held at San Silvestro. This can probably be identified with modern Biblioteca Casanatense ms. 104. Only his concluding section is of independent interest for the thirteenth century, and it is given here because it offers the earliest extant account of the translation of Margherita's relics in 1285, when her followers moved from Mount Prenestino to San Silvestro in Capite, in the heart of Rome. As Mariano neared the end of his biographical treatment, his paragraphs 418 to 425 recounted the miracles and visions found in *Vita II*, chapters 10 to 18. He skipped chapter 16 (since it was not really a miracle) but otherwise simply followed the order as he found it in Stefania's text. His paragraph 426 began as a paraphrase of *Vita II*, chapter 19, but then added new material and continued to describe the move to San Silvestro and the translation of Margherita's relics in paragraphs 427 and 428. Since Mariano had been following

Vita II to this point, it is possible that this description ultimately derives from a now-lost concluding section of that text, but it may also come from other documents that could have existed in the sixteenth century at San Silvestro, or from oral tradition at that monastery.

Lezlie Knox's translation is from Mariano of Florence, *Libro delle degnità et excellentie del Ordine della seraphica madre delle povere donne Sancta Chiara da Asisi*, ed. Giovanni Boccali (Florence: Edizioni Studi Francescani, 1986), 235–37.

THIS WAS A MATTER for admiration: for ultimately the blessed Margherita's holy company, [favored with] such divine gifts, had delayed [making a formal profession due to] her worthiness and ideals, [until] the most ardent Lord Giacomo, [who was] so magnificent in works of mercy and piety that he was like another Moses, led the daughters of Israel out of Egypt into this world and did not abandon them in the desert of penance but rather brought them into the best land like a Joshua.[1] Having remained in that aforementioned place at Mount Prenestino under genuine enclosure, they now made their profession to the Rule of St. Clare under the authority and commission of the pope.[2]

But wishing the virgins to be in a more scrupulous condition, once the most worthy cardinal of Palestrina[3] was elected as Pope Nicholas [IV], just as his blessed sister Margherita had predicted to him,[4] [Giacomo] arranged to move them to the city of Rome [and] to the Abbey of San Silvestro, whose monks had lost their regular observance.[5] It was

---

1. The opening of this paragraph is an awkward series of dependent clauses emphasizing the virtues of Margherita, her followers, and finally Giacomo Colonna, drawn from *Vita II*, ch. 19. From this point, however, Mariano adds new material.

2. The reference to the "Rule of St. Clare" is a misunderstanding on Mariano's part (he regarded all the women he profiled as part of the Order of St. Clare). Earlier (para. 401), he mistakenly identified the Rule of the *Sorores minores* as an adaptation of the Rule of St. Clare, with modifications by Louis IX.

3. That is, the Franciscan cardinal Jerome of Ascoli.

4. It is not clear what "prediction" is referred to here.

5. This was a community of Benedictine monks who had been in residence since the eighth century. Claims that the prior community was lax were common in the case of such transfers (even as there often was little evidence to support such

a very laudable monastery and worthy of veneration, not the least because it was built on the cemetery of Priscilla, where the bones of many martyrs lay. Within its confines were the saintly bodies of Pope Silvester; Aniceto and Marcellino, who were martyrs with Claudio; Carino and Antonio; and Saint Sophia with three of her daughters, and many other relics, including the *Sudarium* of Jesus Christ and the head of John the Baptist.

The aforesaid most reverend cardinal [Giacomo Colonna] transferred the aforementioned Sisters to this worthy nunnery and, acting with his fellow Colonna lords, translated the body of the blessed Margherita at the same time.[6] During this translation, the all-powerful God, wishing to demonstrate to the [papal] court and the Roman people how she was currently shining in heaven, so expressed it with this sign: when the holy body entered the city of Rome and neared the area called Colonna, all of San Silvestro's bells resounded, although no mortal hand had pulled them, only angelic force. This stupendous miracle moved the entire city and court, praising God in his saint.

The aforementioned Sisters were enclosed in that nunnery, and as they increased in their virtues it became a well-known and famous monastery, largely for their perfection and for the renowned Roman women who were imitating the glorious mother St. Clare and blessed Margherita within that monastery.[7]

---

claims!). Emily Graham cites a fifteenth-century Roman chronicle that recalled how the Benedictine monks were basically forced out by Giacomo Colonna in order to install his sister's community there. See Emily E. Graham, "The Patronage of the Spiritual Franciscans: The Roles of the Orsini and Colonna Cardinals, Key Lay Patrons and Their Patronage Networks" (PhD diss., University of St. Andrews, 2009), 226.

6. This reference to the other Colonna lords reflected San Silvestro in Capite's status as a family monastery.

7. San Silvestro in Capite remained a Franciscan convent until 1875.

Rome, Biblioteca Casanatense ms. 104

The two lives of Margherita Colonna are uniquely preserved in Rome, Biblioteca Casanatense ms. 104. Because Oliger's 1935 study provided a competent technical description, we will summarize only the most relevant points here.[1] The manuscript is made up of two discrete halves, one (in a textualis hand) containing *Vita I* and the other (cancellerescabastarda) containing *Vita II.* These two halves evidently once were separate from each other. They were copied on visibly different parchment, though both are in single-column formats with wide margins and light ruling throughout. Both halves were dated by Oliger (and experts he consulted) to the first half of the fourteenth century, and a modern re-examination confirms a fourteenth-century date.[2] Thus neither half can be an autograph, and both must have been copied from now-lost exemplars. It seems virtually certain that both were copied at Rome, very likely at or for San Silvestro in Capite. It is unclear exactly when and under what circumstances the two halves were bound together into a single manuscript, but probably this process took place by the end of the

---

1. *DV,* 4–10. Oliger's plates 1 and 2 reproduce folio 1r (opening of *Vita I*) and folio 27v (opening of *Vita II* after dedicatory letter) of Biblioteca Casanatense ms. 104. Certainly a detailed new study of the manuscript would be welcome; we limit ourselves here to points relevant to the analysis given in the present volume.

2. Dr. Michelina Dicesare kindly examined several digital photos of each hand and confirmed a fourteenth-century dating for both.

fifteenth century. The present binding dates from the seventeenth century, with the Colonna coat of arms stamped in the middle of the front and back covers, flanked by the name "Giulio Cesare Colonna."

The first section of the manuscript, containing *Vita I*, makes up folios 1 through 26 (quiring is 1–10, 11–18, 19–26). Chapter titles, added by another hand (not that of the main scribe), are in red, as are the initial capital letters of each chapter. Capital letters beginning sentences or clauses are sometimes filled in lightly in red as well. Chapter numbers (Arabic numerals) are noted in a faint cursive hand in the margins, but otherwise marginal notes are rare and brief.[3] Several kinds of problems are apparent with the manuscript's transmission of the text. There is a lacuna in chapter 5 (fol. 6r), where text was probably inadvertently omitted by the scribe (who gave no indication of perceiving a problem). At the end of chapter 6 (fol. 9r), two authorial "notes to self" are incorporated into the text and underlined in red. They direct "the corrector" to include two visions that were omitted by the author. The most likely interpretation would seem to be that this interpellation would originally have been a marginal note in the autograph, which was then simply copied in the text at an intervening stage or by the scribe of ms. 104. In chapter 16 (fol. 25r) at least the end of one miracle and the beginning of another are missing. In this case the scribe left a space approximately the size of a single word, indicating that he or she realized something had been lost and thus showing that the omission had occurred at an intermediate stage between composition and this manuscript's creation.

The second section, containing *Vita II*, makes up folios 27 to 38 (quiring is 27–34, 35–38). This section of the manuscript has no rubrics or chapter headings. The text of the dedicatory letter to Giacomo Colonna takes up all of folio 27r. It appears to be in the same hand as the rest of the text, but the margins are smaller, the writing is more cramped, and the ruling and layout are not identical with those of the rest of the text. Throughout *Vita II* space was left for capital letters to begin chapters, but these capitals were never added, except for the "G" that begins chapter 2. Moreover, the text is evidently not complete. It breaks off in

---

3. They range from brief notes indicating themes (e.g., *De abstinentia* on fol. 5r) to a small cross (fol. 5v) or hand (fol. 7r) marking interesting points in the text.

the middle of a word, three-quarters of the way down folio 38v. Because the narrative reaches Margherita's death, it seems relatively likely that only a small portion of the original text is missing, perhaps dealing with her burial. But it is also possible that more substantial portions of the original text were lost. An early modern hand (perhaps sixteenth century) has added marginalia that calls attention to interesting passages, and a sixteenth-century hand has drawn a figure of a man's profile at the bottom of folio 38v.

It is certain that a manuscript described by several witnesses as containing Margherita's "vita" was held at San Silvestro in Capite in the sixteenth and early seventeenth centuries. It was consulted by, among others, Mariano of Florence, whose adaptation shows that in reality both *Vita I* and *Vita II* were present in that manuscript (they were evidently considered as two parts of a single *vita*). Oliger argued persuasively that this manuscript from San Silvestro is in fact the same one that came into the possession of Giulio Cesare Colonna (d. 1681) and eventually entered the collection of the Dominican Biblioteca Casanatense around 1760 (the approximate purchase date is noted on the inside of the front cover, as are early shelf numbers AR.IV.14 and I A.IV.36).

In sum, it seems likely that the two halves of our unique extant manuscript were copied at San Silvestro in Capite in the fourteenth century, then bound together before 1500. The composite manuscript was kept at San Silvestro into the seventeenth century, when it passed into the possession of the Colonna family and then at last came to rest in its current home at the Biblioteca Casanatense.

SELECT BIBLIOGRAPHY

MANUSCRIPT

Rome, Biblioteca Casanatense, ms. 104.

PRINTED PRIMARY SOURCES ON MARGHERITA COLONNA AND SAN SILVESTRO IN CAPITE

Cadderi, Attilio (P. Carlo O.F.M.). *Beata Margherita Colonna (1255–1280): Le due vite scritte dal fratello Giovanni, senatore di Roma e da Stefania, monaca di San Silvestro in Capite. Testo critico, introduzione, traduzione italiana a fronte, da un manoscritto latino del XIV secolo.* Edited by Celeste Fornari and Luigi Borzi. Palestrina, 2010.

Federici, Vincenzo. "Regesto del monastero di S. Silvestro de Capite." *Archivio della Società romana di storia patria* 22 (1899): 213–300, 489–538; 23 (1900): 67–128, 411–47.

Gallonio, Antonio. *Historia delle sante vergine romane con varie annotationi e con alcune vite brevi de' santi parenti loro, e de' gloriosi martiri Papia e Mauro soldati romani.* Rome: A. and G. Donangeli, 1591.

Mariano of Florence. *Libro delle degnità et excellentie del Ordine della seraphica madre delle povere donne Sancta Chiara da Asisi.* Edited by Giovanni Boccali. Florence: Edizioni Studi Francescani, 1986.

Oliger, Livario. *B. Margherita Colonna († 1280): Le due vite scritte dal fratello Giovanni Colonna senatore di Roma e da Stefania monaca di S. Silvestro in Capite.* Lateranum. Nova Series. An. 1, no. 2. Rome: Facultas Theologica Pontificii Athenaei Seminarii Romani, 1935.

———. "Documenta originis Clarissarum Civitatis Castelli, Eugubii (a. 1223–1263) necnon statuta Monasterium Perusiae Civitatisque Castelli (saec. XV) et S. Silvestri Romae (saec. XIII)." *AFH* 15 (1922): 71–102.

Sbaralea, J.-H., ed. *Bullarium Franciscanum Romanorum pontificum, constitutiones, epistolas ac diplomata continens tribus ordinibus minorum, clarissarum, et poenitentium a seraphico patriarcha sancto Francisco institutis, concessa ab illorum exordio ad nostra usque tempora.* 4 vols. Rome: Typis Sacrae Congregationis de Propaganda Fide, 1759–68.

SECONDARY SOURCES ON MARGHERITA COLONNA AND SAN SILVESTRO IN CAPITE

Barone, Giulia. "Le due vite di Margherita Colonna." In *Esperienza religiosa e scritture femminili tra medioevo ed età moderna*, edited by Marilena Modica, 25–32. Acrireale: Bonnano, 1992.

———. "I Francescani a Roma." *Storia della Città* 9 (1978): 33–35.

———. "Margherita Colonna." In *Mein Herz schmiltzt wie Eis am Feuer*, edited by Johannes Thiele, 136–45. Stuttgart: Kreuz, 1988. Translated by Larry F. Field as "Margherita Colonna: A Portrait," *Magistra* 21 (2015): 81–91.

———. "Margherita Colonna e le Clarisse di S. Silvestro in Capite." In *Roma anno 1300: Atti della IV Settimana di Studi di storia dell'arte medievale dell'Università di Roma "La Sapienza" (19–24 maggio 1980)*, edited by Angiola Maria Romanini, 799–805. Rome: L'Erma di Bretschneider, 1983.

Brentano, Robert. *Rome before Avignon: A Social History of Thirteenth-Century Rome.* New York: Basic Books, 1974.

Cadderi, Attilio. *La Beata Margherita Colonna (Clarissa), Palestrina 1255, Castel S. Pietro, 1280.* Rome, 1984.

Carletti, Giuseppe. *Memorie istorico-critiche della Chiesa e Monastero di S. Silvestro in Capite di Roma.* Rome: Nella Stamperia Pilucchi Cracas, 1795.

Furitano, Giuseppe. "Una santa donna del Duecento: Margherita Colonna." In *Fatti e figure del Lazio medievale*, edited by Renato Lefevre, 387–95. Rome: Gruppo culturale di Roma e del Lazio, 1979.

Gaynor, J. S., and I. Toesca. *S. Silvestro in Capite.* Rome: Marietti, 1963.

Graham, Emily E. "The Patronage of the Spiritual Franciscans: The Roles of the Orsini and Colonna Cardinals, Key Lay Patrons and Their Patronage Networks." PhD diss., University of St. Andrews, 2009.

Hubert, Étienne. "Un censier des biens romains du monastère S. Silvestro in Capite (1333–1334)." *Archivio della Società romana di storia patria* 111 (1988): 93–140.

———. "Économie de la propriété immobilière: Les établissements religieux et leurs patrimoines au XIVe siècle." In *Rome aux XIIIe et XIVe siècles: Cinq études*, edited by Étienne Hubert, 177–229. Rome: École française de Rome, 1993.

Kane, Eileen. *The Church of San Silvestro in Capite in Rome.* Genoa: Edizioni d'Arte Marconi, 2005.

Knox, Lezlie S. *Creating Clare of Assisi: Female Franciscan Identities in Later Medieval Italy.* Leiden: Brill, 2008.

Lopez, Bianca. "Between Court and Cloister: The Life and Lives of Margherita Colonna." *Church History* 82 (2013): 554–75.

Montefusco, Antonio. "'Secondo: Non conservare': Per una riconstruzione dell'archivio del monastero di San Silvestro in Capite a Roma." *Archivio della Società romana di storia patria* 135 (2012): 5–29.

Pasztor, Edith. "Esperienza di povertà al femminile in Italia tra XII e XIV secolo." In *Donne e sante: Studi sulla religiosità femminile nel Medio Evo*, 131–49. Rome: Edizioni Studium, 2000.

———. "I papi del Duecento e Trecento di fronte alla vita religiosa femminile." In *Donne e sante: Studi sulla religiosità femminile nel Medio Evo*, 97–129. Rome: Edizioni Studium, 2000.

Solvi, Daniele. "Maria nell'agiografia femminile di area minoritica: Da Chiara d'Assisi a Margherita da Cortona." *Theotokos* 19 (2011): 329–54.

Temperini, Lino. "Fenomeni di vita comunitaria tra i penitenti francescani in Roma e Dintorini." In *Prime manifestazioni di vita comunitaria maschile et femminile nel movimento francescano della penitenza (1215–1447): Atti del Convegno di studi francescani, Assisi, 30 giugno–2 luglio 1981*, edited by Raffael Pazzarelli and Lino Temperini, 603–53. Rome: Commissione Storica Internazionale T. O. R., 1982.

SELECT SECONDARY SOURCES ON THE COLONNA FAMILY

Barone, Giulia. "Niccolò IV e i Colonna." In *Niccolò IV: Un pontificato tra oriente ed occidente*, edited by Enrico Menestò, 73–89. Spoleto: Centro Italiano di Studi sull'alto Medioevo, 1991.

Binski, Paul. "Art Historical Reflections on the Fall of the Colonna, 1297." In *Rome across Time and Space: Cultural Transmission and the Exchange of Ideas, c. 500–1400*, edited by Claudia Bolgia et al., 278–90. Cambridge: Cambridge University Press, 2011.

Bolgia, Claudia. "Ostentation, Power and Family Competition in Late-Medieval Rome: The Earliest Chapels at S. Maria in Aracoeli." In *Aspects of Power and Authority in the Middle Ages*, edited by Brenda Bolton and Christine Meek, 73–105. Turnhout: Brepols, 2007.

Carocci, Sandro. *Baroni di Roma: Dominazioni signorili e lignaggi aristocratici nel duecento e nel primo trecento.* Rome: École française de Rome, 1993.

Gardner, Julian. "Pope Nicholas IV and the Decoration of Santa Maria Maggiore." *Zeitschrift für Kunstgeschichte* 36 (1973): 1–50.

Le Pogam, Pierre-Yves. "La lutte entre Bonniface VIII et les Colonna par les armes symboliques." *Rivista di storia della chiesa in Italia* 61 (2007): 47–66.

Mohler, Ludwig. *Die Kardinäle Jakob und Peter Colonna: Ein Beitrag zur Geschichte des Zeitalters Bonifaz' VIII.* Paderborn: Schöningh, 1914.

Neuman, Richard. *Die Colonna und ihre Politik von der Zeit Nikolaus IV. bis zum Abzuge Ludwigs des Bayern aus Rom, 1288–1328.* Langensalz: Druck von Wendt und Klauwell, 1916.

Osborne, John. "A Possible Colonna Family 'Stemma' in the Church of Santa Prassede, Rome." In *A Wider Trecento: Studies in 13th- and 14th-Century European Art Presented to Julian Gardner,* edited by L. Bourdua and R. Gibbs, 21–30. Leiden: Brill, 2012.

Paschini, Pio. *I Colonna.* Rome: Istituto di Studi Romani Editore, 1955.

Rehberg, Andreas. *Kirche und Macht im römischen Trecento: Die Colonna und ihre Klientel auf dem kurialen Pfründenmarkt (1278–1378).* Tübingen: Max Niemeyer, 1999.

Romano, Serena. "I Colonna a Roma: 1288–1297." In *La nobiltà romana nel medioevo: Atti del Convegno organizzato dall'École française de Rome e dall'Università degli studi di Roma "Tor Vergata" (Roma, 20–22 novembre 2003),* edited by Sandro Carocci, 291–312. Rome: École française de Rome, 2006.

Schmidt, Tilmann. "Eine Studentenhause in Bologna zwischen Bonifaz VIII. und den Colonna." *Quellen und Forschungen aus italienischen Bibliotheken und Archiven* 67 (1987): 108–41.

Vian, Paolo. "Bonifiacio VIII e i Colonna: Una riconsiderazione." In *Bonifacio VIII: Atti del XXXIX Convegno storico internazaionale, Todi 2002.* Spoleto: Centro Italiano di studi sull'alto Medioevo, 2003.

INDEX

LARRY F. FIELD
is professor emeritus of sociology and criminal justice at Western New England University. He is the translator of *The Sanctity of Louis IX: Early Lives of Saint Louis by Geoffrey of Beaulieu and William of Chartres.*

LEZLIE S. KNOX
is associate professor of history at Marquette University. She is the author of *Creating Clare of Assisi: Female Franciscan Identities in Later Medieval Italy.*

SEAN L. FIELD
is professor of history at the University of Vermont. He is the author of a number of books, including *The Beguine, the Angel, and the Inquisitor: The Trials of Marguerite Porete and Guiard of Cressonessart* (University of Notre Dame Press, 2012).

9 780268 102029